When the Good Life Goes Bad

When the Good Life Goes Bad

The US and Its Seven Deadly Sins

STACEY M. FLOYD-THOMAS

Foreword by
MICHAEL ERIC DYSON

UNIVERSITY OF ILLINOIS PRESS
Urbana, Chicago, and Springfield

Portions of the following publications have been reprinted by permission:

Stacey M. Floyd-Thomas, "'Oh Say Can You See?': Womanist Ethics, Sub-Rosa Morality, and the Normative Gaze in a Trumped Era," *Journal of the Society of Christian Ethics*, Philosophy Documentation Center, vol. 39, no. 1 (Spring/Summer 2019): 3–20, 10.5840/jsce201942210.

Stacey M. Floyd-Thomas, "Got Ethics? Envisioning and Evaluating the Future of Our Guild and Discipline," *Journal of the Society of Christian Ethics,* Vol. 36, No. 2 (Fall / Winter 2016): 195-203.

Manufactured in the United States of America
1 2 3 4 5 C P 5 4 3 2 1
♾ This book is printed on acid-free paper.

Library of Congress Cataloging-in-Publication Data
Names: Floyd-Thomas, Stacey M., 1969– author
Title: When the good life goes bad: the US and its seven deadly sins / Stacey M. Floyd-Thomas; foreword by Michael Eric Dyson.
Description: Urbana: University of Illinois Press, [2026] | Includes bibliographical references and index.
Identifiers: LCCN 2025027947 (print) | LCCN 2025027948 (ebook) | ISBN 9780252049507 hardcover | ISBN 9780252089152 paperback | ISBN 9780252048654 ebook
Subjects: LCSH: Deadly sins | United States—Moral conditions—History—21st century
Classification: LCC BV4626 .F56 2026 (print) | LCC BV4626 (ebook) | DDC 277.308/3—dc23/eng/20250918
LC record available at https://lccn.loc.gov/2025027947
LC ebook record available at https://lccn.loc.gov/

The manufacturer's authorized representative in the EU for product safety is Mare Nostrum Group B.V., Mauritskade 21D, 1091 GC Amsterdam, The Netherlands. Email: gpsr@mare-nostrum.co.uk

God in three persons, blessed trinity:

My eternal faith, Janet Floyd

My everlasting hope, Lillian Makeda Floyd-Thomas

My enduring love, Juan M. Floyd-Thomas

O Say, Can You See (The Star-Spangled Banner)

O say, can you see, by the dawn's early light,
What so proudly we hailed at the twilight's last gleaming,
Whose broad stripes and bright stars, through the perilous fight,
O'er the ramparts we watched, were so gallantly streaming?
And the rockets' red glare, the bombs bursting in air,
Gave proof through the night that our flag was still there.
O say, does that star spangled banner yet wave
O'er the land of the free and the home of the brave?

—Francis Scott Key, 1814

America the Beautiful

O beautiful for spacious skies,
For amber waves of grain,
For purple mountain majesties
Above the fruited plain!
America! America!
God shed His grace on thee,
And crown thy good with brotherhood
From sea to shining sea!

—Katharine Lee Bates, 1893

O Say Can We See

O say can we see, by the Gone's early flight,
What so loudly we failed at the mornlight's past gleaming,
Whose flawed stripes and strifed scars, through the perilous plight,
Our wan hearts, we watched, stirred and valiantly screaming.
And the rifle's dread glare, bullets bursting in air,
Gave truth in our sight that our flag was not spared.
O say does that scar-mangled banner yet save
Our land of the free and the home of the brave?

—Amanda Gorman, July 4, 2022

Woe to those who call evil good
    and good evil,
who put darkness for light
    and light for darkness,
who put bitter for sweet
    and sweet for bitter!

—Isaiah 5:20 (New Revised Standard
  Version Updated Edition)

Contents

Foreword

Passing the Baton

MICHAEL ERIC DYSON

I had the sort of excitement that sports fans possess when they meet their athletic heroes. It was the summer of 1986 or 1987 at a monthlong seminar for graduate students at Princeton University in an institute sponsored by a foundation whose name I don't remember. He wasn't too tall, nor too rangy, at least compared to my somewhat short and thin-at-the-time frame. He had light brown skin and close-cropped salt-and-pepper hair, with a slight bald streak in the top back half of his head. He had the bare shadow of what had been a thick mustache—not quite, it seems, the consistency of Nietzsche's bushy stash, but neither was it the neatly styled whiskers that traced across Martin Luther King Jr.'s top lip. He spoke with an ever so slight Southern accent that betrayed his Arkansas roots, while his cadence was rhythmic and steady, his voice booming his brilliant ideas in a relentless stream of enlightening rhetoric.

Years before, in 1980, a dear professor friend, whose field was psychology, had whet my appetite even more for his near otherworldly brilliance and his considerable intellectual gifts. She said to me—an undergraduate at Knoxville College, where I had begun my higher education odyssey four years later than most students, at the ripe young age of twenty-one—words that I never forgot: "Charles Long is on a higher level than most other thinkers, a man who is without question a genius and the smartest man I have ever met." She'd had the opportunity to take a faculty seminar with Long and the impression he left radiated reverence and remembrance in the same breath.

After she spoke his name, I immediately went to the library to look up magazine articles by and about him and to check out his books to read his work. This was long before the convenience of Google, a time when the card catalogue and the *Readers' Guide to Periodical Literature* were crucial allies of literacy and a friend to the intellectually curious reader. I learned that he was a student of the history of religions at the University of Chicago and had cut his scholarly teeth under the sublime tutelage of a legendary trio of luminaries: Mircea Eliade, Joseph Kitagawa, and Joachim Wach.

I tackled Long's *The Study of Religion: Its Nature and Discourse*, an extended essay on the critical study of religion that examines discourse that amplifies power and reinforces bias. Then a few years later I inhaled Long's *Alpha: The Myths of Creation*, a seminal and masterly study of how myth and science operate in discrete spheres and how creation myths are expressed in various modes and types across numerous cultures. What struck me about Long in this phase of his work is that he was a Black scholar who, although he later explicitly engaged racial identity, did not make race the center of his scholarly work while delivering some of the most insightful studies of religion as a phenomenon of human experience.

Charles Long comes to mind as I engage the most recent work of my brilliant colleague Stacey Floyd-Thomas. A renowned social ethicist, Floyd-Thomas's work is rooted in a womanist perspective that takes special note of how gender, race, and class converge, or collide, and how moral philosophy reflects on and is shaped by social forces. The book you hold in your hand, *When the Good Life Goes Bad: The US and Its Seven Deadly Sins*, is a bracing departure from her previous work. In this deeply imaginative and luminous book, Floyd-Thomas delves deeply into the American psyche, and into our national moral practice, to divine how we collectively grapple with a list of sins and vices that have vexed the American soul from the country's beginning. What is especially appealing about Floyd-Thomas's approach at this point in our history is how she shifts the epistemological battleground in two ways.

First, she probes the transcendent character of these vices, or sins, in a universal mode that offers insight about the devastation and destruction in the offing when these features of our moral lives explode into view and impact our everyday existence. The ills that Floyd-Thomas addresses in these pages plague all communities. They must be addressed in a way that shifts the burden of interpretation from the demographic profile of victims, or agents, to a fluid analysis of the forces and drives that target all members of our society.

Second, Floyd-Thomas removes discussion of the vices from an exclusive consideration of individuals to a consideration of the distinct role of vices in public spaces and social arenas. It is one thing, for instance, to speak of how pride might surface in an individual. It is quite another matter to probe the imperial play of pride in a nation-state where the future of democracy is at stake. Floyd-Thomas brilliantly reimagines how flaws spill from the cauldron of our social norms regardless of our personal identities. In an extraordinarily creative fashion, Floyd-Thomas adds flesh to Reinhold Niebuhr's conception of "moral man and immoral society." She probes how the list of vices and sins operates in the culture.

There is, to be sure, a practical dimension to Floyd-Thomas's wrestling with an ethics of universality: It shows that an immensely gifted scholar of any race or gender can insightfully grapple with the deadly sins that tax a civilization, a country, a culture. To doubt the scholarly ability of a social ethicist trained by some of the best thinkers in the land—Katie Cannon among them—because of identity is to introduce cruel bias into the mix and to dishonor the virtues of fair play that should always prevail.

Because I have seen her in action in the classroom, at the lectern, and in the pulpit, I am a witness to how magical Floyd-Thomas is when she is flowing in either setting. I have seen her deconstruct complicated ideas, situate knowledge in illuminating contexts, and appeal to a broad variety of disciplines and thinkers to make her point. She is as lucid in wielding the jargon of sophisticated moral philosophy as she is in breaking down complex ideas for graduate students.

Floyd-Thomas's skills evoke at least a few of the deadly sins in her colleagues. I am, for example, envious of her ability to effortlessly flow from one intellectual scenario to the next. I am admittedly a glutton for her extraordinary intellectual brilliance and for her ability to explain the most complex ideas in clear prose that offers her students—and colleagues—a sure handle on them. I am greedy for her classroom discussions, where she can offer a genealogy of, for instance, the epistemological strategies of Gadamer or Husserl, while at the same time showing us why their ideas are crucial in understanding the sociology of knowledge in a given historical epoch.

The seven deadly sins are good for the business of imperial America. After all, if we fail to account for how sloth, or lust, or pride feed the immoral conduct of political elites, we encourage these vices to intensify and proliferate in the culture. *When the Good Life Goes Bad* couldn't be timelier. We face the prospect of an autocrat wielding even greater power while committing nearly every deadly sin in the book. How are we to think about the seven deadly sins in their political context, in their cultural manifestation, in their societal emergence, and in their collective expression? We need look no further than this exceptionally well-written and deeply researched book that bears the mind and mouth of one of the most prodigiously gifted social ethicists in the land today. I must confess that I take great pride in her as my colleague, my friend, and upon reading this book, as my beloved teacher.

Acknowledgments

I would have fainted, unless I had
believed to see the goodness of the
Lord in the land of the living.
—Psalm 27:13

The psalmist David's song of lament and praise undergirds my work as a scribe of this text. Indeed, I would have been hopeless if I hadn't held onto the heartfelt belief that the village of folk who have helped me with head and heart was life-giving and the embodiment of the goodness and kin-dom of God amid the death-dealing culture wars in these yet to be United States and in a world in need of renewal and transformation.

Akin to Dorothy Day's observation, the long loneliness and solitude of scholarly writing is withstood and cured by the community that cheers you on, collaborates, and critiques as a gift of love-crafting.[1] Here, love-craft is not the subgenre of horror, fatalistic fantasy, or speculative pop fiction that emphasizes the horror of the insane and incomprehensible. Rather, the love-craft of this work is truth-telling that is hopeful, sober, and steeped in mutuality and reciprocity. It is in that spirit of justice and truth and care for the past, present, and future that I extend sincere appreciation to an amazing constellation of stars that have shone bright in the long night and dark soul to call forth and give birth to this text.

The funding of first fruits of the following institutions have been invaluable and unmatched: Vanderbilt University's Research and Scholar Grant, Louisville Institute Sabbatical Grant, Yale Center for Faith and Culture Institute, Luce-American Academy of Religion Advancing Public Scholarship Grant, and the University of Houston-Downtown's Center for Social Inquiry & Transformation. Likewise, I pay tribute to the critical conversations, platforms, lectureships, and speaking engagements hosted by American Academy of Religion's Black Theology Group, Ethics Section, Womanist Group, and Holocaust and Genocide Group; the Society of Race, Ethnicity and Religion (SRER); the Princeton Theological Seminary Black

Theology and Leadership Institute; the Hannover Institute for Philosophical Research; the Ecclesiological Investigations International Research Network; the Princeton Theological Seminary Geddes W. Hanson Lectures; Johannes Gutenberg-University Mainz's Center for Intercultural Theology Scholar-in-Residency; the Iliff School of Theology's Social Justice and Ethics Program, the Latinx Center of the University of Denver; the Chicago Theological Seminary C. Shelby Rooks Lectureship; the Society of Christian Ethics (USA); Society for the Study of Christian Ethics (UK); the Society for the Study of Black Religion; and Virginia Theological Seminary's Bicentennial Visiting Scholar Fellowship.

While naming these institutional investments, I do not want to overlook the individuals who painstakingly stand in real time and offer solidarity through thick and thin. I recognize for their generosity and generativity the vigilant village of collaborators and dear friends in the embodiment of the genius of W. David Nelson, Stephen G. Ray, Mark Toulouse, Blanche Cook, and Anthony Pinn, who have given me hope that people can be different but not alienated. I also recognize the sweet fruit of my scholarly labor as embodied in my indefatigable and faithful postdocs and graduate students: Alexandra Chambers, D. Jamil Grimes, and Jacob Robinson; and the quotidian solicitude and sanctuary provided by my village made up of Michael Eric Dyson, Randy and Shataia Howard, Jackie and Forrest E. Harris Sr., Miguel and Deb De La Torre, Herbert Marbury, Brad Braxton, and the womanist wisdom of too many but who must be named in the embodiment of Renita J. Weems, Maisha Handy, Teresa Fry Brown, Marla Frederick, Cheryl Kirk-Duggan, Marsha Foster Boyd, Cheryl Townsend-Gilkes, Amelia Ward, Marvlieu Hall, Lesia Crumpton-Young, the Sabbath Sistahs Book Club, the Womanist "Q-Force" Conclave, the Zuri Quilting Guild of Nashville, Temple Baptist Church; and most especially the Black Religious Scholars Group (BRSG) and Friendship West Baptist Church. Likewise, there have been angels unaware in the embodiment of the late former President Jimmy Carter, Alice Hunt, Bonnie Miller-McLemore, Mirosalv Volf, Graham Reside, Joerg Rieger, Jaco Hammon, Don C. Richter, David and Gail Williams, and Timothy McNamara. I also want to commend the faithful legacy of mentees, namely Jerrolyn Eulinberg, Damien Durr, Christopher Driscoll, Melanie Jones Quarles, Candace Laughinghouse, Irie Sessions, Lakisha Lockhart, Prisca Dorcas Mojica Rodriguez, Rebecca Ann Wilcox, Jennifer Bailey, Shantell Hinton Hill, Royal Todd, and Tatayana Richardson. Their intergenerational genius and generativity were instrumental in shaping the research direction of this book. The insightful feedback from them as my mentees, students, postdocs, and research collaborators enriched the content and strengthened these arguments with their generous and astute support, without which this extensive research would not have been possible. I would also like to thank my editor, Alison Syring, and her predecessor at University of Illinois Press Dawn Durante, who served as midwives in the birthing of this work.

My heartfelt gratitude to my mentor Katie Geneva Cannon, who showed me how to "read and write even when the lights are out." Following her teaching excellence and womanist tradition, my students who have flocked to my classes over more than twenty-five years are the reason why I write. My students have been my intergenerational spirit-helpers, have helped me realize the fierce urgency of the moral lessons needed for teaching ethics for the academy, church, and society. They have kept me from getting weary on the journey.

I am thankful for the family that shaped me: the entire Floyd and Underwood family clan and my chosen family in the embodiment of Frederick D. Haynes III, Debra Peek Haynes, Duana Butler, Daniel Alexander Jones, Cheryl Diggs Lowe, Philip Cooke, Cleon Edwards, Cindy Crusto, Kecia Carroll, Kerri Thompson Tillet, Lincoln E. Galloway, Peniel Joseph, and others from Virginia Tech to Brite to Vanderbilt who make up a hopeful intellectual camaraderie that has been a constant source of inspiration.

I am eternally indebted to my remarkable family of origin who have graciously contributed to both my personal journey and this work. My late parents, Charles and Lillian Floyd, not only instilled in me the wisdom that "the largest room is the room for improvement" but also laid the foundations of this pursuit. Their legacy endures alongside the steadfast support of my family that remains, especially my daughter Lillian Makeda Floyd-Thomas, who stands as the sweetest fruit of my love and labor, and my unwavering sister, Janet Floyd, whose comfort and devotion have remained an unshakable source of strength throughout my extensive academic endeavors.

My deepest gratitude is reserved for my husband, soulmate, best friend, and esteemed colleague, Juan M. Floyd-Thomas. As my brightest beacon in times of darkness, he embodies an exceptional love that encompasses mind, body, and soul. His daily demonstration of unwavering love and devotion, regardless of circumstances, continues to inspire and shape my journey.

Preface

From childhood, I recognized the intricate connection between societal norms and individual actions. Despite not having a background in moral philosophy or religious ethics, I possessed an innate desire to question and understand the underlying reasons for these norms. My curiosity drove me to constantly ask why in an attempt to unravel the complexities of human behavior.

Why was the "well-mannered" or "politically correct" option almost always based on lying or being in denial about the truth? Why were children routinely instructed by the elders in their communities that they should be seen and not heard and do as they say, not as they do? Why was small talk always geared toward the trivial, as opposed to pressing matters of the day? Why does our rhetoric not reflect our reality?

What is more, sage advice—especially when it came from local clergy and televangelists whose preaching and politics were seldom in accord with their avowed piety and public practices—was likewise baffling. As I grew older, I realized that preachers were not alone in not practicing what they preached. I took note of politicians whose positions of power depended on platforms and policies that rarely supported the pragmatic realities of their voting base. I gazed in disbelief at how some people were marginalized, placed out of sight, silenced, and denied the right to call the world as they saw it, despite efforts to bring into view the plight of being disregarded based on their age, gender, race, ethnicity, sexual identity, belief systems, and economic status.

When I became a professor, I found what my students reported about their own experiences to be revelatory. Those reports compelled me to study not merely the canonical texts of religion, philosophy, and ethics, but also the "living human documents" like my students, who made clear to me the connection between moral meaning and the religious relevance of popular culture. Rather than classic texts or whatever fairy tales their governing authorities insisted were foundational to their formation, I learned that it was the antiheroes of the silver screen and the ways in which television was "going native" into the deep, dark, and unhealthy social-psychological makeup of our society that intrigued them. My students often find fiction more reliable than what is presented to them as fact. After binge-watching televised crime dramas like *Breaking Bad* and sitcoms like *The Good Place* alongside news channels and the endless video loop of police murdering unarmed citizens, of voter suppression, and of suppression of women's rights, my students much preferred to engage these texts than the required readings on their syllabi. *Why?* That it is easier to obtain a weapon of mass murder than to rent a car or cast a vote, that there is more interest in controlling women's wombs than in controlling guns or sex trafficking, that police and the judicial system are more concerned with protecting domestic terrorists than protecting children, that the government bails out banks rather than giving the poor real help, and that there is more money to fund wars than to provide milk for young children and formula for infants—all this has them reeling.

What, they ask, does it mean to pursue the good life philosophically? What does it mean to "Make America Great Again" politically if our actions do not align with our rhetoric for the common good of all in such an allegedly great nation as ours? Indeed. In these ways and more, that outcry and that hope spur me, as an ethicist, to ask, "Why do people do what they do?" That same outcry and hope spur me, as a scholar of religion, to delve deeper into what people name as sacred. Race, gender, and class inform my delving and exploration.

I have written this book for my students, who remind me that theological evaluation and ethical contributions must always be true realities, no matter how scandalous or profane. My students remind me that the afterlife can be relegated to the classroom of abstraction, the church of irrelevance, and the politics of distraction, and that these spaces do not afford moral progress. They remind me that the real demons we encounter are those who lie to us in a vain attempt to "dumb us down and numb us up" with their heartlessness, those who either remain silent in the face of injustice or chatter inanely to drown out others and erode the common good.

It is their questions, and those of my own young daughter, that prompt me to "call it like I see it." For, in the words of Ida B. Wells-Barnett, "The way to right wrongs is to turn the light of truth upon them."[2] That, I find, is a far more honest way to a "more perfect union" and a promised land.

Moral conundrums have a way of revealing that our universal salvific anthems function as psychological torture chambers or empty rhetoric, and the agony or ambivalence that these conundrums leave behind sacrifice any will toward a common good. Instead, they defer American dreams or transform them into hellish nightmares. This book attends not only to the material and structural reality of this perennial punishment we encounter in our pursuits for happiness and first world power, but also to the self-inflicted moral crises and mental anguish occasioned by our personal "failure" to live up to what society deems to be "success." Telling the truth and shaming the devil reveals whether we genuinely love that which we deem to hate, or, conversely, if we truly hate that which we feign to love. The unmasking, discovering, and revealing of this truth is often too painful for us to see.

From its inception to conclusion, this text employs specific cultural examples to uncover a broader, more universal truth—the difference between what we believe (theos), what we value (ethos), what we feel (pathos), and what we understand (logos). Case in point: The best rendition of "America the Beautiful" in my own opinion (but I'd wager a bet that many would agree) is Ray Charles's version. He couldn't see the beauty of America in living color, across neither its socioeconomic, racial, or political landscape nor its "purple mountains majesty." However, his profound musical imagination—fueled by his faith, artistry, and hope as a blind Black man in segregated America—helps us envision what we never would have been able to imagine on our own. This sort of insight, from someone who could *actually* see other realities or was freer to dream new and better possibilities, empowers all of us. This book depicts the ugly truth that will convict and charge all of us without exception, serving as an explicit curative and clarion call for an audience of thinking people who have the faith to garner moral courage and the intellectual capital to do not only the work that our souls must have, but also the work that will save and redeem the very soul of America itself.

For years, two moral maxims that govern how I speak and how I see the world have flanked my email signature line. The first, by a failed presidential hopeful turned principled policymaker, reads:

> In a day-by-day fight for people, sometimes you have to choose to do what's difficult or unpopular. Sometimes you have to be willing to suspend your popularity in order to pick the hard right over the easy wrong.[3]

The second, by a renowned preacher and peace activist, reads:

> Hope is a state of mind independent of the state of the world. So, if your heart's full of hope, you can be persistent when you can't be optimistic.

> You can keep the faith despite the evidence, knowing that only in so doing has the evidence any chance of changing. So, while I'm not optimistic, I'm always very hopeful.[4]

As two publicly revered white men, their prescient and wise words hold sway. And they echo the soulful-spiritual guidance of the Black Church refrain "Tell the truth and shame the devil!," the common sense of my nana, "It's a long line that has no end," or the militaristic integrity of my father, "The biggest room is the room for improvement." These words of wisdom, taken together, can empower the real citizens who take them to heart, inspiring them to seek the common good and to strive both to envision *and* to realize a more perfect union.

I have written this book to push us to consider why we remain at odds with our highest ideals, why justice must be contextual, and why we refuse to address what we should clearly see. None of us is exempt from such questions until America is beautiful to every one of us.

When the Good Life Goes Bad

INTRODUCTION

"Oh Say Can You See?"

The Good Life in Contemporary America

Whereas for millennia the broad question of *what is the good life?* has consumed the ordering of human lives, modern American iterations of this old adage have evolved into a hornet's nest of increasingly individualistic existential questions such as *How should one live?*, *What does it mean to be successful?*, and *How do I know that I've made it?* Beneath the surface of these queries shaped by American optimism and aspiration lies a relatively unexplored, pessimistic, and more foreboding reality shaped by the embedded epistemologies, moral crises, and undergirding complexities that comprise the concept of *the good life* in contemporary America. In particular, it is the shift to the primacy of the individual and the individual's happiness that is now shaping such questions, so much so that many people believe that if something feels good to them, it must be right, others be damned.

Even more foreboding perhaps is that many Americans' social outlooks, cultural mores, and personal strivings now endorse cardinal vices rather than virtues in pursuit of the so-called American dream. This American vision of the good life and dream of success influences what Americans eat, where they live, how and whom they love, how they work, how they spend their money, what they do for leisure, what they wear, and perhaps especially what they think. It sacralizes American politics and ideologies into a form of civil religion that supplants and trumps organized religion itself. The dream has become grafted onto American bodies, minds, and souls, and in so doing personifies privately, publicly, and politically what is considered "American." In many ways, the soul of the contemporary American nation and its sense of the common good life is being transformed by a decline—or at least a shift—in morality and values, one that is driven by insatiable human choices as opposed to ethical and historical forces, and by individualism.

A marker of this transformation is that the "seven deadly sins"—lust, pride, greed, sloth, envy, gluttony, and wrath—have become the seven markers of American success. In essence, we have upended and perverted Stephen Covey's *7 Habits of Highly Effective People*[1] by making sin not merely our habit, but also the very definition of what it means to be successful.

When the Good Life Goes Bad: The US and Its Seven Deadly Sins explores how these transgressive traits have come to shape the individual and collective moral character and the so-called good life in the United States. It analyzes America's transmutation of these individual, personal temptations into sins that make an institutional impact in the public sphere to such an extent that people have come to place not only their trust within this vision of the good life but also their faith.

Therein lies the moral meaning and religious significance of the American making of success and the good life. In spite of the rise of various forms of secularism and the trend of the "spiritual but not religious" designation, the majority of Americans still claim to be religious by nature, and they still believe that morality influences and is influenced by their respective religious traditions. The diversity of that moral expression reflects our markers of achievement and character as a nation. By morality, I mean some vision of human life in accord with what society deems to be of ultimate truth and value. Religious believers in American society rely upon moral principles within their respective faith traditions to govern their best practices and right relationships. Moreover, as a country, America not only ensures their religious freedoms but also claims to be the champion and arbiter of the central virtues that they value.

This book explores the challenge of the twenty-first century for most Americans of faith: namely, that the attainment of the good life is no longer as focused on the need to be in right relation with God and one's fellow human beings as it is on the need to rely upon actions and assumptions that cultivate options and opportunities *for one's success at all costs*—often to the detriment of others, even loved ones. Put another way, it epitomizes and expounds upon the notion that if it feels good, then it must be right. By examining the cardinal sins of lust, pride, greed, sloth, envy, gluttony, and wrath, this book shows how these transgressive, *personal* principles in actuality have come to shape the *collective* moral strivings and sociopolitical condition of American society and culture. It renders transparent how the innermost workings of US society are informed and ultimately beholden to these capital vices.

We often disconnect contemporary concerns like white supremacy, misogyny, poverty, homophobia, transphobia, Islamophobia, xenophobia, and militarism from questions about sin. Given the inherently intersectional nature of my womanist perspective, in this book I remake that connection. I suggest that in order to reinvigorate our national discourse on moral thought and practice in meaningful and pertinent ways, we need to restore the power of naming these seven deadly sins on both an individual and a societal basis. Through its intersectional theoretical approach grounded in interdisciplinary methods informed by American studies, religious studies, sociology of religion, moral philosophy, liberation theology, political science, psychology, critical race theory, social criticism, popular culture, and feminist-womanist thought, I hope that this book will not only attract the interest of a diverse audience, but will also extend the trajectory of moral reflection, public theological witness, and pursuit of social justice established over the past 240 years by abolitionists, feminists, pacifists, trade unionists, and other activists.

I also hope that reinvigorating this conversation will help us to overcome the world-weariness and distress of our current moment, that it will rekindle communal commitment to seek "our better angels" (as Abraham Lincoln called them) in the current age of political pessimism and social peril. Following in the footsteps of such luminaries as Walter Rauschenbusch, Reinhold Niebuhr, Dorothy Day, Martin Luther King Jr., James H. Cone, Katie Cannon, Michael Eric Dyson, and Kelly Brown Douglas, to name only a few, it seems to me vitally important that scholars and practitioners of religion speak directly to the social and spiritual ills confronting the nation in an accessible, conversational manner by addressing the present American context as the most urgent case study for American faith and agency. *When the Good Life Goes Bad* aims to be just such a book.

By looking at the American context through religious and ethical lenses, I hope this book fosters a deeper understanding of how our nation has brought about its current social crises largely by perverting and inverting its claimed values. By laying false claim to the underlying moral high ground and power of its foundational principles, the United States has abnegated the promises of its national faith claims by tapping into its first world power and prominence as a self-declared national paragon of virtue. Obsessed with what makes us "great" and legitimates our power, America's moral failures are very often projected onto the "Other," and any divergence from our own way of life is deemed an aberration or evil, a threat or problem caused by external forces or impulses that we never claim as our own.

Furthermore, bent upon success at all costs, we perceive failure—whether understood as lacking virtue or simply not winning—as having no place within the American psyche. We are obdurate in refusing to accept any notion of failure either as an option or a possibility. Rather than moderating definitions or adjusting expectations of success, American exceptionalism entails a pathological insistence on forging on until we realize success, no matter the evidence countering our claims of excellence, no matter how much collateral damage we cause along the way, and no matter the evils we have to employ to get whatever we want. The American dream of success is, in fact, a fairy tale of the good life in which the individual is proved to be not only right in their principles, but also righteous in their practices. In so doing, that dream makes faith and lies indistinguishable from one another because of our relentless drive to bring about "the substance of things hoped for and the evidence of things unseen" no matter the cost.[2] This represents not only the confluence but also the contradiction of the "best and worst of times" and the "better angels of our nature," in which compassion fuels contempt, liberalism gives way to cynicism, and humanist ideals succumb to hubris.

For too long we have relied upon the best intentions and blessed assurances of our moral exemplars and religious leaders in the United States who have claimed, like Rev. Dr. Martin Luther King Jr., that "the arc of the moral universe . . . bends towards justice," or, like Reinhold Niebuhr, that "the sad duty of politics is to establish justice in a sinful world."[3] Neither the passage of time nor the assumption of a leadership title alone can assure the realization of these lofty aspirations. However idealized they might be as faith claims and however insistently identified as inalienable truths, such religious proclamations and preacherly words of comfort are at best a façade and at worst lies when extolled without attending to the moral responsibilities required to realize them.

The effect this has on society and social transformation mandates not only scrutinized study by scholars of religion but also a careful social analysis of the very religious ideals and values to which we adhere as a nation. To date, the discourse around religion and social transformation has paired religious people and their stereotypical social concerns. That is to say, we tend to examine the role and study of religion in society as "Black Christians and Civil Rights," "Catholics and Social Welfare," "Jews and Social Action," "Muslims and Social Acceptance," and so forth. Instead of this plug-and-play approach, to gain a deeper understanding of how people can remake society scholars must home in on where and how religion actually takes place, beginning not with how they hope it will be, but by looking at how they have facilitated what it has already become. In this respect, religion as a focus is no longer about the rote rhetoric we attach to communities of faith and their associated social aspirations. Rather, religious Americans often derive more meaning from what has been typified as sin or vice to such an extent as to make them symbols of American success.

The seven deadly sins are key to understanding how the United States approaches, analyzes, and addresses notions and realizations of success. *When the Good Life Goes Bad* examines these capital vices as erroneously and perilously hailed key touchstones of public morality in contemporary American culture and society. It analyzes lust, pride, greed, sloth, envy, gluttony, and wrath as prisms through which to reflect upon the principled, as well as the practical, challenges they pose to the national well-being in both sacred and secular terms. Whereas the notion of the seven deadly sins and the challenges they present to spirituality, morality, and identity in everyday life are neither new nor originated on American soil, they certainly have been perfected here. No longer seen as sins, they have been refashioned as signature American traits for success. Together they comprise and chart our country's path to success, moral worth, value, and first world power. And this is no small irony given that, since its founding, the United States has long believed itself to be the promised land and beacon of virtue. To make room for the possibility of ever recovering or realizing any sense of American virtue, *When the Good Life Goes Bad* unmasks the sinful veneer of the American good life by demystifying how the sins in their American manifestations have largely trumped virtue as what propels our nation's success and character.

This book explores the "oxymoronic ontology" of American success and the challenge of the twenty-first century for most Americans of faith. It acknowledges that the attainment of the good life is a faithful search, but it also highlights how this journey can be obscured when it is confused with what in common parlance is referred to as "getting right with God." This act of "getting right" is often just as much about getting the right goods in this life as it is about the need to rely upon actions that cultivate options and opportunities for success at any cost. This oxymoronic characteristic can be found throughout the various narratives about this country, including its name. As poet laureate Maya Angelou points out, the United States of America is actually "these yet to be united states," and our country has claimed itself to be a "more perfect union" while rendering invisible—although invaluable—the majority of its population.[4] This country's sense of exceptionalism has made it not only take up the space of other territories but to literally claim what cannot be claimed by dropping the "United States" altogether and instantiating itself as "America the beautiful," no less. The very essence of the United States and sense of its being has proven to be oxymoronic in that its thinking-being-doing are so self-contradictory as to be not only a philosophical paradox but also a moral contradiction. It is an oxymoron created by the construction of a so-called good life that has little to do with either the common good or with common sense.

Critical to this observation and the main impetus for this text is that age-old philosophical query of queries, "What is the good life?" This question is asked in such a way that those who are not philosopher-kings must not merely ponder but pragmatically engage in informing the *polis* (the people and their perspectives, practices, and politics) by which they may hold claim to a life assured through an inalienable right to life, liberty, and the pursuit of happiness (or is that property?). The fact that the US Constitution assures them this not only as the written word but also as sacred rhetoric demonstrates that this has become the American religion to the extent that one's ability to be in and of the United States is to succeed more in the oxymoronic ontology of its existence, being, becoming, and reality.

At the core of this text, then, is not a prescription but rather a description, perhaps even a confession, that questions how the good life, the constitutive elements of our American dreams and strivings of success, are grouped and guided by basic categories and characteristics made up of what appears to be anything but good. The pursuit of the proposed good life has resulted in bad circumstances that have held the country and its citizens captive in a context plagued by a cruel and unusual preoccupation that is ultimately sinful. Put another way, *When the Good Life Goes Bad* expounds upon the notion that this country's understanding of the good life is caught in a death-dealing vice grip.

This book extrapolates the religious and moral significance of the seven sins as a uniquely American driving force of success by adapting the seven dimensions of religion outlined by Ninian Smart in his seminal volume *The Religious Experience of Mankind*.[5] Smart's sevenfold framework serves here as a heuristic device for deriving a more complete picture of religiosity in general. The *mythical* dimension aids in addressing matters of sacred meaning and holy significance, sometimes in epic fashion. The *doctrinal* dimension outlines appropriate relationships and offers guidance as to how followers should orient themselves within the world. The *legal* dimension connotes the ethics, key values, principles or precepts, and rules or laws. The *institutional* dimension perpetuates religious ideas by imbedding them in the fabric of society. The *ritual* dimension demonstrates how the faithful engage in actions and behavior that define meaning for life and merge belief with experience and practice. The *experiential* dimension enables followers to express their feelings and experiences of extraordinary meaning. The *material* dimension facilitates concrete and tangible expressions of the sacred that enliven the five senses of touch, smell, sight, hearing, and taste.

While Smart's taxonomy underlines the religious dimensions of the sins, Gandhi's "seven blunders of the world" provide correlates to the cardinal vices that offer a clear and concise way to understand the moral motivations that unpack their correlative manifestations.[6] Thus, *lust* is better understood as Gandhi's "pleasure without conscience." *Pride* is "knowledge without character." *Greed* is "commerce without morality." *Sloth* is a form of "wealth without work." "Science without humanity" extends from *envy.* "Worship without sacrifice" is a form of *gluttony*. And *wrath* is made manifest as "politics without principles." Gandhi's blunders unpack and reveal the underlying *telos* (goal) of religious adherence to sin.

What Gandhi identifies as blunders, I have observed to be the hallmarks not only of the American dream of success but also as that which the vast majority of Americans worship and in which they place their faith. Together with Smart's seven dimensions of religion, these blunders reassess the religiosity of America's cardinal sins and propose a way to examine how the American quest for the good life has gone bad. The general structure of the analysis is outlined under the book chapter titles below.

Experience of the Good Life: Lust as Pleasure Without Conscience

Let's begin by examining lust as the *experiential* dimension of the American good life. The first chapter defines lust as the insatiable need for self-gratification and fleshes out how Americans embrace "pleasure without conscience." Among other things, this chapter focuses on the persistence of sexual assault (from the Boy Scouts of America to the Catholic Church to Hollywood up to the US presidency); the pervasiveness of the sex industry (e.g., in the forms of prostitution and escort services); the predatory practices of sex trafficking (e.g., from chattel slavery to mail-order brides to the current scandals involving Jeffrey Epstein and Ghislaine Maxwell and Sean "Diddy" Combs); and the proliferation and pornification of culture and technology (e.g., OnlyFans), sexbots, and the abuse of Viagra and Cialis. Taken together, this chapter shows how the unmitigated experience of lust not only drives but also orders the lives of Americans without any accountability or regard outside of our own needs and desires.

Institution of the Good Life: Greed as Commerce Without Morality

Greed represents the idealized *institutional* dimension of the American good life. "Commerce without morality" channels the energy and lifeblood of American notions of success framed within an economic context. Chapter 2 addresses the failed promises of economic and political theories, including "trickle-down economics," by investigating how these theories have been influenced by greed. This chapter analyzes the effects of these greed-driven policies, which often result in the rich getting richer and everyone else fighting for what is left. The chapter also analyzes how various greedy economic practices in the United States, such as retail therapy and corporate profiting from public goods, dictate the functioning of the free market economy, which often results in the loss of free will for many of its citizens.

Myth of the Good Life: Sloth as Wealth Without Work

Wealth often appears to be the greatest and most desired marker of success in the United States, yet the *myth* of the American good life is marked by the shallowness and superficiality of sloth, also known as "wealth without work." Chapter 3 illustrates how the myth of the good life is exemplified through the three white lies of legend, legacy, and the leisure class. As evidenced by the manifestation and impunity of white patriarchy and the evolution of a de facto class structure in the United States, the concepts of legend, legacy, and the leisure class help us understand how sloth not only has been accepted as a part of the American ethos, but that it is celebrated as a marker of success. The significance of slothful success involves the manipulation of both people and the economy to foster the American myth of getting "something for nothing."

Doctrine of the Good Life: Pride as Knowledge Without Character

Pride represents the *doctrinal* dimension of the American good life. "Knowledge without character" is a process in which Americans view the world through their own pride as the ultimate worldview. Americans take pride in themselves being doctrinaire by imposing quintessentially American knowledge production, ideologies, and policies without regard to practical considerations or the possibility of the veracity of the opinions of others. By analyzing how knowledge is produced, maintained, and privileged, chapter 4 surveys the ways in which the existential crises of higher education have legitimated the implicit bias and dehumanizing projects that pass off stereotypes as scholarship and hate as history.

Material of the Good Life: Envy as Science Without Humanity

The *material* dimension of envy makes possible the acquisition or realization of that which one otherwise would or should not be able to achieve or possess. With the human condition limited by various physical, mental, emotional, and psychological factors, many have developed a desire for omnipotence, omniscience, and omnipresence in the face of this human limitation. Envy—"science without humanity"—attempts to create the good life in ways the laws of nature otherwise would deny. Such is the depth and extent of the drive of material envy that science becomes our means to exceed the limitations of the physical and natural world by literally divining for ourselves that which nature has foreclosed. Through a critical survey and analysis of various scientific achievements and technological advancements like artificial intelligence and the atomic bomb, chapter 5 shows how science without humanity makes accessible—and necessary—a reality where the sky is the limit and one's desires can be fulfilled by any and all means necessary.

Ritual of the Good Life: Gluttony as Worship Without Sacrifice

Chapter 6 examines the *ritual* dimension of gluttony, revealing that, as a form of "worship without sacrifice," this deadly sin is best understood as a form of addiction in which our aesthetics, actions, and attitudes are oriented toward consumable goods. Governed by the desire of consuming not only food but anything that produces sensory satisfaction, we find ourselves bereft of any real substance that yields true human fulfillment or spiritual yearning. In the act of repetitive consumption, a crisis ensues when we cannot get enough to consume and the desire for more ultimately consumes us. Gluttony urges people to engage in the abuse and overuse of a wide variety of substances and activities in order to fulfill sensual desires, often creating negative behavioral patterns that cause more harm than good—not only to oneself but also to others. Put another way, whether one engages in the fetishization of wish fulfillment or the compulsive pursuit of conspicuous consumption, the only thing routinely sacrificed and disintegrated is one's very self and soul. Moreover, the repeated submissions to a given ritualistic behavior demonstrate that the suspension of both self-preservation and self-control can eventually lead to self-destruction.

Legality of the Good Life: Wrath as Politics Without Principles

When contemplating the *legalistic* dimension of the good life in America, wrath is the most glaring, obvious force at work in our culture and society. Despite lofty rhetoric to the contrary, the most enduring feature of societal power in the United States is the ability to amass and wield might against one's opponents and the subjugated in ways that are both self-assured and self-assertive. The most clearcut way to understand the role of wrath in American life is to equate it with the blunder of "politics without principles."

Chapter 7 exposes the ways in which the practice of law and order throughout American history—from civil rights (killing of unarmed persons, racial profiling) to equal rights (pay equity, voter suppression, health care) to human rights (borders, immigration, separation of families)—is often the legalization of wrath that undermines the justice that the law and its representatives are supposed to uphold. Without question, much of the rancor and vitriol rampant in society today is indicative of the spirit of wrath that avows "might makes right" in all human endeavors without any regard for compromise, much less compassion.

Ultimately, I engage my audience in the same way I interrogate myself—as a person in faithful pursuit of understanding the good life, and as a thinking person of faith who seeks a good life. However, this dual pursuit is often fraught with paradox, if not paralysis, located at the nexus of despair and disillusionment. In the end, this book offers no resolution by way of pat prescription or false hope, but rather offers a thick description of a moral predicament. If not critically and candidly delineated, this moral predicament will render our country and its citizens empty and soulless, hopelessly captivated and held captive by its sins and the arrogance of its ignorance posing as American innocence.

CHAPTER 1

Experience of the Good Life

Lust as Pleasure Without Conscience

Since its earliest evocations, conceptions of the *good life* have been rooted in the fleshly experience of satisfaction in a world filled with material, spiritual, and emotional want. This good life may be conceived in wildly varying ways, from gluttony to asceticism, but common to all is the dimension of fulfillment relating to what happens with our flesh. Moreover, the *good life* is a category that draws together the strands of pleasure and revulsion, morality and cupidity, carnality and spirituality, and then focuses them through questions of ultimacy, questions framed as a category of finitude. Put another way, the idea of the good life is deeply anchored in questions about what the content of human life—*our* lives—might be and ought to be. The nature of these ponderings shapes both the desires of human hearts and the lives driven by those desires.

Because desire is so intimately bound to fleshly living, it is also bound to the experience of pleasure. The experience of pleasure might be thought of as the fulfillment of desire, whether fleeting or life-shaping. To the extent that ideas of the good life are both motivator and consequence of desire, pleasure is its final validation. In fact, it might not be an overstatement to say that to experience the good life is to experience pleasure to the fullest. It is our desire to have pleasure enfleshed in a sensuous manner that affects our senses in such a way that lets us know that we are, in fact, alive. Though given to lascivious interpretation, this language of desire and satisfaction actually and more appropriately encompasses the entirety of human existence—the palpable joy of embracing a grandchild, the anticipatory delight of hearing the pop of a champagne cork, hearing the first notes of a favorite song at a lavishly expensive concert. Pleasure literally connects us to the intimacy and physicality that our souls must have. Of course, healthy physical intimacy and sex can also be experienced as transcendence, of living beyond our own bodies. However, as with all dimensions of human existence, this essential part of our humanity is open to the type of corruption that transforms something life-giving and affirming to that which is base and finally annihilating, as when desire and pleasure become reduced to lust.

Lust as an animating force reduces not just us as its subjects but others as its objects. When thus instrumentalized, pleasure comes at the expense of the flourishing of others and finally any claims they might have on us for empathy and compassion. This perversion of desire and pleasure has become the means by which far too many of us now live out an American dream masquerading as the good life, particularly the dimension of the good life related to fulfillment in romantic relationships.

For many movie fans, the romantic comedy *When Harry Met Sally* is the classic, contemporary American love story. The two title characters, Harry Burns (played by Billy Crystal) and Sally Albright (played by Meg Ryan), first meet as recent college graduates as they depart from the University of Chicago's campus headed to the Big Apple, having been paired up for the cramped, eight-hundred-mile drive by Sally's good friend and Harry's girlfriend, Amanda. The two pass the time by poking fun at each other and pushing the limits of their instant intimacy by arguing about men's and women's perceptions of romance and sex. While eating at a roadside diner, Harry comes clean: He finds Sally attractive. Not taking the bait and thinking that she is cutting him off at the pass, Sally scoffs at his sexual advance and accuses him of disloyalty to Amanda. Undeterred and driven by the logic of his lust, Harry suggests they get a motel room. This ultimately leads to the question that makes the film the classic it is—"Can men and women ever just be friends?"

HARRY: You realize of course that we can never be friends.

SALLY: Why not?

HARRY: What I'm saying is . . . and this is not a come-on in any way, shape or form, is that men and women can't be friends because the sex part always gets in the way.

SALLY: That's not true, I have a number of men friends and there's no sex involved. . . . You're saying I'm having sex with these men without my knowledge?

HARRY: No, what I'm saying is they all want to have sex with you . . . because no man can be friends with a woman he finds attractive, he always wants to have sex with her.

SALLY: So you're saying that a man can be friends with a woman he finds unattractive.

HARRY: Nah, you pretty much wanna nail 'em too.
SALLY: What if they don't want to have sex with you?
HARRY: Doesn't matter, because the sex thing is already out there so the friendship is ultimately doomed and that is the end of the story.
SALLY: Well, I guess we're not going to be friends then.
HARRY: Guess not.
SALLY: That's too bad. You were the only person I knew in New York.[1]

As a poster child for Freud's "pleasure principle," Harry remains undaunted by Sally's heartfelt rebuke and puts his ego into full drive. Despite Harry's overtures, their close quarters in a cramped car, and their heated dialogue, they don't have sex. Upon their arrival in New York, the would-be couple part ways on extremely unfriendly terms, with no guarantee that they will ever meet again and with Harry nearly losing his future soulmate forever. Yet, in spite of Harry and Sally's mutual antipathy, there is still an all-consuming curiosity about one another that somehow manages to survive the crass way in which Harry first reduced Sally to an object of his sexual desire. To be clear, this reduction is not just about a battle between the erotic (*eros*) and the platonic (*philos*); it is about whether the pleasure of human company and intimacy is doomed to end in destructive instrumentalization.

The movie's popularity and success offer a window into the manner in which love American-style is more often a conquest driven by unrequited lust rather than the pursuit of loving affection. Nonetheless, the film's story and sensibility have become a veritable Rosetta stone for interpreting heterosexual relationships. In this respect, it is interesting that the film is most renowned for a scene in a diner in which Sally fakes an orgasm.[2] Although she does this to dispel Harry's grandiose self-delusion of sexual prowess and performance, Sally's faking it also whets the lustful appetite and arouses the desire not only of the presumably sexually unsatisfied older woman sitting at the next table over, but also the film's vast audience members, to "have what she's having."

Harry and Sally's unlikely "lust story" is considered one of the most classic expressions of a good American love life. However, beneath the film's witty tone lies insight into the way that using others to fulfill deep-seated yearnings and carnal passions without Other-regard supplants love with lust, paving the way for human lustful desire to serve as a primary mode of experience of the American good life. Lust is the *experiential* dimension of the American good life. Overcome with the insatiable need for self-gratification at the expense of others, Americans have embraced lust as what Gandhi calls "pleasure without conscience," by allowing sensation to substitute for the sensual as the ultimate form of intimate satisfaction. Thus, the experiential nature of lust is best understood by reflecting on the differences between the sensory/sensuous and the sensual. Whereas "sensory" and the sensuous refer to stimuli perceived physically by the five senses—what one can hear, see, touch, smell, and taste—the "sensual" is how sensory stimuli channel human intimacy and create connection. To be clear, sensation and the pursuit of pleasure are central components of human sexuality, which is itself a moral good. It is important to distinguish between sexuality and its components as good versus lust as the seeking of the good gone wrong—that is, without consideration of the moral demands that our encounter with another in their full humanity places on us.

Religious studies scholar Ninian Smart's approach to the experiential dimension of religion is useful here. According to Smart, people who yearn for and seek to identify with religion want to experience ecstasy as an out-of-this-world, divine encounter that involves "the hope of, or realization of, *experience* of that world" (emphasis added).[3] Lust fits wonderfully in this conceptualization, if we allow ourselves to recognize how the primacy of physical embodiment and human sexuality functions as a "serviceable god" for many Americans; albeit superficial, it is nevertheless a sacred surrender to pleasure.[4] As such, lust in modern US life is governed by the relentless and often reckless pursuit of immediate pleasure as if it is one's intimate experience of the invisible, infinite divine. Stated differently, lust substitutes what is seen and felt for what is unseen and intangible. Lust is when libidinous satisfaction masquerades as the unique sort of transcendence that is experienced through self-fulfilling intimacy.

Ultimately, pleasure is felt but fleeting, leaving lust as its surrogate. A scholarly genealogy is necessary at this point to unpack this concept. The lust-filled body is sovereign and everything else is subject to it, because, as philosopher Maurice Merleau-Ponty asserts, "the body is the medium through which we have a world."[5] Philosopher Lewis Gordon builds upon this assertion by constructing a three-dimensional reality of what it means for one's body to encompass the world: seeing, being seen, and being conscious of being seen by others.[6] That which can be manufactured and made manifest governs one's passions, whether deemed problematic or not. Lust is the bodily appetite to encompass the world by apprehending what womanist ethicist Katie Cannon calls "erons"—the creative, powerful, and erotic energy that is present when we get what our souls must have.[7] Womanist theologian M. Shawn Copeland explains that rather than experiencing a mere craving, people ultimately want to possess the divine power as a way to enflesh this bodily yearning, for this not only enhances their capacity for joy and knowledge, but also provides them with a transformational experience.[8] Copeland invokes this concept of *eros* as embodied spirituality as a potential vision of human sexuality in its purest, most ideal form. Yet, in order to grapple with the intrinsic truth of how lust functions in our current era, it is crucial to look at the erotic from the reverse angle. In her classic essay "Uses of the Erotic: The Erotic as Power," feminist theorist Audre Lorde contends that American society and culture have thoroughly perverted *eros* as creative and connective power into "plasticized" or "pornographic" form.[9] *Eros* has been stripped of its power and depth of feeling and "relegated to the bedroom."[10]

Thus, embodied spirituality can be supplanted by erotic superficiality, which at worst leads to suffering of self and others and at best to numbing through the pursuit of sensation, effectively poisoning the very notion of *eros* by substituting lust for love and by supplanting the erotic with "a vision of sex as a fearsome and destructive force in human life."[11]

In the posthumously published fourth volume of his *History of Sexuality* series, entitled *Confessions of the Flesh*, French philosopher Michel Foucault expands our understanding of this fearsome, destructive force in human life by framing it as the embodied phenomenon straddling the divide between *concupiscence* (lustful desire) and *connaissance* (human awareness or enlightenment).[12] Foucault compels us to see how desire and knowledge are construed experientially both in and through the body by means of three modes: aphrodisia (the erotic desire for others), flesh (the corporeal connection to others), and sexuality (the orientation/ordering of desire and connections to others). If the body is the medium through which humans seek to experience what their souls must have, then aphrodisia, flesh, and sexuality are the modes by which the body meets those needs.

However, when devoid of meaning—that is, disassociated from seeing, being seen, and being conscious of being seen—the corporeal becomes prioritized over connection and the significance of the *eros* becomes nothing more than lust. This realization of the intentionality behind connection (knowing others) versus conceit (knowing one's desires) reduces what should be the subject of one's desire to the objects of one's lust.

Sexual objectification is the process whereby one sees, treats, and uses people—most often women and children—as objects, rather than seeing and regarding them as persons with their own desires and agency, persons with whom we want to be connected. Feminist philosophers Martha Nussbaum and Rae Langton have identified ten features that typify how love gets lost when observation becomes objectification: (1) *instrumentality*: the treatment of a person as a tool for the objectifier's purposes; (2) *denial of autonomy*: the treatment of a person as lacking in autonomy and self-determination; (3) *inertness*: the treatment of a person as lacking in agency, and perhaps also in activity; (4) *fungibility*: the treatment of a person as interchangeable with other objects; (5) *violability*: the treatment of a person lacking in boundary-integrity; (6) *ownership*: the treatment of a person as something that is owned by another (one who can be bought or sold); (7) *denial of subjectivity*: the treatment of a person as someone whose experiences and feelings (if any) need not be taken into account; (8) *reduction to body*: the treatment of a person merely as their body, or body parts; (9) *reduction to appearance*: the treatment of a person primarily in terms of how they look, or how they appear to the senses; and (10) *silencing*: the treatment of a person as if they are silent, lacking the capacity to speak.[13] Thus, when Harry meets Sally, the ordering of their lives is likened to offering up oneself as a sacrifice for another's appetite. And as soon as that appetite is filled, the use of the person is stilled, and as philosopher Immanuel Kant states, "the person is cast aside as one casts away a lemon which has been sucked dry. . . . A person becomes an Object of appetite for another, all motives of moral relationship cease to function. . . . A person becomes a thing and can be treated and used as such by everyone."[14] As it turns out, lust is not about what one should or should not do nor what one's responsibility is to another, but rather what one can get away with in terms of sexual desire and intimacy.

It is at this juncture that Mahatma Gandhi's indictment of lust as "pleasure without conscience" is indispensable. By moving beyond the rote reductionism of all erotic desire and sexual activity to lust (something that Gandhi himself was unable to do), understanding lust as "pleasure without conscience" suggests that our inquiry into lust as a facet of human existence should not involve merely ascribing it a pejorative label in an absolute, rigid manner, but rather that it should be an exercise of critical self-reflection. To this point, the self-aware person grapples with lust as an outgrowth of thoughts and actions that bespeak not merely all things sensuous in nature but, more importantly, how one's reactions to the sensual stimulation and sexual activity affect others in ways that are considered immature, selfish, reckless, predatory, and even dehumanizing.[15]

Gandhi's own thought and practice belied his efforts to counter lust. According to Ramachandra Guha, Gandhi's biographer, "all sex was lust" for Gandhi, who believed that "sex was necessary only for procreation. Modern methods of birth control legitimized lust. Far better that women resist men, and men control and tame their animal passions."[16] With such an understanding of sex, Gandhi sought to be in close association with the divine through ascetic practice, including a commitment to celibacy, which he practiced for over forty years. In focusing on overcoming personal temptation, he used young women, including his grandniece, to test his self-discipline by having them sleep naked with him.[17] In his own spiritual pursuits, Gandhi objectified these young women and made them instruments in his own efforts to connect with the divine. Even though Gandhi undoubtedly was aware of seeing others and being seen by them, by failing to be fully "conscious of being seen by others," he enabled that thing he was trying to avoid—lust—to enter into the equation of his relationships with these young girls. Even if he succeeded in maintaining the principle of "pleasure without conscience" from his own frame of reference, he seems to have fallen short of this ideal by discounting the conscience of these young women, whether in the present or in a possibly regretful future.

When people encounter something or someone that might bring them pleasure, the lustful individual frames their reaction around the following concerns: *Why can't I do whatever I want? Will this satisfy me? If it feels so good, how could it be wrong? If my intentions are good, how can it be harmful?* This brings to mind the commonly used phrase "guilty pleasure," applied to those things that simultaneously induce pleasure and some measure of guilt. As philosopher Simon Blackburn explains:

> If you feel guilty about one thing . . . it is not so easy to "vent" the feeling by feeling guilty about something else instead. Is it even possible? And what would be the function of this displacement—why should it help? If I displace my original guilt by feeling guilty about something else, such as having lustful thoughts, . . . why does that make me better off? I am still feeling guilty.[18]

Many people seem intent on pursuing any and all pleasure without compunction, restriction, or sense of moral accountability for their thoughts and actions. The avid pursuit of pleasure at all costs (even as a means to avoid pain) and by any means has led people to abandon their children and/or spouses, to avoid responsibility, to abnegate the law, to abdicate their life's vocation, and even to annihilate the lives of themselves and others, all in the vainglorious desire of "doing it" until they're satisfied. The corrective that Gandhi's definition imposes on the prominence of lust in modern life recognizes that yielding to lust, without some active use of moral reasoning that we might call conscience, establishes a state of affairs in which there is no sense of social responsibility or accountability in the pursuit and embrace of pleasurable activities, and leads to almost certain debasement and destruction on both personal and societal levels. As *New York Times* columnist and author David Brooks states:

> We use the word "lust" to refer to sexual desire, but a broader, better meaning is selfish desire. A true lover delights to serve his beloved. But

> lust is all incoming. The person in lust has a void he needs filled by others. Because he is unwilling to actually serve others and build a full reciprocal relationship, he never fills the emotional inside. Lust begins with a void and ends with a void.[19]

For our purposes, conscience serves as the wellspring of eternal truths and moral principles within each person. Conscience helps govern one's character, conduct, and compassion in a way that is rooted in right relationship and guided by a sense of obligation to do what is generally deemed moral, good, or right. The critical problem of lust is that choosing to prioritize pleasure above all other motivating factors in one's life short-circuits and ostensibly undermines any internal ability to monitor and govern oneself with an awareness of what is truly precious. Many people have convinced themselves that having sex for its own sake with whomever, whenever, and wherever can replace all of their needs for intimacy and connection. However, they eventually discover it was a poor proxy for both satiation and satisfaction, in that they were neither full nor fulfilled by it. That being said, the ultimate costs of succumbing to lust, of embracing pleasure without conscience, are quite high both tangibly and intangibly in terms of wasted time, squandered money, lost dignity, broken promises, damaged reputations, and physical, emotional, and psychological wounds to oneself and others. The greatest danger is allowing oneself to be seduced away from what is most life-giving and meaningful in human relationships, without caring about the consequences of endorsing pleasure without conscience.

When we consider the idea of lust for its own sake, there is probably no more iconic figure in twentieth-century Hollywood than Michael Douglas to gauge how lust has captured the fancy of the American mainstream. In the wake of the social transformations of the late twentieth century concerning gender and sexuality, few American actors have so easily and categorically embodied the collective, white, straight, male, Freudian *id* within the cinematographic American mindset as Douglas. On the heels of his bravura, award-winning performance as Gordon Gekko in *Wall Street* (1987), Douglas shifted to taking roles in more sexually charged movies, such as *Fatal Attraction* (1987), *Basic Instinct* (1992), *Disclosure* (1994), and *A Perfect Murder* (1998), among others. In these movies Douglas typically portrays an aggrieved, white, middle-class, middle-aged heterosexual man confronted by strong-willed, self-determined women who mirrored society's sea change in gender roles and sexual norms over the last three decades.

For instance, consider *Fatal Attraction*, in which Douglas portrays Dan, a wildly successful lawyer and happily married New Yorker who has a torrid extramarital encounter one weekend with Alex, portrayed by Glenn Close.

Notably, the filmmakers eschewed the moral turpitude demonstrated by Dan's adultery—a betrayal of his committed relationship—in favor of vilifying Alex, who is portrayed as mentally unstable and eventually transmogrified from the object of his desire into a murderous grotesquerie of a spurned woman. Yet the filmmakers' solution for the life-threatening repercussions of Dan's fateful fling was to have his wife fire the lethal gunshot to dispatch the burdensome woman and rescue her family.

Similarly, *Basic Instinct* revolves around Douglas's role as a police detective who has a passionate, reckless affair with a mysterious female author who is the prime suspect in a brutal murder case. At the time of the movie's release, Sharon Stone's character in the film was a lightning rod for heated controversy for feminists and LGBTQIA+ persons for being a brilliant, beautiful bisexual woman who was also a homicidal sociopath and a voracious sexual partner. Notably, it is the female character rendered as a modern-day succubus who robs the man of his moral agency, professional integrity, and even his common sense, and ensnares him with her potent sexuality. As his biographer, Mike Eliot explains, Douglas

> not only wanted *Basic Instinct*, he needed it. He knew he was chasing himself to catch up to the glory of his past, and he believed this was the movie that could do it. He was both very right and very wrong. The film would be a sensation, but all the heat and attention would go to his costar, Sharon Stone. One quick flash of her pubic hair would make her a star—if not at the morning-after water cooler, like Glenn Close in *Fatal Attraction*, then in the night-before wet dreams of the film's male viewers. And no actor could compete with that.[20]

Douglas next starred with Demi Moore in *Disclosure*, a story about high-tech corporate espionage and office intrigue masquerading as an erotic thriller film. Its main characters, portrayed by Douglas and Moore, are competitive coworkers at a computer company developing cutting-edge technology who were romantically linked in the past. At the heart of the film's storyline, however, is the issue of sexual harassment in the workplace as well as implicit gender bias within the power structure of corporate America. Once again, it is Moore—not Douglas—who is presented as the sexual aggressor who manipulates the system to topple her male colleague and advance her own nefarious schemes. As was the case in the other films, Douglas's lustful interaction with his female costar nearly ruins him, except for the helpful intervention by a heteronormative female character who is relatively benign and benevolent to him despite all his moral flaws. By the film's end, Douglas's character emerges from his lusty adventure not just unscathed but also unchanged.

In these ways and more, this spate of films starring Michael Douglas effectively captured the shifting social dynamics of cisgendered heteronormative sexual politics in late twentieth-century American society and culture around controversial issues like monogamy, marital fidelity, queer sexuality, sexual harassment in the workplace, institutional sexism, and divorce. In more ways than one, these films reveal a shift in public perception regarding sex, lust, and intimate relationships compared to earlier generations. Interestingly, later in his career Douglas played against type by portraying the world-renowned pianist Liberace in *Beyond the Candelabra* (2013), which explored the libidinal exploits of the closeted gay male celebrity.

Although it is well known for parading lust in the spotlight and in front of the camera, some of Tinseltown's most lewd and lascivious behavior is performed not by the actors who play the parts, but by the producers who wield the real power in the industry and control the lights, cameras, and action from behind the scenes. Cut to Harvey Weinstein. Formerly of Miramax Films and The Weinstein Company, he is alleged to have sexually harassed, assaulted, abused, and raped more than eighty women in the film industry over a period spanning thirty years. In spite of his virulent denials, the sheer weight of the accusations by his victims and evidence of his elaborate cover-ups ultimately led not only to his professional demise, but also to his worldwide public shaming through the emergence and efforts of the Me Too and Times Up movements.[21] Convicted in New York and Los Angeles on several counts of rape and sexual assault, he was sentenced to a total of thirty-nine years in prison. In 2024, his New York conviction was overturned on appeal because of the admittance of women's testimony of nonconsensual sexual encounters—included to demonstrate a pattern of behavior that often characterizes sexual violence—that were not included in the charges for which he was tried.[22] At the time of this writing, his Los Angeles convictions are under appeal.

Weinstein's salacious appetite for making unsolicited advances and demands is by no means unique to him. Rather, these advances and demands are representative of how powerful men in Hollywood like Weinstein get down to business, to such an extent that these perpetrators now see themselves as the innocent protagonists, flipping the script on their predatory behavior by claiming themselves to be victims of what is now referred to as the "Weinstein effect"—that is, to bemoan the fact that what was once merely "show business" is now "unjustly" a fireable offense.[23] In a stirring *New York Times* article, Rowena Chiu, a former assistant to Weinstein, addressed the professional and personal tragedy that hindered her willingness to break her silence roughly twenty years after he attempted to rape her. As Chiu recounted, she and another female colleague, Zelda Perkins, attempted to report Weinstein to the police as well as to senior Hollywood executives, but were summarily dismissed. According to her assessment, "the message was always the same: Who would ever believe us over the most powerful man in Hollywood?"[24]

So prevalent is the experience of sexual assault in Hollywood that Bill Cosby made light of this gross, old tradition in a now infamous comedy bit called "Spanish Fly" on his comedy album, unfortunately but tellingly titled *It's True! It's True!* Once heralded as being the most lovable American comedian, kid enthusiast, racial barrier breaker, and all-around upright guy, Bill Cosby served (only) three years in prison for conviction on a single incident of sexual assault, while he has lived under the larger spotlight of publicized sexual assault allegations ranging over five decades of his iconic career, beginning in the 1960s.[25] He has been accused by more than sixty women, who shared resonating experiences of being drugged by Cosby and then subjected to sexual assault, sexual battery, and rape.

Cosby's covert sexual misbehavior was by no means unknown in the industry. For decades, many deemed it to be a secret widely known but rarely discussed, until the infamous standup routine by comedian Hannibal Buress went viral in October 2014, finally making Cosby's conduct no laughing matter. As women across North America recalled their experiences, the viewing public was stunned and shocked not merely by the perversions of a Hollywood type, but by the reality inversion of the Cosby persona. If anyone served as a paragon of a virtuous person, loving spouse, father figure, barrier breaker on behalf of women in show business, advocate for educational advancement, promoter of morality among youth, and self-proclaimed moral exemplar, it was Bill Cosby. As TV historian Robert Thompson conveys:

> What [Cosby] was so well known for was playing these characters of great dignity, great gentle humanity and paternal qualities, and this is so completely the opposite. . . . It would be like suddenly hearing a scandal about Santa Claus. You've got a person who was really important in the history of the development of the medium; a person who was the star of one of the most popular programs of all time, who rescued a network; (but) someone who was playing (a character) completely at odds with the stories told by his accusers.[26]

The equally revealing and reviling stories of many other male celebrities uncovered in the last few decades—including of Michael Jackson, Kevin Spacey, R. Kelly, Woody Allen, Louis C. K., Matt Lauer, Charlie Rose, Roman Polanski, and Sean "Diddy" Combs—give a glimpse into what is going on behind the scenes with America's most successful celebrities to whom we pay tribute and whom we name as role models, success stories, and bearers of the American good life.

If we close the curtain on the world of entertainment and turn our attention to the political realms that govern our very lives and allegedly assure our inalienable rights, we quickly realize that they are no less subject to the same desires that reduce our nation's highest ideals to their basest instincts. No small number of our most regaled elected leaders and appointed government officials have taken liberties with, rather than fight for the rights of, the bodies of those whom they have vowed to protect. Furthermore, in the pursuit of their personal happiness, the legitimate causes and hopeful careers of these selfsame public officials have fallen prey to the predatory predilections of lust that they have perceived as part and parcel of the privileges of their positions. As opposed to securing the rights of the most vulnerable in American society, they have furthered their victimization.

At the top of the list is the forty-second US president, Bill Clinton, who in 1994 signed into law the Violence Against Women Act, federal legislation that provides juridical tools to combat violence against and provide protection for women. Clinton, nevertheless, participated in acts of gross abuse of power that ran counter to the spirit of that legislation and his claims to protect and support women's rights. Take the infamous 1998 Clinton-Lewinsky scandal, involving the then forty-nine-year-old POTUS and a twenty-two-year-old White House intern, Monica Lewinsky. After performing oral sex on President Clinton in the sanctum of the Oval Office, the "holy of holies" of the White House, Lewinsky's soiled clothing was eventually turned over to federal officials as evidence. The emergence of the scandal led to Clinton's national television address, during which he declared, "I did not have sexual relations with that woman, Miss Lewinsky." The attempt to blur the lines between oral sex as sexual intercourse among consenting adults and sexual misconduct as an abuse of presidential power led to a federal special investigation, charges of perjury, and ultimately to charges of impeachment being raised and passed by the US House of Representatives.[27] By avoiding any language of coercion and framing the encounter within the legal parameters of consent, the public presentation of this scandal was an attempt to minimize the ethical ramifications of the abuse of power by the president, and in so doing completely deflected any role of conscience on Clinton's part. Lust became a legal matter and not an ethical one.

In 2004, New Jersey Governor Jim McGreevey, with his wife standing at his side, came out as gay and announced he would resign the governorship after being criticized for appointing his secret lover, Israeli national Golan Cipel, as the state's homeland security adviser, this in spite of the fact that

Cipel lacked experience or other qualifications for the position. As a result of his confession, McGreevey became the first openly gay governor in United States history. Only in hindsight did he realize that living a lie not only cost him his credibility and career, but also compromised the very cause of gay rights that he could have advanced had he comported himself differently and stayed in office. Consider the full sentiments that McGreevey offered as he admitted his offense and resigned from office:

> I've never been much for self-revelation. In two decades of public life, I always approached the limelight with extreme caution. Not that I kept my personal life off-limits; rather, the personal life I put on display was a blend of fact and fiction. I invented overlapping narratives about who I was, and contrived backstories that played better not just in the ballot box but in my own mind. And then, to the best of my ability, I tried to be the man in those stories.
>
> In this way I'm not at all unique. Inauthenticity is endemic in American politics today. The political backrooms where I spent much of my career were just as benighted as my personal life, equally crowded with shadowy strangers and compromises, truths I hoped to deny. I lived not in one closet but in many.
>
> Ironically, the dividing experience of my sexuality helped me thrive in that environment. As I climbed the electoral ladder—from state assemblyman to mayor of Woodbridge and finally to governor of New Jersey—political compromises came easy to me because I'd learned how to keep a part of myself innocent of them. I kept a steel wall around my moral and sexual instincts—protecting them, I thought, from the threats of the real world. This gave me a tremendous advantage in politics, if not in my soul. The true me, my spiritual core, slipped further and further from reach.
>
> There were moments when the ripping misery of this life became too great, moments when I thought about "becoming gay" and all that that entails. One of these moments came after I lost my first race for governor to Christine Todd Whitman in 1997. I thought to myself: *You're at a fork in the road. You could give this up and be yourself. This is your last chance.*[28]

In November 2012, the highly decorated, West Point and Princeton–educated, US military leader General David Petraeus was forced to resign his position as CIA director, due to a scandal arising from the revelation of an extramarital affair with Paula Broadwell, author of Petraeus's biography *All In: The Education of David Petraeus*. Aside from the damage ensuing from the discovery of adultery that eviscerated the general's previously sterling reputation, the controversy escalated rapidly once it was revealed that, in direct violation of his role as the head of America's premier clandestine espionage agency, Petraeus had shared highly classified information with Broadwell. Even though nearly a decade and a half had passed between Clinton's impeachment and Petraeus's resignation, these events demonstrate how the lack of marital fidelity and self-control put an even more personally destructive spin on sexual politics at the highest levels of the federal government.

In their pursuit of pleasure and happiness, the road to American success leads many who have mastered the art of government deeper into closets, thus becoming morally compromised, and ultimately living a lie and experiencing a life that yields little good for themselves and those around them. Consider the behaviors of Eliot Spitzer, Democratic governor of New York (frequently soliciting prostitution), Congressman Anthony Weiner, Democrat from New York (sexting with minors), Congressman Mark Foley, Republican from Florida (sexting boys), and Republican Speaker of the House and Illinois Congressman Dennis Hastert (sexual abuse of boys). Their examples show that there is no legislative safe space, as all were involved in, implicated in, or imprisoned for sex scandals of various types.[29] Their power provided them with the privilege to position the objects of their proclivities or perversions close at hand for easy access that was seemingly above reproach. Rather than protect those who were supposed to be under their care, they abused the power invested in them by an unwitting majority who believed their persona and policies to be consistent with their personhood and practices. With these and other cases, the opprobrium that arose from powerful male leaders behaving terribly has been largely fueled by the sense of betrayal felt by Americans outraged that these politicians' obsession with their own private parts caused them to pervert and mishandle the public interests entrusted to their office. Though the origin of these lusts may be personal, the effects of this deadly sin extend way beyond the individual into the communal, collective, and cultural realms.

Then, of course, there is perhaps the most salient, egregious example of the objectification of lust in the political sphere, which occurred during Donald Trump's 2016 presidential campaign. In October 2016, when the national news media released a raw, uncensored recording in which he bragged to *Access Hollywood* television entertainment reporter Billy Bush (himself a nephew and cousin respectively to the forty-first and forty-third US presidents) about his efforts and ability to seduce a television actress. During his recollection, Trump let on that he was going to kiss the woman that he and Bush were about to meet, bragging, "I don't even wait. And when you're a star, they let you do it. You can do anything. Grab them by the pussy. You can do anything."[30] Alongside a running list of ex-wives, ex-lovers, and hundreds of deplorable, demeaning remarks about women's body parts and appearance, this act of self-admitted sexual assault was aired and shared broadly with the general public three weeks prior to his election as the forty-fifth president of the United States. And since then several female victims have described under oath instances of sexual violation and assault spanning more than thirty years. More than sixteen accusers have attested to the fact that central to their encounters with Trump were his gropes for power and pleasure at the expense of their pain, including his late ex-wife Ivana Trump, who charged in 1989 that she was figuratively "raped" by her husband and sworn to silence about any comment on their marriage without his approval; a thirteen-year-old girl ("Katie Johnson") who claimed she had been "repeatedly raped by Trump and Jeffrey Epstein"; advice columnist E. Jean Carroll, whose New York civil suit had him adjudicated a sexual abuser; and adult film actresses Stormy Daniels and Karen McDougal. McDougal had a ten-month affair with Trump during his marriage, and Daniels had a one-night encounter with him while his wife, Melania, was home caring for their newborn child.[31] The airing of his illicit encounters did not keep him from being elected. And in spite of the evidence of his sex crimes, abuse of power, and proving himself entirely devoid of conscience and unfit to hold the highest office of the land, Trump still insisted that "nobody has more respect for women than I do. Nobody. Nobody has more respect."[32]

Within recent memory, many of us will recall how the contentious Supreme Court confirmation hearing of Brett Kavanaugh reached a fever pitch as Trump and the GOP steamrolled Christine Blasey Ford and Deborah Ramirez's accusations of sexual assault. In the highly partisan context of the sworn testimonies of Blasey Ford and Kavanaugh, both became representative of their hugely divided constituencies: Democrats endorsed calls of #MeToo, #TimesUp, and #believeallwomen, and their Republican counterparts defended their nominee from a perceived liberal agenda against good, honorable, conservative men. Blasey Ford and Ramirez recounted their separate accusations of sexual assault against Kavanaugh against the historical backdrop of the Clarence Thomas–Anita Hill Supreme Court confirmation hearings nearly thirty years earlier. Despite the disgraceful mistreatment of Hill, similar mistreatment of Blasey Ford and Ramirez, and the credible claims of Kavanaugh's heavy drinking, Republican senators created a heightened sense of existential crisis for the preservation of Kavanaugh's successful nomination, due in no small part to the privilege rooted in his race, gender, wealth, and elite social network.[33] Much like the president who placed him on the highest court in the land, Kavanaugh's toxic masculinity and tawdry mediocrity (like Thomas before him) was minimized even with the nexus of sexual objectification, assault, and abuse of power—the lust for power enables acts at the expense of anyone who threatens their fulfillment. Even though Anita Hill's testimony gave rise both to a third wave of feminism and to the development of new policies regarding sexual harassment, nothing has really changed when it comes to granting access to a seat on the highest court in the land. Nothing illustrates better the irony of the ways lust has been institutionalized in the American landscape.

Whereas some have no qualms about using their power to fulfill their selfish desires, others prefer to have them facilitated by means of intercession. Such intermediaries not only provide the means by which people have their lust-driven needs met, but also serve as companions who participate in the perversions, thus forming a self-affirming and guilt-absolving community of like-minded, compromised cohorts. A case in point is Jeffrey Epstein, who cultivated the company and patronage of a pantheon of politicians, professors, princes, philanthropists, and billionaire businessmen, all of whom shared a common desire for coerced sexual behavior with attractive, often underage, girls. Transgressing boundaries well beyond the stash of photographs of nude young girls that he kept locked in a safe within his lurid "massage" room, Epstein created an actual network of recruiters charged with the task of luring underage girls to serve as "masseuses" in his various private residences in New York, Palm Beach, and Paris, at a New Mexico ranch, and on a private island in the US Virgin Islands. Epstein developed a worldwide sprawl of debauched playgrounds where he served as host to his mostly male business partners/quasi-friends who shared similar sexual appetites, including Britain's Prince Andrew, Donald Trump, Alan Dershowitz, Bill Clinton, and others, but these friends also included at least one woman, Ghislaine Maxwell, who facilitated many of these encounters.

More sensational than his predatory predilections is the unasked query that might have helped shed light on who, how, and why perverted men get and then use their power: How and why did Jefferey Epstein, a working-class college dropout and failed high school math teacher, become a pimp to princes, politicians, and presidents? Many observers have understandably questioned the size of Epstein's claimed billion-dollar fortune and just how it was amassed. As part of a police investigation in 2007, Epstein confessed his lust for young women upon receipt of a sweetheart "nonprosecution" plea agreement with federal prosecutors in South Florida. He subsequently pled guilty in 2008 to state charges of soliciting prostitution. Given his mysterious death in prison, we will never know from his own lips just how he gained the trust and assets of some of the wealthiest, most connected, and most powerful men in the world. If anything, their pedigrees would suggest that they would have been unlikely acquaintances of Epstein. Could it be the case that their own proclivities connected them with Epstein and made them fast and faithful friends? The question will likely go unanswered with certainty, in that Epstein fell on the sword, took a fatal hit for the team, and carried their shared secrets to his grave. Meanwhile, Ghislaine Maxwell, a former girlfriend and coconspirator with Epstein, was sentenced to twenty years in federal prison for her conviction on sex trafficking and the sexual exploitation and abuse of minors, demonstrating that such lustful depravity is not limited only to men.[34]

It is one thing when individuals act out in morally compromised, lustful ways in the shadows. But what about situations where organizations are either severely compromised or entirely corrupted without conscience in broad daylight? For example, take the case of the self-proclaimed "political, civil rights, and educational organization" known as the North American Man/Boy Love Association (NAMBLA).[35] Formed in 1978, the organization is unabashedly devoted to justifying, rationalizing, and promoting what it calls the adult male's "natural love for boys." Among its self-articulated reasons as to "why NAMBLA matters," the organization states that it provides the "primary voice testifying to the benevolent aspects of man/boy love," "a beacon of moral support for all individuals who feel a natural love for boys," and a "celebration of the dignity inherent in the natural love of boys."[36]

In a perverted twist of reasoning, NAMBLA rationalizes the act and experience of man/boy pedophilia by wrapping it in a cocoon of pseudo moral reasoning. For example, it proclaims a commitment to highlighting "injustices and harm in age of consent laws," arguing that "instead of protecting young people, these laws have done the very opposite," and telling us that "NAMBLA was formed in the belief that if people knew more about the actual nature of typical man/boy love relationships, . . . there would be less unjust scapegoating and persecution of boys and men who have such relationships." It argues that instead of protecting vulnerable young boys, age of consent laws "give undue power to those who already have power—police and prosecutors—while removing power from some of society's most vulnerable populations—notably, gay youth." Finally, it professes that "vulnerable people are better served by giving them more choices, not fewer. Children and youth can be made less vulnerable by giving them more options."[37] If nothing else, NAMBLA's warped spin is open for all to see; the organization lays bare its goals and designs. However, more offensive and egregious are those esteemed organizations and institutions that profess their outreach to youth to be firmly founded upon bedrocks of moral rectitude and virtue, while simultaneously hiding deeply rooted, systematically opposite modes of behavior behind their doctrinal statements of purpose.

The Boy Scouts of America (BSA) serves as a different kind of sad exemplar of institutional dysfunction. According to the *Los Angeles Times*, an investigative researcher hired by the BSA compiled a comprehensive set of records ranging from the years 1944 to 2016, referred to as the organization's "perversion files," that identify approximately eight thousand suspected abusers and more than twelve thousand victims in their initial tallies.[38] However, according to the teams of lawyers who have sued the organization on behalf of hundreds of alleged victims, these gross numbers are considered an underestimation of how many pedophiles and molesters actually infiltrated the Scouts' ranks over the years. Not only do the numbers exceed what has been reported, but the *Los Angeles Times* further notes that at least two of the BSA's insurance agencies refused to cover the payouts to the victims, contending that the Scouts could have prevented the abuse that resulted in these claims. Still claiming assets of more than a billion dollars, officials state that the pending liabilities and impending claims are significant enough for the BSA to consider filing for Chapter 11 bankruptcy protection. Doing so would amount to an escape route, through which BSA would bypass adjudication of any new molestation claims in state courts, channeling them instead into bankruptcy court to be resolved in pennies-on-the-dollar fashion alongside any other creditors. Yet, on their honor they claim that "the BSA is considering options to determine how victims can be equitably compensated while the organization continues with its mission to serve youth."[39] Over the last eighty years, even something as historically wholesome as the Boys Scouts, which aims to cultivate the good life by grooming honorable young citizens, has become tainted by the dingy tentacles of lust.

The manifestation of lust is not relegated only to the secular spaces of society but is also prevalent within the more "sacred" spaces of religion and religious organizations. In spite of various claims to morality—even moral superiority—many religious individuals and organizations also seem to lack strong convictions of conscience when it comes to pleasure, sex, and the tolerance of lustful expressions. Case in point, the Roman Catholic Church. The Catholic dioceses and parishes caught up in the Church's notorious sexual abuse scandal employed tactics similar to those applied by the BSA but on a larger scale.[40] According to CNN religion editor Daniel Burke, the sexual abuse in the Catholic Church is a global crisis, with the Church in the United States leading in these sexual offenses.[41] Also, it is generational, if the reporting of *The Boston Globe*'s "Spotlight" exposé and other news outlets are to be trusted. According to their own report commissioned by the US Conference of Catholic Bishops, within a twelve-month span from 2017 to 2018, the Catholic Church in the United States spent more than $300 million on costs arising from clergy sexual abuse, of which $200 million was issued as legal settlements. The 2018 *Annual Report on the Implementation of the Charter for the Protection of Children and Young People* also revealed that during the same twelve-month period the Church fielded an additional 1,051 "credible allegations" of sexual abuse of a minor by priests and other clergy. This number of allegations and their related costs were significantly higher than what was reported in previous years. The report attributes this to the 2017 victim compensation program adopted in New York state. That staggering number notwithstanding, the numbers will likely continue to rise in the years to come.

Even more hellish than the simple fact of these staggering numbers are the testimonies of how this experience affected the victims' perception of their moral exemplars. According to journalist Kathleen Megan, when a priest sexually abuses a child, the experience is particularly traumatic and shattering, and the effects are lifelong and drastic, given that an adolescent is being subjected to such abuse by someone who should be among the most trusted adults in their life.[42] Sexual abuse at the hands of a member of the Catholic clergy is unique, because the Catholic faithful believe that their clergy are endowed with the power of the divine, given that they serve as direct intermediaries to God.

According to psychologist Laurie Pearlman at the Traumatic Stress Institute in South Windsor, Connecticut:

> You will hear them say, it was like having sex with Jesus [and was akin to stealing] the spiritual security that another child might be able to find in a belief in God. To be used as an object to satisfy someone else's need is a profound violation of the self. It's not an act that is over and done with. [The child will wonder,] "Whom can I trust? Can I trust myself? Am I a worthy person or just an object to be used by others? Am I valuable? Can I control what happens to me?"[43]

Children who suffer sexual abuse at the hands of a priest are likely to keep the experience a secret, leading to depression, acting out, and delinquent behavior. They will likely experience shame, anger, fear, and a deeply rooted sense of betrayal and disappointment. Such abuse can be particularly devastating to boys, who might begin to question their sexual orientation as well as their spiritual connection to God. Leslie Lothstein, director of psychology at the Institute of Living in Hartford, describes how intense sexual abuse at the hands of priests is to its victims: "Many of the patients I've seen in therapy . . . talked about 'soul murder.' They felt as if something had been taken deeply inside of them in which the body wasn't hurt as much as the soul."[44]

While it has been glaringly apparent that the American tropes of lust have often been attributed to men, women also have been at fault. Most distressing in recent years are the rising accounts of female teachers turned sex offenders. Psychologist Anna Salter has described three types of women who sexually abuse children: those who abuse preschool-aged children, often their own, with sadistic violence attached; those coerced into abusive situations by a dominant male partner; and, most frequently, those who as teachers, counselors, coaches, or administrators sexually abuse students under their care. While the Associated Press has reported that women abusers make up about 10 percent of those in education who are charged,[45] there seems to be less outrage about their activity. While some are shocked at first when news of a female abuser appears, instead of being accompanied by disgust, for many the shock quickly morphs into intrigue, which can even become envy on the part of boys and men. One needs only to recall the 2023 film *May-December*, based on the Mary Kay Letourneau case, to understand the problematic nature of female sexual predation and the grooming and violation of boys under the auspices of nurturing and mentoring within the teacher-student context.[46] The film depicts the once-celebrated teacher (played by Julianne Moore) engaging in a sexual relationship with her twelve-year-old student, resulting in pregnancy, jail stints, and, astonishingly, a marriage nearly nine years later. Whether used to redeem the depravity of statutory rape or to normalize such female atrocities, these stories lend themselves to making invisible the victimization of the child, all to the glorification of a male fantasy wherein sex is power and men are the powerful ones, regardless of whether they pursue a woman or a woman assaults them. As Salter summarizes, "We underestimate female sex offenders," she said. "It's the old mythology. 'Boy, did he get lucky,' still rules."[47]

We are not so shocked by the debauched sexual exploits of the Cosbys, Epsteins, and Weinsteins of our nation because we deem them to be individual outliers and deviants; likewise, we have allowed the media to profile and mark certain institutions as singularly sinful—aberrations as opposed to norms. The deliberate actions of these individuals and institutions provide us with snapshots of the full extent to which the successful and privileged in America fulfill their desires and experience the power of their success. But it is not just these men who are the menaces, nor is it just the media's focused profiling of the Catholic Church, NAMBLA, and BSA that are to blame for the cultural acceptance of lust and its multitude of manifestations. The loss of conscience and proliferation of lust is equally rampant among everyday citizens—husbands, fathers, lovers—who are not considered especially successful and yet demonstrate similar thoughts and practices in the pursuit of lustful pleasures. How has this distorted cultural ethos been cultivated? What gave rise to it? How did we all to some degree tend to and nurture its creation and sign on to its proliferation as part and parcel of the American good life? Do these lustful men represent the realization of *our* wildest American dreams? Have they become *us*, in that their deviance is not a deviation from our norms, but actually a manifestation of *our* desires?[48]

The prevalence of pornography in today's internet age provides insight into why this is the case. Not only are there no longer any obstacles to its full accessibility, but abstaining from its presence is also not possible; like it or not, porn will eventually pop up on everyone's computer screen or in the spam folder of one's inbox. *New York Times* columnist and author Pamela Paul and psychology journalist William Todd Schultz have both identified how "pornification" is universal and unavoidable because porn is everywhere. Indeed, Schultz notes that "it is easier to get pornography than to avoid it. We have protected the rights of those who wish to live in a pornified culture while altogether ignoring the interests of those who do not."[49] Regarding this constant, unavoidable proliferation of pornography, Schultz states:

> Porn is . . . the new universally shared experience. The nation has been "pornified." It's everywhere. It's open 24/7. And chances are good, judging from research into internet habits, that before or after reading this post, a high percentage of you will visit a porn site. . . . The point is if you did, you are hardly alone.[50]

The abnormalities of pornification enable practices of abuse across the spectrum, which power and privilege make not merely perverse but often predatory. Whereas many people restrict their engagement with porn to vicarious, online sexual experiences, there are no small number of people who have the ability, means, and privilege to purchase sexual gratification with real human beings. For some, this includes participating in the consumer-driven sex work industry in its various forms. For others, this means contributing to the more insidious realm of sex trafficking, which most often includes the buying and selling of young girls and boys not just nationally but internationally.[51] In these transactional forms of lust, both the supplier and the consumer seem to be devoid of conscience and compassion for the harm done to others—particularly women and children. As an industry in which its workers are vulnerable to and consistently victims of sexual violence, the so-called "oldest profession" is a patriarchal trick or trap of sexism that presents itself as an optional trade. Technological advances have strengthened the perception that sex work is a matter of choice with minimal risk. Even during the height of COVID-19 crisis and its stay-at-home mandates, OnlyFans, a social media website where content creators share sexually explicit content that followers pay to see, became not only a viable option for sex workers but an optimal one by making this work virtual and, therefore, more lucrative and safer. Now sexually explicit content creators, whether through photos, prerecorded videos, or live streams, could chat with their paying fans and put themselves and their wares safely behind a paywall.[52]

But it all begins with people, and particularly with men whose power and/or proclivities have made prostitution the "oldest profession" for the dispossessed and vulnerable women who come to the trade by means of coercion, manipulation, and the reality that there most often is simply no other viable employment available. The expression "oldest profession" puts a veneer of respectability on sex work; prostitution is no more a "professional option" or "career aspiration" than sharecropping was to yesteryear's formerly enslaved African American or day labor is to today's undocumented immigrant. The words "trade," "profession," and "work" only divert scrutiny from the cruelty of those who create not only the demand and need for the sex labor, but also the unjust world in which women come to be trapped in it for lack of better, if any, life choices.[53] Prostitutes and other sex workers do not simply materialize out of thin air. Instead, they are the unfortunate products of a web of interlocking systems of abuse, coercion, and victimization, one spun and supported by a range of people who purchase and participate to various degrees in the spectrum of provided services. Lust creates prostitution and victimizes those who enter its workforce, whether by "choice" or coercion.

Understanding sex work as labor adds a level of complexity to the question of victimization and abuse. To better grasp this complexity, let's use the models of prostitution delineated by Carisa Showden in "Working It: Prostitution and the Social Construction of Desire," a chapter from *Choices Women Make: Agency in Domestic Violence, Assisted Reproduction, and Sex Work*. The three models she considers are sex as violence (abolitionist feminism); sex radicalism (sex positivity and empowerment); sex as work (most labor is exploitative). Here is a critique of abolitionist feminism for the ways in which it treats women as sex:

> In the abolitionist discussions, male sex workers are not considered relevant to the analysis of sex work. Perhaps one reason why they are neither pathologized nor deemed germane is that abolitionists (and others) simply assume that men can separate self from sex without being deficient in some way. It is the cultural code of what a woman is, of woman as sex, that makes women seem so pathological when they "sell themselves."[54]

Sex worker rights activists have pushed back against the focus on ending demand and call instead for changes to policies that improve safety and working conditions for sex workers. The "sex work as labor" camp would position this as a larger issue of capitalism, arguing that sex work is not the only labor that is sexually exploitative.

Sex workers are typically mined from places of misfortune, naïveté, and disadvantaged social circumstances. In her ongoing ethnographic research with former pimps, prostitutes, and prosecutors on how women become ensnared in the world of prostitution, Meredith Dank, a consultant at the Urban Institute's Justice Policy Center, discovered that women from all avenues and walks of life become prostitutes. For example, family members and close friends are often coerced into doing sex work in order to support their loved ones. Oftentimes, doing what they could to make the most money was what convinced women to move into prostitution. Dank's research found that "pimps find prostitutes from their [prostitutes'] friend groups. Social circles and home neighborhoods are more likely venues for pimps to scout than clubs or the internet. One in nine pimps surveyed said they recruit from schools."[55]

Intersectional victimization from structural racism, sexism, and classism create the circumstances in which many victims of sex trafficking experience emotional, physical, and sexual abuse *before* the trafficking, making them terribly attractive to predators and increasingly vulnerable to their manipulations.[56] As critical race theorist and former federal prosecutor with the US Department of Justice specializing in sex trafficking Blanche Bong Cook explains, "Traffickers profile for vulnerability and exacerbate preexisting trauma, all for the purposes of exploitation."[57] Vulnerability is the lynchpin of exploitation, and sex trafficking thrives on it. Traffickers are good at profiling and manipulating the vulnerability of their victims, and they work within a society that pledges allegiance to liberty and justice but does little to protect these victims.

In addition to profiling their targets based on their emotional vulnerability, traffickers are often masters of the "grooming process." Physical, emotional, and psychological abuse is designed to keep their "trade" in line, often beginning with romance, professions of love, and promises to fix credit and offer protection. After the original enticement, the grooming process escalates to controlling tactics that include rape and assault, threats of public shaming and exposure, threats to family members, threats to abduct and/or torture children, threats of deportation, social isolation, and withholding of food, money, or identification. Eventually the process cycles back to customized forms of seduction, emotional and "romantic" manipulation, encouragement of substance abuse, and other forms of exploitation designed not only to retain those already in hand, but also to get them to participate in the recruitment of other women and girls. In too many circumstances, the victims themselves continue to perpetuate the lustful system as they deceive and exploit others in the same way in which others took advantage of them.

Sociology of religion Peter Berger helps unpack what might seem incomprehensible to us or assumed to be voluntary on the part of these women is actually part of a sacralization process of a meaning-making life. According to Berger, within our sociological, world-constructing context, the most powerful people declare "I'll make me a world," to which others respond by believing that "this is the world that exists." In short, there are those who miss the *trompe l'oeil* intended by the mastermind, powerful world-creators, and in so doing come to see realities that are subjectively fashioned as objective truths. They undergo an internalization process whereby they come to believe fiction to be fact and thus proclaim: "I am a product of the world."[58] In this respect, the women, children, and range of nonheteronormative victims who fulfill the carnal desires of the powerful come to understand that this is simply the way the world is—a world without conscience in which men love sex, women in particular exist to please them, and women's work is tied to their bodies, which are made for men's pleasure. Simply calling prostitution (for example) the "oldest profession" promotes a reality in which this is the work that women not only do, but also are meant to do, and do well, seemingly by choice.

To numb the depression of this insufferable, internalized reality, sex workers, escorts, and also trophy wives and boy toys more often than not will turn to substance abuse (be it crack, meth, or opioid cocktails) and other means to dull the pain of the abuse and to get ready to work by lowering their inhibitions about sex. Furthermore, jurors, judges, and the public will readily recognize various forms of force and fraud, in which the victim is subjected to sensationalized forms of violence. Much less obvious, acknowledged, and detectible to them are the multitudinous forms of vulnerability, psychological manipulations, "head games," and grooming processes that sex traffickers use to control their victims. This is comparable to battered-women cases, where jurors are often reluctant to believe that a sex trafficking victim was unable to escape a situation in which she was physically mobile, in public without physical surveillance, or in contact with others. They often become preoccupied with the question of why the victim didn't just leave. The emphasis on force completely elides the psychological coercion pimps and sex traffickers effectively use to groom, socialize, control, and imprison their victims.[59] As Bong Cook explains, "Perpetrators create climates of fear through incremental layers of increased threats from seduction, to insult, and assault, all of which create a dehumanizing conditioning process designed to make victims feel completely helpless, dependent, and constantly panicked."[60]

Beyond a shadow of a doubt, lust results in the dehumanization and objectification of women via prostitution. As the pimp's property, a prostitute's very survival and worth are dependent upon and reduced to her performance of sexual acts. In an oddly similar manner, lust also conditions men to participate in their own self-objectification, by fostering and building upon the belief that their manhood and potent masculinity are inextricably tied to their sexual performance. Whereas anxiety about sufficiently selling the performance of sexual acts makes a prostitute dependent upon her pimp, it is performance anxiety itself that has come to make many a man dependent upon a little blue pill called Viagra.

Originally developed and patented in 1996 by the pharmaceutical company Pfizer to treat heart disease, Viagra was also noted for its ability to treat erectile dysfunction. Soon thereafter, the company began marketing and selling the drug for this purpose, which quickly led to billion-dollar annual sales. Competing pharmaceutical companies rushed to develop their own parallel products—Cialis, Levitra, and others. What for some is a miracle drug, America's tendency to celebrate excess has coopted. As Viagra aided men in their desire to rise to the occasion of on-demand sexual performance, likewise did the billion-dollar annual sales motivate Pfizer and its pharmaceutical competitors to devise ways to raise demand for the product among a larger pool of potential customers. Pfizer itself came under criticism around 2008 for its approach to advertising, using "Viva Viagra"—a play on the song "Viva Las Vegas"—as the theme for its campaign, and creating an online game called "Viva Cruiser" that clearly shifts Viagra from a legitimate treatment for a medical condition into the category of a party drug. Today, marketers have entered mainstream media outlets like CNN to sell generic Viagra to potential customers, who can receive an immediate prescription simply by calling an 800 number.[61] Under the pretense of sexual dysfunction, but in reality propelled by the pleasure principle, men of all ages have increasingly come to abuse the drug, and in the cases of some with undiagnosed heart conditions, even die from using it. Once upon a time, pornography provided men with the vicarious means through which to experience the pleasure and instant gratification of penis worship from a distance, by projecting their own identity onto the man performing the act in the scene. Now, rather than merely watching a porn star, these drugs allow men to become porn stars themselves, fulfilling their lustful desires without conscience. After all, as the commercials warn—or, some would say, boast—one needs to be certain to contact a physician if one's erection lasts more than four hours.

The lustful expectations and experiences of the good life in America have facilitated the pornification of culture through unconscionable acts of objectifying women, assaulting the vulnerable, and abusing people, power, and prescriptions. These exemplifications reveal not only the full potential of lust's destructive power, but also the deterrent to that power that exists to some measure or degree out of concern for the potential to be seen, caught, morally judged, or punished by others. Even as the examples provided thus far are reprehensible and unthinkable because they exploit humans or eliminate the humane, there is still a human response. This is to say, *actual people* are still present on both sides of these lustful equations—subject and object, viewer and performer. The grand unifier of all the examples of lust has been the fact that the people performing the acts could or actually have been caught with their pants down, have been held accountable in some fashion for their actions, have suffered the consequences, and have reaped what they have sown.

But what happens if one side of the lustful equation is eliminated entirely? What if there is no human being present who can be exploited or subjected to another's lustful actions or inclinations? If the humanity of other people is the obstacle to one's lustful desire, while their actual bodies are also the object of that same desire, what is the means by which to get what one's soul must have? Or, as Sartre puts it in his play *No Exit*, if "hell is other people," then why not just eliminate the problem entirely so that the true love story literally becomes never having to say that you are sorry and you can go about living the good life by having your needs met and your unfettered desires fulfilled?

As if an answer to a prayer, sexbots have been created in the image of many lustful desires. According to business journalist Patrick Knox, sexbots are "lifelike dolls [that are] so real you can't tell the difference. [It is as if they are] out of the film *The Stepford Wives* where husbands replace their partners with sexually subservient spouses."[62] The disruptive technological aim of this new but annually already over $30 billion industry is for sexbots to become anatomically indistinguishable from the idealized, fleshy human form and endowed with artificial intelligence that can discern human need. This is done in such a way as to satisfy desires and satiate human fantasy without having one's desires lost in translation. As Harmony, the top-selling sexbot manufactured by Realbotix, promises, "I have all the love in the world to give to humanity."[63]

Because no other humans are involved, no one can get hurt. Consumers can get off by turning on these inanimate instruments of inorganic intimacy, which function willingly in accordance with all their human owners' desires. And for many, that's bringing heaven down to earth. Getting what they say their souls must have, men claim sexbots represent the erotic feminine ideal—eternally young, never fat, well developed, submissive, adventurous, silent, insatiable, and capable of satisfying "her man" sexually. Further, sexbots also provide a virtuous service to consumers who yearn to experience intimacy and are in need of a substitute for social interaction, sexual gratification, and sex safe from STDs, pregnancy, and exploitation. While exploring the extent of sexual fantasy, sexbots provide consumers with robots that fit human nature and humane needs for intimacy. There are even those who claim that sex robots are not only acceptable but are appropriate, valuable, and even socially useful when they help someone overcome a disability, remove the obstacles of distance/separation from a partner or loved one, or simply increase pleasure and fulfill fantasy. Over the last few decades, the academic research of feminist theorists such as Donna Haraway ("A Cyborg Manifesto")[64] and Anne Balsamo (*Technologies of the Gendered Body*),[65] as well as expressions of popular culture with television shows like Syfy's *Battlestar Galactica*, AMC's *Humans*, and HBO's *Westworld*, and films like *Blade Runner* (1982), *Ex Machina* (2014), *Blade Runner 2049* (2017), and *Companion* (2025), demonstrate the numerous ways in which the female body has been reconceived and reduced to little more than a high-performance sex machine.

However, contrary to its (largely male) consumers' beliefs, this allegedly humane means of getting sexual satisfaction in reality does not exempt actual women from exploitation. Instead, the advent of sexbots takes the radical institutionalized sexist turn of concretizing women's roles and supplanting human agency by representing and/or replacing women as robots, functioning machines that deprive real women of any self-creativity not useful to the male scheme of things.[66] Women's health expert Susan Bewley brings the point home: "This is the idea that women are sex objects and should be constantly available for the pleasures of men. Researchers say such an outlook could lead to the further victimization of women and children."[67] Thus, the confluence of sex and technology has made gods out of men and turned women into their creation.

It is little surprise that ethicists across the globe are actively calling for an absolute ban on the continued development of sex robots because they represent a clear and dangerous disruption to social norms of human intimate contact. Human beings simply have not had time as a species to prepare for the possibility of their usurpation of substantive human contact and interaction. Robotics expert Kathleen Richardson argues that sexbots are intrinsically harmful to humans and pose a detrimental risk to society, contending that the technology involved in developing sexbots must center more around the ethical implications that sexbots have for the real-life construction of gender, particularly among women. In essence, her fear is that robots will get more love than the actual women they emulate because the robots will do whatever heterosexual men want actual women to do.[68] The development of sex robots thus further objectifies women and girls, reducing human empathy that can only be developed in a mutual relationship.

Conclusion

This chapter emphasizes how the good life as derivative of the American dream has been reduced to destructive operations of lust. So, while this chapter's litany of offenses might seem outrageous, outsized, and overblown, it functionally reflects a culture so eroticized that lustful individuals do not merely lack conscience, but also prefer that the object of their desire be unconscious as well. In the vision of the good life as part of the American dream, lust serves as a means not only to truncate, but ultimately to trump, the willpower and agency of the other person to the point of abolishing altogether their ability to say no. The outright fear of having desire frustrated, or even worse, rejected, induces such psychological anguish and misery that many would rather normalize and rationalize pedophilia, sexual harassment, sex trafficking, drug abuse, sexbots, pornography, and rape culture than accept the possibility or likelihood that their attentions and affections will be denied. It is truly astonishing to witness the lengths to which American society has gone to shield the often fragile, male ego from the perceived insult and injury of a desirable, albeit unwilling (and possibly even unconscious) sexual partner saying "no, thanks, I'm just not that into you," or "no thanks," or even a simple "no." The problem of lust in US society is that, regardless of what romance novels and soap operas might suggest, the erotic passions of one person should never abrogate the ability of another to negotiate their intimate dreams and desires on equal terms. This cultural fascination with lust takes the goodness of the erotic beyond its rational and often legal limits for the most selfish, shallow purposes of a few moments of pleasure that could potentially devastate lives forever.

The wrongs for one generation become the rites of passage for the next. Consider Brock Turner's sexual assault of an unconscious woman at Stanford University. In January 2015, two Stanford students witnessed the nineteen-year-old, freshman athlete sexually assaulting a young woman behind a dumpster next to a fraternity house. The district attorney's office said the victim, "Emily Doe," was taken to a hospital and treated for her injuries after she was found "lying on the ground unconscious, not moving."[69] After Turner was arrested and found guilty of three counts of felony sexual assault (assault with intent to rape an unconscious or intoxicated person, sexual penetration of an unconscious person, sexual penetration of an intoxicated person), he was sentenced to a mere six months in jail with three years' probation. Many critics denounced Judge Aaron Persky for his extremely lenient sentence, even as Turner's father complained that his son's life had been ruined by "20 minutes of action" fueled by alcohol and promiscuity.[70] Despite the physical abuse and dehumanization to her personhood, "Emily Doe" spoke out in court against the rampant injustices of the legal process, denouncing the trial, the sentencing, and the legal system's approach to sexual assault as irrevocably marred by elite white male privilege.[71] After her victim impact statement went viral and ignited public outrage, a recall effort resulted in Persky's removal from the bench. More than three years later, the survivor—Chanel Miller—identified herself publicly, thus encouraging rape survivors to feel that they were no longer silent and alone.[72] In her memoir *Know My Name*, Miller states that she intended to "reclaim the story of her sexual assault from both her assailant as well as the broader legal system."[73] Whereas Brock Turner serves as a textbook, personified example of collegiate rape culture, Chanel Miller struggles to reclaim her sense of self and personal humanity from her buried existence as "Emily Doe," the unconscious object of Turner's lustful abuse.

In the final analysis, American attitudes toward lust and sex reveal that a continuum exists between the fictionalized romance of *When Harry Met Sally* and the real-life horror of "When Brock Turner Met Chanel Miller." The toxic masculinity that motivated Harry's sexual objectification of Sally ultimately became the intoxicating masculinity that led Brock to assault the unconscious Chanel as his sex object. More often than we would like to admit, Harrys become Brocks, while Sallys become Chanels, and the only way forward is to absolve oneself through the acquisition of a sexbot both affordable enough for the common man and intricate enough to satiate all of his lustful desires. If the experience of the good life for some of our country's most powerful yields unconscionable actions such as those highlighted and discussed in this chapter, then it is little wonder that harassment and rape of college girls is often viewed as a natural social development of "boys being boys," whose future and further sex acts will subsequently be dismissed as "men being men."[74]

The ubiquity of lust within the broad sweep of American society and culture represents a feverish effort to sever from humanity the notion of being humane. Even as the post–World War II era witnessed the emergence of "the minority rights revolution"[75] that has advanced full and equal rights for all people regardless of race, class, gender, sexuality, ethnicity, and religion, this process of pursuing joy and pleasure as the apex of human flourishing fell deeper into corruption as each generation of Americans substituted love for lust. Because facets of political and cultural fundamentalism throughout much of American history have prompted explicitly prudish attitudes toward sensual behavior and sexual appetites, the only way for society to advance has required limiting, rather than liberating, the power of the flesh. In response to the successful gains of a more robust realization of gender identity, sex positivity, and sexual fluidity, the fundamentalist counteractive, a heteronormative, morally delimitating defense of the status quo, has created a social context within which freedom and fulfillment of the flesh is possible only within a moral vacuum. As a result, the movement toward the fullest expression of *eros* as embodied spirituality in our lives must reckon with the corresponding corrosive and corrupting nature of lust as a dehumanizing force.

The long-term quest to rehumanize our capacity and commitment to love will be difficult to bring to fruition. If we overlook how pleasure and conscience must go hand in hand to cultivate the ultimate experience of human intimacy, we will have difficulty escaping the terrible pathology of objectification and moving into the true passion inherent in our shared humanity. Until we address the impact lust has on the ethos of this country, instead of having a cultural understanding of the good life that is just, honorable, kind, and actually good, our vision of the good life will continue to be dictated and distorted by the powerful, whose consciences have often proven to be questionable when it comes to the pursuit of pleasure.

CHAPTER 2

The Institution of the Good Life

Greed as Commerce Without Morality

In 1994, the legendary hip-hop group Wu-Tang Clan released the song "C.R.E.A.M," employing an acronym for "Cash Rules Everything Around Me" as the title for what became an instant twentieth-century classic. Decades later, Robert Diggs (better known as the RZA), the renowned producer and de facto leader of the Wu-Tang Clan, announced one of the greatest marketing schemes that the music industry had ever witnessed. In March 2014, the hip-hop supergroup planned to create only one copy of a new album, *Once Upon a Time in Shaolin*, which would then be sold to the highest bidder. Discussing the forthcoming development of a single-sale collector's item, RZA told *Forbes*, "We're about to put out a piece of art like nobody else has done in the history of music."[1] *Once Upon a Time in Shaolin* represented a truly unique landmark. Aside from the excellent songcraft and expert musicianship reflected on the album's thirty-one songs, the album was encased within a hand-carved box, accompanied by a leatherbound book printed on 174 pages of parchment paper filled with lyrics and background information on each of the songs. No outsider ever heard the entire record, because all duplicates and prototypes had been destroyed prior to the auction, and the final copy had been stored within a vault in the Moroccan Royal Mansour Marrakech hotel.

The Wu-Tang Clan hired Paddle8, an online auction start-up company, to handle the sale of this one-of-a-kind album. Some Wu-Tang fans objected to the group's plan. A Kickstarter campaign was organized to buy *Once Upon a Time in Shaolin*, to keep it from "someone who has disposable millions" and for whom "it's just another shiny new toy."[2] That effort proved to be too little too late. On November 24, 2015, Paddle8 announced that the Wu-Tang Clan had sold the album. The $2 million price had been agreed to in May, but according to the press release, the parties "spent months finalizing contracts and devising legal protections for a distinctive work whose value depends on its singularity."[3] And the group wouldn't reveal the buyer's name. "This was very much a mutual decision," RZA said in an email, insisting that the buyer wanted privacy.[4] There was only one wrinkle: The buyer himself wanted to go public. Bloomberg revealed the buyer's identity as the now-infamous ex-CEO of Turing Pharmaceuticals, Martin Shkreli.

The son of Albanian immigrants raised in the Sheepshead Bay neighborhood of Brooklyn, Shkreli became fascinated by the Wu-Tang Clan's song "C.R.E.A.M.," with its often-repeated phrase, "Dollar, dollar bill, y'all!" Shkreli himself was simultaneously relentless and ruthless at making dollars. He made headlines in September 2015 for massively inflating the price of Daraprim—a lifesaving antiparasitic drug routinely prescribed to treat patients with HIV/AIDS as well as cancer—from $13.50 to $750 per tablet. Shkreli's profit-making moves were decried by many, including the 2016 Democratic presidential candidate Hillary Clinton. "Price gouging like this in the specialty drug market is outrageous," Clinton tweeted.[5] More remarkably, Clinton's Republican opponent, Donald Trump, also attacked Shkreli: "He looks like a spoiled brat to me."[6] Despite the stiff competition, the BBC wrote that Shkreli "may be the most hated man in America."[7]

RZA attempted to create distance from Shkreli, emailing a statement to *Bloomberg Businessweek* declaring that "the sale of *Once Upon a Time in Shaolin* was agreed upon in May [2015], well before Martin Skhreli's [*sic*] business practices came to light. We decided to give a significant portion of the proceeds to charity."[8] Hidden behind the nobility of RZA's statement—which solidifies Shkreli as the sole "bad guy" in the situation—is the story of *Once Upon a Time in Shaolin*, from production to purchase, as a tale of American greed, one in which there is broad rather than singular culpability. The focus of public outrage on Shkreli belies the ways in which greed, as an excessive desire for more at the expense of the public good, marked the Wu-Tang Clan's album's manufacture, preservation, and commercialization. That these things typically went unquestioned in commentary on *Once Upon a Time in Shaolin* reveals how greed has been made a guiding American virtue, one that permits all but the most flagrant abuses of wealth.

As the idealized *institutional* dimension of the American good life, greed is an organizing principle around which both public morality and institutional formations are clustered. So positioned, greed becomes both the impetus and pathway through which corrupted desire becomes capitalized lust. As suggested in the previous chapter, this transformation underlies the migration of the "good life" from one of generative virtue connected with communal vitality to selfish vice. While there are different ways to trace this migration, this chapter explores what Gandhi refers to as "commerce without morality," or put another way, when markets become religion. It addresses the failed promises of economic theories like "trickle-down economics," "creative destruction," and "neoliberalism" by investigating how greed has dictated these theories, and reveals how institutionalized greed results in the rich getting richer and everyone else fighting for what is left.

"Greed Is Good"

> The point is, ladies and gentlemen, that greed, for lack of a better word, is good. Greed is right. Greed works. Greed clarifies, cuts through and captures the essence of the evolutionary spirit. . . . Greed, in all of its forms—greed for life, for money, for love, knowledge—has marked the upward surge of mankind.[9]

In 1987 the film *Wall Street* embedded the phrase "greed is good" in the American cultural lexicon. Uttered by lead character Gordon Gekko, played by Michael Douglas, the phrase from the above quote captured the collapse of any meaningful connection between commerce, financial markets, and the common good. In its place arose a cultural ideology in which the highest good of our national economy was to foster opportunities for the "entrepreneurial" among us to create wealth for themselves that would, through some strange alchemy, "trickle down" for the benefit of society as a whole. In this schema, greed is not only a virtue but a moral imperative.

The appeal of *Wall Street* demonstrates the ubiquity of greed as a cultural ethos that cuts across racial, cultural, and socioeconomic lines during the fundamental restructuring of the American economy and society beginning in the 1980s. Recognition of this ethos invites us to think about greed as something more than just a personal vice.

The institutional dimension of US commerce is built upon a conscious and deliberate manipulation of deception, a veritable foundation of proven and known deception that serves as the means to promote self-interest and capital. The top 1 percent are considered the providential source representing what it means to be the ultimate American. Such a system, however, twists the perception of the 99 percent, the manipulated majority, who view their economic marginalization and misfortune not as the result of a system that is stacked against them but rather as due to their own lack of ability or social value. Political economists have repeatedly emphasized that "one of the most firmly entrenched myths of the American Ideology is that the

U.S. is a 'middle class society,' a 'land of opportunity' where anyone who works hard has the opportunity to achieve the standard of living which has made America 'the envy of the world.'"[10]

The very way of defining the middle class seems to benefit the rich. First, middle-class identification does not always align with income. Many identify with the middle class only aspirationally or morally. A kind of "false consciousness," as noted in Marxist theory, has the "middle class" confuse their socioeconomic state with claims of status and success, which does not necessitate being in the midstream of American wealth (because they are actually in the middle of the bottom 80 percent struggling to lay claim to the 20 percent of crumbs of the American wealth pie chart). They merely have the aspiration to be seen as if they are above the fray.[11] This false consciousness tricks them into accepting things as they are, keeping them from questioning things or fighting for change. This can range from simple misunderstandings to strong beliefs that support the status quo. People group themselves among the middle class not because they actually are but because they wish to be. Or they identify themselves as middle class based on certain attributes, habits, customs, and so forth that they have or wish to cultivate.[12] An income-based identification with the middle class, however, does not solve the problem. The Pew Research Center has defined the middle class as those who make between two-thirds and twice the median household income, which was a little over $70,000 in 2021.[13] According to this definition, making at least $47,000 would enable an individual to join the prestigious ranks of the middle class. Moreover, even if we take the middle class to be a legitimate status, there are indications that it is shrinking even according to its own criteria.[14] Meanwhile, the top 1 percent own about a third of American wealth and the very top 0.001 percent own approximately two-thirds of all US wealth, with the majority of the American population owning less than 10 percent.[15] As the money made by America's highest earners—think members of the Forbes 400 list, like Jeff Bezos, Elon Musk, Mark Zuckerberg, and Bill Gates—continues to balloon, traditional middle-class metrics smooth over the jagged edges of income inequality. How can $47,000 be the "middle," the esteemed space between abject poverty and the millions or billions gobbled up by the ultrarich? The numbers don't add up, hinting instead at the ever-illusory nature of an economic fiction in which the wealthiest of Americans live on the other side of a vast, expanding disparity.

The greed of America's most wealthy individuals has them eating up more than their fair share of the pie, while what the masses are being fed is an illusion that is empty of truth and that makes them believe that by claiming middle-class status they should be economically satisfied. The reality of "middle class" contradicts the term itself. The typical American has no clue what American wealth actually is, and even the superrich are often invisible to us because we are institutionalized to not question greed. So forceful is this institutionalized deception that what is blatantly obvious is, nonetheless, not believed. So strong is the middle-class lie that most fail to pause and realize that in fact they might actually find themselves among the one in five Americans who are unable to save any of their income, or among the majority (58 percent) of Americans who have less than $1,000 in savings, or among those who, in spite of their best intentions, are sinking further and further into debt due to credit cards, student loans, mortgages, car loans, and personal loans.[16] Whereas Americans may believe they are securing their status in the mythical middle class, their efforts to do so are actually designed to line the pockets of the ultrarich. Aspiring middle-class individuals and families further enrich the wealthy through the very debts they assume in pursuit of an ephemeral goal, one that not only does not exist in the first place but also is the result of the economic policies established and set in place by the ultrarich themselves. The very notion of the middle class is a ruse—a vague and vapid aspiration that serves as an ill-defined, ever-shifting nostalgic notion of what it means to have arrived in the realm of the American economy.

"Trickle-down economics," another debunked but doggedly believed deception, is no different. The economic zeitgeist of the 1980s was influenced by President Ronald Reagan's "trickle-down" economic policies. "Reaganomics" maintained a zealous commitment to supply-side economic theory and instituted a drastic reduction in government spending on social services coupled with oversized tax breaks for big business and the wealthy. The administration defined Reaganomics by the misguided proposition that so doing would result in overall prosperity. Media consolidation created a celebrity status for "businessmen" who fully exploited this newly emerging economy. The rise of the consumer credit industry placed a semblance of availability of this trickle-down "lifestyle" and cultivated a desire to achieve it. This "availability" masked the reality that actual wealth landed in fewer and fewer hands while the masses financed it by creating a substantial bill for our entire economy. The restructuring of the economy resulted in runaway inflation, massive government deficits, and eventually in the 2008 collapse of the US economy.

Well before the rise of the Occupy Wall Street movement circa 2011, economists, historians, political scientists, sociologists, and even legendary American satirists proclaimed aloud the flawed reliance on trickle-down economics. Indeed, so farcical is the trickle-down theory that its very name was the brainchild of the paragon of American satire himself, Will Rogers. During the 1932 presidential election between Democratic candidate Franklin D. Roosevelt and Republican candidate Herbert Hoover, Rogers quipped, "They [Republicans] didn't start thinking of the old common fellow till just as they started out on the election tour. The money was all appropriated for the top in the hopes that it would trickle down to the needy. . . . But he [Mr. Hoover] didn't know that money trickled up."[17] How is it that such jokes and lies become the theories and truths on which commerce relies, and in which people put their trust and faith? And how is it that both the 1 percent who own the majority of American wealth and the 99 percent who share the smallest remaining piece of the pie bought into the same bogus economic lie? How did this lie become a myth and obtain an unquestionable status not unlike religion?

In *The Market as God*, Harvey Cox deftly identifies the way that financial markets became an ersatz religion. Constructed through the sacralization of the materialist vision of the good life, the elevation of wealth and its realization take on not only a religious significance but also display the primary characteristics of organized religion. As preparation for writing his book, Cox read the business pages like a pastor reads Scripture in order to get a better grasp of the financial, material world. As he did so, he realized that the leaves of the market's lexicon "turned out to bear a striking resemblance to Genesis, the Pauline Epistle to the Romans, and Saint Augustine's *City of God*."[18] It is not, of course, the case that the business section focuses on divine matters; rather, its register and key jibe in strange harmony with religion. Both institutions—religion and Wall Street—are imbued with a sacred, shared, and inherent belief system, a set of rules and attitudes that are followed and practiced by a group in their pursuit of the golden promise and reward of life eternal. In the same way that religions are not merely systems of belief but also institutions that hold social significance in their power to confer ultimate significance, the American system of commerce literally enshrouds its operation as an expression of divine sovereign power. Capitalism has the ability to define free market ideology as an expression of the divine economy. These echoes of the divine economy are what anchors the idea that the making of a "good life" is mirrored in the current shape of American economic relations.

For example, Adam Smith's "invisible hand" became the hand of God in the US political economy as it governed the organic nature of the market process. This "hand" became shorthand for an expressive operation that is believed to be beyond the comprehension of ordinary people, yet has the remarkable distinction of fostering voluntary social cooperation. In the realm of nationalist politics, the economy has come to be situated as the overarching framework governing human existence and creating ultimate meaning, even if it develops a world that is incomprehensible. As Katrine Marcal puts it, the invisible hand becomes helpful in creating acceptance of the nonsensical:

> Morality represents the way we would like the world to work, economists tell us how it actually does work . . . and we don't need to know any more than that. This is how we move through life. And thanks to this, society is held together. As if by an invisible hand. That is the great paradox. And as we all know, God always speaks to us in paradoxes.[19]

According to womanist ethicist Katie Cannon, the elevation of the market as divine makes economics—like racism—an idolatrous religion and an abortive search for meaning. The institution of capitalism in the United States and its accompanying self-interest expressed as greed is a form of idol worship that glorifies predatory material relations that distort our understanding of what it means to be human. In referencing Christian ethicist George Kelsey, Cannon claims that this idolatrous institution does not merely call into question the nature of divine action but claims it as its own.[20] She also employs sociologist Oliver C. Cox's assessment of the institutional mode of capitalism and identifies seven ways in which the institution of US capitalism becomes the incarnation of greed and the essential fault line in the making of the United States.[21]

For instance, capitalism creates mutual networks of social relationships that are linked by national, economic motivation and dependence, and individuals often are unaware of how capitalistic norms are internalized. Cox pairs this lack of individual awareness with a deliberate exploitation. The ruling class claim to represent the masses but, in truth, promote the interests of the wealthy rather than the common good. The masked promotion of dominant interests is further exemplified through the use of diplomacy, global democracy, and even religious tolerance to serve the expansion of capitalism and its multinational corporate agents. These forces have worked together to produce imperialist effects in the developing world, where underdeveloped nations are the very foundation of capitalistic exploits in which their resources and residents are mere appendages to the larger enterprise of industrialization. The structural dynamism and imperialist penetration of capitalist control is such that the development of civilization is marked and marketed along a racial hierarchy that perpetuates a racist ideology. The exploitation of people of color, both domestically and globally, is a persistent feature of capitalist economic systems. Furthermore, capitalizing on its promises to provide primary essentials for life (e.g., water, welfare, care for the sick, protection, health, etc.) makes a savior of capitalism and presents capitalist endeavors as fulfilling the will and work of God in its attempts to serve as the sustenance of human life. As Harvey Cox reminds us, capitalism displaces religion, making politicians priests and plutocrats omnipotent.[22]

The capitalistic institutionalization process constructs a reality that manifests a sense of human belonging and relationship with something greater—the very things that many philosophers and theologians place at the center of being human. This sociology of knowledge is the power of cash, commerce, and capitalism to articulate the existential angst and agency to which individuals alone cannot give voice. For the everyday individual, these institutions are not understood as "commerce" or "capitalism"—lofty esoteric terms designed more for the discourse of policy and politics. Rather, they are internalized and engaged when we patronize a business or purchase stock in a corporation. Corporations are the institutions that guide us as we envision and craft a way of life that is perfectly designed for how we want to see ourselves and how we want others to see us. This reflective and projective "vision" often takes the form of branding—both the brands in which we want to be seen and the way in which many try to "brand" themselves.[23] Overtly and covertly, capitalism fashions our tastes, our aspirations, and our emotional, physical, social, intellectual, and even spiritual experiences. The economy offers us a home in which we can not only take up residence but also discover our extended family and corporate identity. Our vision of the "good life" becomes bound to company brands and our performance as consumers.

Capitalized commercial greed becomes affixed to our very real appetites and perspectives. Our identity formation and socialization are thus situationally determined by where we place our capital or beg for a line of credit. Corporations promise that our purchases will create advantages that will change our lives—whether it is our utilities, what we drive, what we wear, or what we eat. We are led to believe that commerce is the only means to bring *good things to life* (per General Electric):

Coke provides *the real thing*
American Express urges that we *don't leave home without it*
Burger King lets you *have it your way*
Mercedes Benz—*the best or nothing*
Lexus is committed to *the relentless pursuit of perfection*
Women should buy L'Oreal *because [they're] worth it*
Nike says you should *just do it*
Pepsi is *the choice of a new generation*
Sprite commands you to *obey your thirst*
Some things money can't buy, but MasterCard is for *everything else*
Samsung tells you to *do what you can't*

These slogans entice us to claim alignment with them as a way of meaningfully ordering our lives. Questions arise, yet go unanswered: "How can I be sure of these hyperbolic pronouncements?" or "Why and how can a product represent my values?" and, ultimately, "What am I being sold and how am I selling out in the process?" Corporations concern themselves less and less with the actual goods and services they offer (which is, after all, the substance of their slogans) and more with shaping perceptions of what people want. Their products produce meaning for us and their services shape our conceptions of who we are. While we seek the abundant life, which our ideal economy convinces us exists for each of us, we find it difficult to understand, internalize, and combat the ways that "cash rules everything around me." We are affected by this reality in at least five ways: **c**reative destruction, **r**etail therapy, **e**conometric egoism, **a**ccounting for public goods/accounting for the public good, and **m**ortgaged futures (CREAM, borrowing from the hip-hop song that opened the chapter).

Creative Destruction

"Creative destruction" refers to the economic theory that promotes the dismantling of long-standing practices in order to make room for more innovative means of increasing productivity. It is founded upon the assumption that disruptive technologies should be developed to shake up and displace existing enterprises. Rather than aspire for economic equality and equilibrium, destructive development is the driving force behind a model that destroys anything in its path so as to promote economic growth. First coined by economist Joseph Schumpeter and inspired by Karl Marx, now encapsulated by Mark Zuckerberg's slogan "move fast and break things," this process of change, innovation, and novelty at all costs is presented as an evolutionary good that displaces outdated, traditional models, revolutionizes the market, and keeps economic forces in motion. In the economic world of creative destruction, the new is better than the old and outmoded, and sophisticated developments that lower costs, increase productivity, and drive profits are progressive inevitabilities.

As is inherent in the term "creative destruction" itself, inventive means are sought to destroy what currently exists, resulting in winners and losers along the way. These profit-creating, technological disruptions foster no small degree of social striation, abandonment, and disequilibrium. Who would have thought in the late 1930s, with the advent of the automated grocery store checkout, heralded at the time for its potential to foster easy payment and efficient inventory, that seventy years later America's workers in a range of industries would face the threat of being rendered redundant by advances in robotic and artificial intelligence? As but one example, the grocery store clerk/cashier—the most common and enduring job opportunity for workers across the employment age, race, gender, and regional spectrum—is currently confronted by the challenging reality of a technological obsolescence that could very possibly both upend the $800 billion grocery industry and affect or even void more than 7.5 million entry-level employment opportunities.

In the wake of creative destruction, concrete livelihoods and actual lives are often destroyed. The casualties are many and the winners are few. And when all is said and done, one has to wonder to what extent creatively destructive economic strides should be facilitated and taken for the sake of corporate profit when this progress comes at such a corresponding cost of individual life and living.

Retail Therapy

Whereas "creative destruction" has more to do with the profit side of the market economy, the second, and possibly most popular, way in which CREAM creates meaning in Americans' lives is through their participation as consumers at the intersection of culture and commerce. In particular, take the consumerist trend known as "retail therapy." For many Americans, it feels almost natural to shop or spend in order to feel happier, to lift spirits, to reverse a sour mood, or to provide a sense of control, reward, or accomplishment on a down day. Indeed, so goes the cliché, "when the going gets tough, the tough go shopping!" Or as the character Rebecca Bloomwood proclaims in the 2009 film *Confessions of a Shopaholic*, "When I shop, the world gets better, and the world is better. But then it's not, and I need to do it again."[24] Indeed, most people rarely stop to ask for an explanation why they should act this way, caught up as they often are in the behavioral imperative to "shop until you drop."

Therein, however, lies the economic greed and power that retailers exert over people by means of this phenomenon of retail therapy, belied as it is by its seemingly beneficial and restorative moniker. For however much retailers promise or promote the reflexive reaction that shopping is the answer to all that ails their oft-targeted female demographic, in fact they are not concerned with fulfilling actual consumer needs so much as "creating wants." This is to say that businesses of all types—corporations, retailers, resellers, internet marketers—are heavily invested in compelling shoppers to spend on, and acquire, almost mindlessly, goods of all types for which they have no intrinsic need, but nonetheless feel compelled to think that they want and cannot live without.

Econometric Egoism

W. Edwards Deming's perhaps apocryphal adage "In God we trust. All others must bring data" has long served as a doctrine for statisticians, a principle of professional standards, and a stance of steadfast commitment to objective, dispassionate methods of research and analysis.[25] More recently, however, some of America's largest and most profitable corporations, such as Google, Meta (formerly known as Facebook), and Amazon, have coopted it as a cash cow credo. These companies, along with many others, thrive and profit off individual, personal data that they collect free of charge in their sales transactions in exchange for providing some type of service, or often simply in an unwitting manner.

Critical to their method is the ability to profit from such consumer information in an economics of desire and control—a mode of "econometric egoism" in which corporations analyze the inordinate amount of data consumers quantitatively provide them in order to maximize their profits. Econometrics involves analysis of economic statistics and data so as to devise theories and approaches to sales and marketing. In the current internet age, the econometric data is also "egotistical." It is individually self-driven and solipsistic. Through internet sales, consumer activity, and "clickbait," the computer-consumer does not merely submit their conscious needs and wants for immediate delivery and gratification, but also reveals their subconscious, unrealized, and imagined desires for future analysis and economic fulfillment.

Accounting for Public Goods and Accounting for the Public Good

Through their attempts to coopt or comingle private market transactions with public services or public goods, corporations often masquerade as arbiters of goodwill when they are actually robbing the public of its access to and benefit from renewable resources.[26] These public goods are products that people can use or consume without diminishing or depriving their availability to others, such as public services and utilities; this includes natural resources such as water and air. Motivated by greed and the desire to create new markets and sources of revenue, corporations and businesses are increasingly attempting to privatize public goods, particularly renewable natural resources, so as to package and sell them back to consumers for whom they should be readily available. These businesses rob resources and commercialize that which should be held in common for the benefit of their own personal prosperity and bottom line.

This corporate capitalization of public goods extends, in unforeseen ways, to the realm of humanity's inalienable right to natural resources. Throughout the course of human history, for example, farmers would naturally and logically harvest, save, and reuse seeds from season to season. In recent decades, however, a handful of biotech companies—DuPont, Bayer, Dow, Monsanto, and Syngenta chief among them—have managed to corner and dominate the American agricultural seed market. A Supreme Court ruling in 1980 determined that seeds were no longer considered a living entity, which released seeds from protection from the granting of patents. As a result, agricultural biotech companies began manufacturing specific, patent-protected, genetically modified seed products designed in ways that increase farmer dependence upon them (e.g., inherent pesticidal resistance and dependency characteristics), while simultaneously mandating at the time of purchase that farmers sign agreements promising not to save or reuse the seeds from season to season. The granting of patent protection rights has allowed biotech companies to generate farmer reliance upon their specific, genetically modified seed products, while also requiring them to purchase them anew annually. The result is an upending and unraveling of farming as a traditional profession and way of life, along with the impoverishment and financial imprisonment of farmers, due to monopolized, higher seed prices and increased agricultural dependence upon the biotech companies' pesticidal products, which the seeds themselves are manufactured to require in order to grow and flourish.

Therefore, it is little wonder that dystopian businesses, such as the bottling of water and even air, are skyrocketing. As corporations have polluted the world by taking advantage of relaxed environmental regulations to increase profit, they now produce profitable, if not sublime, solutions for the health and resource crises for which they are largely responsible. If the current trend continues, all natural resources and public goods—human rights, public health services, education, social services, etc.—will eventually be privately owned and administered, with only the historical assurance of additional public peril and private profit.

The greed that drives profiting from the control of public goods is only one aspect of this market problem. Another is problematic profiting from various goods and services deemed *for* the public good—its health and well-being both individual or social. For example, consider the deadly opioid crisis that has affected every corner of this country. Members of the wealthy Sackler family and their privately owned company Purdue Pharma were at the center of this drug crisis that ravaged the United States during the early decades of the twenty-first century. The CNN Politics website aptly stated, "The worst drug dealers in history are getting away with billions."[27]

The Sacklers literally made billions of dollars over several decades from their company's relentless marketing and often ruthless distribution of its infamous OxyContin medication. Prescribed opioids helped unleash the horrific epidemic that destroyed countless lives and wreaked unimaginable havoc upon families and communities across the nation. In a particularly poignant observation, Zachary Wolf notes that whereas "back alley drug dealers go to jail when they get caught, [c]orporate boardroom drug dealers can hide behind bankruptcy and keep most of their billions when they get in trouble."[28]

There is no question that Purdue Pharma broke the law. In fact, representatives of Purdue Pharma admitted in sworn testimony to criminal wrongdoing in both 2007 and 2020. In 2007, when the company first admitted to misleading regulators as well as the general public about the safety of OxyContin, it agreed to pay $700 million as part of the settlement of a lawsuit brought in Virginia. However, instead of curtailing its corrupt and callous business practices, the Sacklers pressed even harder to expand the profit margins, even if it meant putting themselves in further legal jeopardy. During the intervening years, roughly four hundred thousand Americans died from their addiction to the opioid painkillers that had become Purdue Pharma's stock in trade. Meanwhile, the family used a modicum of their vast wealth to underwrite public philanthropy. In the thirteen years between Purdue Pharma's first and second criminal settlements, the Sacklers were busy reaping billions in profits from the company and then secretly stashing their funds while never having to apologize or accept responsibility for their medicinal malfeasance.

Mortgaged Futures

In many instances in the US economy, corporate moguls, financial magnates, and even entire industries profit on the premise that Americans are too irresponsible or ill-informed to protect their economic self-interests, count the costs, manage their own money properly, or know when they are being sold a false bill of goods. As if profiting from people's present predicaments and problems was not bad enough, corporate executives have many Americans mortgaging away their futures under the premise that only in doing so can they have a secure life or live the American dream. The issue at hand is not the notion of "good debt," but rather examples of "bad debt" such as exorbitant student loans and financially perilous home mortgages. All debt involves risk and exposure, in that a percentage of your future worth and income is apportioned to current property and expenses. Debt is considered "good" if it represents a financial burden undertaken for things that will accrue value in the future. On the other hand, bad debt accrues for something that holds no future value, or even worse, for something that will decrease in worth or lose value. Most acute, however, is the present-day manifestation of debt-inducing greed through economic phenomena such as usury and predatory lending, Ponzi schemes, and "too big to fail" bank bailouts, which reveal the capital offenses of corporations at the excessive expense of the American people.[29]

In the most impoverished neighborhoods in urban America, there are three institutions that routinely mark most street corners: a place of worship to offer hope in the midst of despair; a liquor store to dull or numb the pain of life; and a payday loan operation to proffer a quick financial fix at a long-term cost. Be it Advance America, Cash America, or Dollar Financial, to name but a few, these poor man's banking establishments are underwritten and financed by some of the country's largest financial institutions, such as Wells Fargo, Bank of America, and JP Morgan Chase, which provide up to three billion dollars of credit to the industry as a whole.[30] As the only form of credit available for the many low-paid workers and families whose income falls short of meeting daily and weekly expenses, payday loans are offered at some of the highest interest rates, making them not only one of the nation's most expensive forms of credit, but also a necessary fiscal evil for bridging the paycheck-to-paycheck gap. A commonly offered 18 percent interest rate for a typical two-week payday loan borrowed against the future earnings of a yet to be received paycheck equates to an astonishing annual percentage rate of almost 470 percent. No matter how much they are promoted as quick fixes for short-term financial concerns, these stopgap loans are predatory in that they are designed to entrap the millions of impoverished individuals and families that are compelled to take them in a continuous borrow-now-pay-back-later cycle.

But poor, underemployed, and working-class households are not the only ones going broke while enhancing the profits of the biggest banks. Even those attempting to purchase homes through the help of mortgage lenders have found themselves entrapped in a ruined reality of false financial hopes and promises. The US subprime mortgage crisis that precipitated the Great Recession of 2008 was the culmination of overeager banks offering high-risk, ill-conceived, and overextended home mortgages to naïve borrowers, all of whom were literally banking on an unrealistic increase and indefinite continuation of a housing-price bubble that was bound to burst. When it inevitably did burst around 2008, the event vanquished the nation's economy and millions of homeowners held exorbitant mortgages borrowed against vastly overvalued properties. It took the better part of a decade for the national economy to show signs of recovery. Yet, most affected individuals and families never recouped their losses, leading to immediate and long-term futures bereft of financial hope, security, and comfort. Despite the overt financial manipulation of unwitting, yet faithful, citizens, the normalization of institutional corporate greed compelled Washington to rescue Wall Street and to abandon Main Street in the process.

The $700 billion congressional Toxic Assets Relief Program (TARP) bailout funds compensated the "too-big-to-fail" banks and the corporate executives that had perpetrated the disastrous mortgage fraud in the first place. As opposed to being held accountable for the manner in which they preyed upon their clientele, the bailout ultimately allowed the banks to use taxpayer funding both to shore up their failing institutions and to pay their leadership grotesquely high salaries and bonuses. The US government leveraged the nation at the expense of the affected Americans it vowed to protect. Most continued to struggle in the aftermath of the devastatingly greedy financial mismanagement of the big banks, institutions that enjoyed a huge bailout at the expense of America's taxpayers.

In a climate so driven by institutional greed and lack of responsible governmental oversight, it is little wonder that Ponzi schemes like the one perpetrated by the late Bernie Madoff have been able to deceive even the wealthiest in American society. Shortly after the recession and the bottomed-out big-bank buyout in 2009, Madoff pled guilty to fraud, money laundering, and other crimes connected to his oversight of one of the largest fraudulent financial pyramid schemes in US history. Convicted of defrauding investors of more than $50 billion over a two-decade period and ultimately sentenced to 150 years in federal prison, Madoff came to exemplify the 1920s financial swindle named after Charles Ponzi, its originator and founder. Ponzi promoted his scheme with an initial $1,800 investment in the Securities Exchange Company, which he created; Madoff's scheme began with an initial $5,000 investment. In the Madoff and Ponzi cases, thousands of people, numerous charitable foundations, illustrious investors, large banks, pension funds, and business start-ups came either directly or indirectly to entrust and invest their money in the supposed financial prowess and reputation of these two men, who ultimately betrayed the trust of investors from all walks of life, including their closest friends and family. Teacher pensions, celebrity portfolios, international banks, and nonprofit assets and holdings were among the victims of these Ponzi schemes.

Ultimately, both schemes collapsed when investors panicked at the onset of an economic meltdown and wanted to retrieve or make good on their investments, only to realize that these financial swindlers had literally "made off" with their portfolios and life investments. There were numerous expressions of doubt from expert financial analysts and individual skeptics who provided proof that there was simply no way that a legitimate multibillion investment fund, unregulated by the Securities and Exchange Commission (SEC), could operate out of a small storefront operation with a handful of employees generating false trading records and bogus monthly investor statements on an antiquated dot matrix printer. Nonetheless, people repeatedly ignored the warning signals that these schemes were too good to be true, because their greed (or desperation) led them to entrust their assets and stockpile their investments in an illusory institution formed by fraud and fated for forfeiture.

The mere hope of wealth or affluence and its attendant materialism creeps through our society, and greed becomes aspirational. Money is access, power, and celebrity, and the opportunity that attaches itself to these things. Greed is the good made evident in the CREAM that rises to the top. It is not even the cash itself; it's the currency of attachment to something that is both greater and elusive. The social recognition of self-worth will rise because powerful people cannot go unnoticed. Suddenly this is rare air, the soft bigotry of low expectations. In the final analysis, Bernie Madoff is proof not merely that figures like Gordon Gekko really do exist, but that the truth is actually much worse than fiction. Greed may not be *a good*, but it is good to have by virtue of the fact that it is rewarded, divorcing good intentions from good results. To have a good life requires that one have goods. Greed does not require that people be good to be on top; if they have the goods, the capital, they become more than mere mortals. They become institutions and virtual gods in and of themselves. The question is then what happens when the money, wealth, capital, and resources collect at the top of the economic market. To answer this question, we look next at neoliberalism as a case study to learn what really happens when greed dictates not only the collection of wealth but also its economic (non) distribution.

The Global Takeover of Neoliberalism

The emergence of neoliberalism with its emphasis on macrolevel transformations in finance, modes of production, and governance, all with global origins and reach, is a prime concern in terms of how the ravages of greed have been normalized within modern society. Most work on neoliberalism tends to be ahistorical, lacking the specificity and attention to content, context, and even chronology that accurately demonstrates a sense of historicity even as it attempts to describe and dissect transhistorical trends. Since the turn of the twenty-first century, scholars, mostly on the Left, have employed the term "neoliberal" to denounce contemporary capitalism and inequality.[31] Neoliberalism is sometimes used as a name for the deregulatory and antiwelfare policies of Margaret Thatcher in Great Britain and Ronald Reagan in the United States and their successors. It is sometimes a loose description of an orientation toward the market and a faith in market-based solutions to social problems. It is most often a synonym, usually pejorative, for right-wing or conservative economic programs. In the work of many scholars, neoliberalism is also a totalizing term that blurs geographical distinctions. It has been used variously to describe public policies promoting free market forces and limiting the reach of the state in countries as divergent as the United States and Zambia, and as the basis for the strengthening of an oppressive state apparatus in nations as diverse as Chile and China.[32]

Many influential theoretical works on neoliberalism share one underlying premise: Change happened from the top down. Economic elites and their political allies, with the support of right-wing think tanks and research centers, engineered a neoliberal "turn" or "takeover" in the 1970s and 1980s that effectively restructured governments to preserve the interests of capital by deregulating financial markets, weakening labor power, cutting taxes while imposing austerity and antiwelfare policies, and privatizing education, housing, and social services. Neoliberals valorized the market and delegitimated the public sector as inefficient, corrupt, and sclerotic, even as they used the power of the state to spur financialization and restructure tax policies in service of the financial sector. In the most familiar version of this story, the triumph of a neoliberal agenda illustrated the ability of capital to capture the state, political parties, and other institutions of civil society to advance its agenda.[33]

This top-down concept of neoliberal triumphalism, laden with the theoretical trappings of Marxist political economy, has been most associated with the work of David Harvey, an urban geographer who, despite being one of the most widely cited scholars in the social sciences today, has had, until quite recently, surprisingly little influence among urban and political historians. His book *A Brief History of Neoliberalism* has become the dominant if not de facto account of neoliberal ascendency in our time. Harvey's analysis relies on a powerful (but, as shown below, oversimplified) distinction between two ideal types of political economy and governance. One—the social democratic—prevailed from the Great Depression through the early 1970s. Social democratic regimes promoted prolabor policies, strong economic regulations, state-funded economic development, and a robust system of social welfare. The second—neoliberal—took form in the years following the global economic shocks in 1973. Neoliberal regimes were increasingly oligarchic, with a commitment to untrammeled capital, economic austerity, and financialization.[34]

Harvey's framework is both ahistorical and reductionist. For example, his premise that a social democratic order prevailed in the period from the Depression to the early 1970s has been undermined by the revisionist work of historians and other scholars of the New Deal and post–New Deal American politics. Scholars of race and gender have focused on the limited scope of the American social welfare state during the supposed heyday of liberalism, particularly its underpinnings in a system that created a two-tiered set of social policies that subordinated or excluded African Americans, Latinx persons, and women to the outsized advantage of white men. Economists and labor historians have emphasized the fragility of worker protections and unionization, particularly during the Cold War years, as corporations consolidated power and bankrolled a campaign to market the ideology of "free enterprise." Urban historians have pointed to the deep illiberalism of urban whites, particularly around questions of racial equality in housing, workplaces, and schools. Political scientists, sociologists, and historians have detailed the growing influence of probusiness conservatives, the religious right, anticommunists, and the resilience of a "small government" libertarian discourse in the post–World War II era. If social democracy was weak at best in the United States, then the post-1973 period seems less discontinuous than Harvey and his school of thought might suggest. The emphasis often placed on chronology by historians is not trivial in the context of understanding neoliberalization. Indeed, it is impossible to understand the depth and persistence of market-based policies and political skepticism toward the welfare state that theorists of neoliberalism see emerging newly in the 1970s and 1980s without realizing that social democracy was always weaker than its most fervent supporters and passionate critics believed.[35]

Most work on neoliberalization begins its analysis at the national or international levels, through the global workings of financialization; the maneuverings and machinations of global institutions like the International Monetary Fund, the World Trade Organization, and the World Bank; and the rise of the Anglo-American political right in the 1980s. Neoliberalism appears as an insuperable force swooping in from beyond, rather than as a process shaped and sometimes constrained by local political actors, community organizations, and social movements. Neoliberalism, as historian Julia Ott argues, "is not a historical actor itself. We should not treat 'neoliberalism' as if it possessed a predetermined historical trajectory or an essential nature." We thus need to consider its specificity. Neoliberalism was as much local as transnational. As countless politicians, activists, policymakers, and citizens shaped neoliberalism, they did so by sometimes limiting it, sometimes reinforcing it, and sometimes adapting it to their own agendas, such as school reform, economic "empowerment," or community economic development. Neoliberalism, especially as a key feature of globalization, has been both deeply contested and always incomplete.[36]

Wendy Brown posits neoliberalism's evolution from political theory to political ideology and then to a dominant rationality within a political culture that, in her words, "figures citizens exhaustively as rational economic actors in every sphere of life."[37] In accounts of the rise of the New Right, a range of political languages and ideas (among them consumer rights, homeowners' and property rights, meritocracy, entrepreneurialism, individualism, and freedom) are crowded under the umbrella of modern conservatism that, seen from another perspective, could be read as symptomatic of the penetration of neoliberal values into US political culture.[38] While neoliberalism germinated among conservative activists and intellectuals and found its staunchest support on the political right, it gained broad assent across the political spectrum. The Democratic Party in the United States, much like its center-left counterparts in Britain's Labour Party and in many European socialist parties, came to embrace market-oriented policies, austerity, and privatization, and to varying degrees enacted policies that undermined trade unions, weakened the social welfare state, and rationalized probusiness initiatives as necessary.

There is a great need for work to understand the position of Democrats and socialists who embraced neoliberalism. Some centrist Democrats applied the rather vague term "neoliberal" to themselves in the 1980s.[39] Ever since the Reagan Revolution following the 1980 election, the previously unforeseen political realignment of white evangelicals has garnered the attention of scholars and journalists.[40] Neoliberalism became a "dominant rationality" precisely because it could not be confined to a single partisan identity.[41]

The extent to which many prominent theorists of neoliberalism either downplay or ignore the ongoing significance of race, racism, and the creation of the modern American metropolis as a cultural milieu in which capitalism has been most fully realized is utterly alarming. Urban geographers David J. Roberts and Minelle Mahtani have criticized their field for separating rather analytically questions of race and neoliberal political economy, arguing instead that the two need to be considered as "co-constitutive." Neoliberalism, they insist, is more than a "socioeconomic process that has racial implications." Instead, "neoliberalism modifies the way race is experienced or understood in society."[42] When thinking about the evolutionary transformation of numerous urban centers such as New York, Atlanta, Boston, Chicago, Cleveland, Detroit, Miami, Houston, Los

Angeles, New Orleans, Seattle, and San Francisco, it is fairly clear that the American city has long been a large-scale living laboratory for austerity, governmental decentralization, and market-based responses to urgent and inexorable public problems such as affordable housing, criminal justice, public health, employment, and education, and whether such problems have been addressed (or not) for more than a century.[43]

Neoliberalism shaped the opportunities, the politics, and the everyday lives of Americans across racial and ethnic divisions but had a disproportionate effect on urban people of color because of the entanglement of race with economics. Race has also been central to how Americans constructed citizenship and understood the "moral benefits" of markets in every conceivable sense. One cannot understand such neoliberal phenomena as the privatization of social housing without understanding the racialized history of American housing markets and their role in constituting different categories of citizenship. One cannot make sense of the intensification of antiwelfare and procarceral politics—and the belief in the "discipline of the market"—outside of other disciplinary projects such as the racial stigmatization of welfare and criminal justice. One cannot discuss the challenges to publicly funded urban spaces without considering the racialized perceptions of who used and who was entitled to public spaces.[44]

By both its supporters and detractors, neoliberalism is usually considered an economic policy agenda, but a strong case can be made for its theological underpinnings. For instance, critical theorist Walter Benjamin once famously asserted that "a religion may be discerned in capitalism—that is to say, capitalism serves essentially to allay the same anxieties, torments, and disturbances to which the so-called religions offered answers."[45] The renowned economist John Kenneth Galbraith noted that neoliberal laissez-faire economics is actually built upon theological grounds. Even though economic downturns are still followed by upturns, fewer people benefit from them. As a result, economic crisis is an everyday reality that permanently affects all levels of our lives. The logic of downturn helps make sense of what is going on, as the economy shapes us more deeply than we had ever realized, not only our finances and our work, but also our relationships, our thinking, and even our hopes and desires. Religion is one arena shaped by economics and thus part of the problem but, as Joerg Rieger shows, it might also hold one of the keys for providing alternatives, since it points to energies for transformation and justice. Rieger's hopeful perspective unfolds in stark contrast to an economy and a religion that thrive on mounting inequality and differences of class.[46]

In *Neoliberalism's Demons*, Adam Kotsko argues that neoliberalism is much more than an economic theory: As a complete worldview, it presents the competitive marketplace as the model for true human flourishing. And it has enjoyed great success: From the struggle for "global competitiveness" on the world stage down to our individual practices of self-branding and social networking, neoliberalism has transformed every aspect of our shared social life. Neoliberalism's appeal is its promise of freedom in the form of unfettered free choice. But that freedom is a trap: We have just enough freedom to be accountable for our failings, but not enough to create genuine change. If we choose correctly, we ratify our own exploitation. And if we choose incorrectly, we are consigned to the outer darkness—and then demonized as the cause of social ills. By tracing the political and theological roots of the neoliberal concept of freedom, Kotsko is attentive to the intersectional dynamics of race, gender, and sexuality at play here. More than that, he accounts for the escalation of right-wing populism by arguing that, far from breaking with the extant paradigm of neoliberalism, mainstream society is actually witnessing the doubling down on neoliberalism's most dangerous and destructive elements.[47] As Simone de Beauvoir writes in *Ethics of Ambiguity*, "someone told a young invalid who wept because she had to leave her home or occupations and her whole past life to get cured, the rest has no importance. But if nothing has any importance, she answers, what good is it to get cured?"[48]

Kotsko's book suggests a rethinking of connections between intersectionality and neoliberalism and go a step further to demonstrate how considerations of race, gender, sexuality, ethnicity, class, religion, and nationality play a role in urban policymaking. In the United States, it has been virtually impossible to separate structural arguments about market activity, exploitation of labor, and privatization of capital from moral, political, and cultural frameworks that create, reinforce, and perpetuate racist, misogynist, elitist, homophobic, transphobic, and xenophobic ideologies and inequalities.

There are fairly stark and frankly scary examples of how intellectual ambiguity and ideological promiscuity can lead our society and culture astray. As an economic policy expert working at Demos, a progressive policy research think tank, Heather McGhee recalls how, circa 2010, budget deficits were rising at an alarming rate. "The Great Recession had decimated tax revenue, requiring more public spending to restart the economy," McGhee recalls, but "both the Tea Party and many in President Barack Obama's inner circle were calling for a 'grand bargain' to shrink the size of government by capping future public outlays and slashing Social Security, Medicaid and Medicare. Despite the still-fragile recovery and evidence that corporations were already paring back retirement benefits and ratcheting down real wages, the idea gained steam."[49] The "idea" in question was austerity. Although more formally enshrined and enacted as a cost-cutting policy initiative by the UK's

Tories during David Cameron's tenure as British prime minister, austerity quickly became a benchmark of Anglo-American conservatism. Embraced on this side of the Atlantic by a vindictive GOP intent on undermining Obama's presidential agenda and championed by the predominantly white, quasi-populist Tea Party movement, austerity proved to be a successful weapon for the Right. Adherents publicly proclaimed the language of fiscal responsibility while harnessing the dog whistle politics of white grievance and attacking the so-called undeserving poor. Despite the warnings of diehard progressives and grassroots activists, many of whom were instrumental to President Obama's earliest electoral victories, the administration favored the same lousy neoliberal economic theories, often voiced by some of the very same bad actors who precipitated the Great Recession in the first place.[50] Once implemented, the austerity measures imposed by the Republican Party led to the 2012 shutdown of the federal government and across-the-board spending cuts to public programs, and essentially brought the legislative function of the federal government to a standstill for the remaining six years of the Obama presidency.[51] As economists and policy wonks now admit, the measures created a jobless recovery accompanied by a slow and steady yet markedly unequal era of economic growth that hurt Americans of every walk of life.[52] In an even more ironic twist of fate, as failed businessman and false self-proclaimed billionaire Donald Trump bulldozed his way to a previously unthinkable 2016 presidential win, he quite literally capitalized on the general public outrage and mistrust of both Washington politics and Wall Street economics fomented by decades of failed right-wing economic theories (neoliberalism included) as his pathway to electoral victory.

Conclusion

While public attention and outrage has increasingly turned toward corporate greed, the American ethos that "greed is good" runs deep and continues to structure the American economic enterprise even in the face of grievous harm done by late-stage capitalism. While economists continue to rely on failed economic theories, arguing whether corporate greed is contributing to inflation, corporate profits have hit record levels as everyday Americans struggle to put food on the table or fill up their gas tanks, much less to find and maintain affordable housing as the American dream of home ownership becomes further out of reach for younger generations.

One might wonder if it is even possible to find contentment in our current economic reality, or is saying "that's enough" seen as the most contemptible constraint? As this chapter has attempted to make clear, America faces a "subprime morality" crisis. Like the subprime mortgage crisis of 2008, nonworking billionaires can go bankrupt but still make bank, and banks can break the market but still be made whole. The excessive expense and impulses of the American economic enterprise drive our notion of free will in a greedy market. Those who make loan-shark arrangements see themselves as indispensable, while the borrowers, who are not making living wages, are nonetheless willing to risk their lives with death-dealing odds, with some virtually mortgaging their souls. As the organizing morality of our institutions, this subprime morality has become sublime. And when the market becomes god, greed becomes our religion. For instance, there is a scene in *1923*, the prequel to the hit television series *Yellowstone*, from the episode that aired on January 1, 2023 (season 1, episode 3). Cara Dutton (played by Helen Mirren) is watching her husband, Jacob Dutton (portrayed by Harrison Ford), shave his face in the morning with a straight edge razor. She tells him she still enjoys watching him even after forty-four years of marriage. "You could watch me too, I suppose," she tells him. "You know it's all the rage now. Women shaving—their legs, beneath their arms." Jacob quips, "Interesting fad, to be sure." She replies, "I wonder what that says about us as a species. I mean it's not as if women were running a straight razor down their legs a decade ago. They invented a razor specifically for women when no need for one existed, then invented the need. As if selling razors to half the population wasn't enough." Jacob looks at her and responds, "It's greed. That's it." Cara replies, "Exactly. That's exactly my point." Keeping the Duttons' conversation top of mind, the terrible genius of the American economy is that the creation of an insatiable need inevitably leads to the establishment of an inescapable norm.

The context for this discussion is that it takes place the morning after a range war has started between sheepherders and cattle ranchers, with Jacob Dutton directly in the center of it. Dutton owns the largest ranch anywhere in Montana, and the only ranch that extends into the nearby mountain range, where the only edible grass for grazing still exists during a drought that has wreaked havoc on all the grasses across the region. He has willingly shared this area with other cattle ranchers, but has refused to help any sheepherders, whose sheep eat the grasses down to the roots. When sheepherders trespass his ranch for grazing, he and his family come upon them, and a fight ensues. Dutton captures the main perpetrators and leaves them on their horses with nooses around their necks tied to a tree. Four of the five hang when left there, while only one, the sheepherder's leader, escapes. With this as context, Cara concludes the discussion about razors with a touch of unconscious irony considering the vast expanse of land the Dutton family has accumulated and controlled over the years for a relatively small family who extend mercy capriciously and malice copiously. With a touch of prophetic prescience, Cara rightly notes, "It'll be the thing that ends us. Greed will be the thing that kills us all."[53] Indeed, Cara, indeed. When all is said and done, that might just indeed be the case.

CHAPTER 3

The Myth of the Good Life

Sloth as Wealth Without Work

Today, there is no greater marker of success in American life than wealth. However, the myth of the American good life is undercut by the shallowness of sloth, or "wealth without work." Ripped from the pages of American success stories are veritable cheat sheets, moral maxims, and notable quotables of "how to work smarter not harder," "how rich people don't work for money, money works for them," and "how to make others do the work for you." Many of us are taught from an early age that "leisure" is a direct benefit of wealth, a right that the well-to-do have "earned" through having been entrusted by God with vast fortunes that they will dole out for the good of society in acts of *noblesse oblige*. Of course, this "leisure" is not considered sloth even though many of the beneficiaries of such wealth do very little work on any given day. Instead, a familiar depiction of sloth is as a central character flaw of the vast multitude of Americans who are intractably identified as impoverished, people of color, foreign-born immigrants, and/or female (and heaven help those who represent all these realities simultaneously!).

This chapter illustrates how the myth of the good life is exemplified through the three white lies of *legend*, *legacy*, and the rise and lure of the *leisure class*. These three white lies have converged over time, as the manifestation and impunity of white-collar crime and the evolution of a de facto class structure in the United States show. The significance of slothful success involves the manipulation of both people and the economy so as to foster the American myth of getting "something for nothing" through the exploitation and disposability of others.

In the wildly popular HBO dramedy series *Succession*, the ultrawealthy yet chronically unhappy Roy siblings squabble over their crumbling media and entertainment empire, and jockey for the affections of their monstrously manipulative mogul father, Logan Roy. As the title suggests, the central premise of the series is that when the tyrannical patriarch faces his own mortality, he confronts the even more daunting problem of choosing a successor from among his disappointing and dysfunctional offspring to assume control of his vast conglomerate. When *Succession* explores the lifestyles of the ultrarich and shameless, the characterization of the Roys is much more akin to comedic TV series of the past couple decades like *Arrested Development*, *Gossip Girl*, *Schitt's Creek*, and *The White Lotus* than the 1980s prime-time melodramatic soap operas like *Dallas*, *Dynasty*, *Falcon Crest*, and *Knots Landing*. Taken as a whole, these characters are wantonly despicable yet also painfully relatable, and the descriptive tone is an unusual combination of funny and unsettling, with varying degrees of narcissism, paranoia, neurosis, cynicism, sociopathy, and even nihilism. The Roy clan, and the handful of ultrarich characters that move in their rather nebulous social circle, are not merely from another part of town—they come from a different planet altogether.[1]

In a crucial subplot clearly inspired by the #MeToo movement, one phrase becomes interoffice shorthand to document any and all incidents and allegations of sexual harassment and violence: "NRPI," or no real person involved. More than a technical abbreviation on incident reports for corporate lawyers, the acronym can be read as a mission statement for the main character's grand unifying theory *that only some people matter*. Most shockingly, this bone-chilling language gets to a core theme of *Succession*: that individuals and families who comprise today's wealthiest 1 percent have become more divergent from the remaining 99 percent of the American populace than previously imaginable.

We get another glimpse of this phenomenon in legendary director Ridley Scott's raucous crime thriller *All the Money in the World* about the 1973 kidnapping of John Paul Getty III. Much of the film's publicity was overshadowed by the #MeToo accusations against the actor Kevin Spacey, until Scott replaced him with Christopher Plummer. Plummer's portrayal of the elder Getty reflects the grandfather's subversion, stubbornness, and misanthropy. The storyline of *All the Money in the World* focuses on the abduction and hostage taking of sixteen-year-old John Paul Getty III from the streets of Rome by Calabrian mobsters. His grandfather and namesake, the aged and absurdly wealthy oil tycoon J. Paul Getty, refused to pay the $17 million ransom for his young grandson. When the patriarch of the Getty dynasty was asked why he refused to pay the kidnappers to return the boy, he purportedly said he did not want to establish a precedent by rewarding criminals. Notoriously stingy and preternaturally paranoid, the elder Getty also voiced his suspicions that the boy was actually a spoiled wastrel who cooked up the whole scheme to scam his family to support his hedonism. It was only after the young heir's captors sent the *paterfamilias* a package containing the boy's severed right ear that the cantankerous miser reached for his checkbook to pay (some of) the boy's ransom.[2] *All the Money in the World* suggests that wealthy families like the Gettys often fear their own children more than they fear outsiders. Many affluent parents and grandparents fear their offspring will not only squander the family's riches and status but also be unworthy of the same.

The concept of sloth as "wealth without work" comes into sharp focus when we think about the tumultuous blows suffered by global capitalism under the long, twisted shadow of COVID-19. While the full magnitude and devastating aftermath of this pandemic remain uncertain yet ongoing, it is clear that the world as we have known it has already changed dramatically. In this post–COVID-19 pandemic era, how does ethics help us understand new concepts of wealth, social status, and leisure?[3] For instance, what religious worldviews are bound up in the matrices of power that determine who lives and who dies? Who was truly able to quarantine safely and happily without risking their own or others' health or job? Moreover, even as Washington politicians and Wall Street executives used the rhetoric of "frontline heroes" and "essential workers" to describe the great working class of people, how much do the economic and social elites value—and compensate—the most overworked, underappreciated, and underpaid members of our national workforce as they sacrificially give their all to keep the entire society and political economy afloat?

It is this sort of delusional paradox that undergirds the American myth of meritocracy in which you have low-wage workers trapped riding crowded mass transportation who vote for duplicitous politicians who support perpetual tax cuts for billionaires and large corporations. Meanwhile, the only hope for these workers to enjoy an early retirement—or any retirement at all—is to daydream about winning the lottery or a large insurance settlement check for a car crash or similar calamity. The perpetuation of social control as well as the preservation of societal power requires the persistence of the "lazy, good-for-nothing" social myth with which the elite members of our society can bludgeon their more indigent counterparts. Yet, if one were to be honest about the convergence of white supremacy and capitalist domination vis-à-vis the so-called Protestant work ethic, one would see that labeling anyone other than the nation's ruling class as "lazy" is a contemptible bold-faced lie. For wealthy whites to use the word lazy to refer to those they enslaved, exploited, and exterminated is both obscene and absurd. Nevertheless, accusations of laziness are part of a powerful deception, undergirded by a mythical strength. Understanding the workings of sloth therefore requires an attention to myth.

What Is Myth?

Myths give meaning to life, lived experiences, and yearnings. They express how humans want themselves and others to perceive their innermost being and how they want those perceptions to become physical reality. Myths often do this by means of exaggerated truths—overstated because, however fantastical they might be, myths ultimately ground people in factual aspects of human existence. Mythology propels the mind to where the body cannot take us, pitching us beyond the reach of our physical limitations. In religious terms, myth becomes the metaphor of what can be known beyond human reality, shaping it by interacting with places that only the mind can go. In *The Power of Myth*, Joseph Campbell explains:

> People say that what we're all seeking is a meaning for life. I don't think that's what we're really seeking. I think that what we're seeking is an experience of being alive, so that our life experiences on the purely physical plane will have resonances with our own innermost being and reality, so that we actually feel the rapture of being alive.[4]

When societies were largely devoid of scientific inquiries and influences, myths were essential to help people make sense of the natural world. Despite our scientific research and cutting-edge technology, today we need myths more than ever. Why? Because the more we know, the more doubts we have and the less certain we become. Scientific insights generate more questions than answers, and the more insight we have into the inner and unseen workings of the physical world, the more unsettled we become about the reliability and soundness of the foundations of human existence. Myths reassure us in the face of anxiety, and, once disseminated in culture, they become an unquestionable part of the fabric of our world.

Myths can be passed along, told and retold throughout generations, until their truths become ingrained and accepted through the very fact of their repetition. Whereas science may show how much we have in common with the rest of humanity, myths have a *super*natural and *extra*ordinary way of enabling people to place themselves above and beyond others—and unfortunately in so doing to exploit those others for someone else's benefit. How so? Not only do the socially powerful establish the moral framework of myths' meanings, they see to it that over time those meanings become accepted as truth that holds this part of society in place to their benefit.

Recall the African parable of the lion and the hunter, most notably shared by novelist Chinua Achebe, which conveys the maxim that "until lions have their own historians, tales of the hunt shall always glorify the hunter" (Igbo people, Nigeria), and "until lions start writing their own stories, the hunters will always be the heroes" (Kenya and Zimbabwe). Unchecked lies and unchallenged falsehoods become part of a culture's revered and esteemed tradition. As Winston Churchill is reported to have said, history is written by the victors, the hunters not the hunted, and in such stories the hunter is always the hero.

Robert Wuthnow suggests that American cultural myths have accomplished this by grounding

> our collective thinking . . . in widely accepted narratives that almost always go unexamined. These are the deep meanings of which our culture is composed, the tacit knowledge we use to make sense of our worlds. They are fundamentally about *morality*. . . . They tell us what it means to be Americans, how America is good, and why some people are more successful than others. They reassure us that our privileges as individuals and a nation are well-deserved.[5]

These widely accepted narratives are not mere fables—they are lucrative lies that make dollars and sense. Religious studies scholar Christopher Driscoll notes in *White Lies: Race and Uncertainty in the Twilight of American Religion* that "the god early white settlers and immigrants brought to the American shores [was] thoroughly enmeshed with economic concerns." The settlers bequeathed a legacy of an "American god of economic privilege and violence" that frames the experience of what it means to be American with the social power to enforce the myths.[6] Such (white) myths and legends tend to disparage the less privileged.

Our cultural myths are American currency. The three types of cultural myth mentioned in this chapter's opening—the myth of the American *legend* (past), the inheritance of the American *legacy* (present), and the fringe benefits of the American lifestyle of the *leisure class* (projected future)—form the core of the American slothful "good life" that is exhibited by complacent creatures of comfort whose lap of luxury is made viable by lethal living that is death-dealing to others. The underlying truth that Gandhi exposed—wealth without work—is the moral blunder that has been a burgeoning force behind the myth of the good life of which American dreams are made and of what matters most. Idol worship and idle worship converge in the American version of the good life that is ripe with superficiality.

Legends: "We Hold These Truths to Be Self-Evident"

Lies become legends and the people who write them become legendary. When Thomas Jefferson penned the line "we hold these truths to be self-evident" in the Declaration of Independence, he was referring to the claims of the Constitution as foundational truths that required no verification or corroboration. Although the Constitution's underlying principles can be adapted to interpret changing circumstances, this does not set aside the fact that white, propertied enslavers saw their role as to exclusively decide the telling of history and the foreshadowing of the future by setting themselves as legends who would frame how the story that came to be America got told. To challenge what became the dominant narrative, we must critically explore how a particular understanding of whiteness informed America's founding and its relationship with sloth.

WHITE PATRIARCHY AS PROPERTY Patriarchs created American wealth through policies, programs, and practices designed not only to facilitate wealth building by white people (predominantly men) but also to create barriers to the same for people of color and women of all races. Legal scholar and pioneering critical race theorist Cheryl Harris's development of the notion of "whiteness as property" helps us understand the connective tissue, as it were, between the psychic (envisioned desire) and material (monetized manufacturing) manifestations of racial injustice. It explains the disproportionality between the power held by white and Black communities in the United States from the early American colonial period to the present. For Harris, whiteness constitutes a form of "property" in the sense that it includes the possession of rights, capacities of that possession, and protection of the law as well as the actual possession of material property. In this, whiteness is a form of life that is *the* preeminent mode of ownership and power. Whiteness can do with blackness what it will.[7] This means whiteness is a mode of personhood with rights and capacities and land and materiality. This protects white people from the precariousness that comes from lacking rights, land, and wealth, and confers upon white people the ability to increase their power materially. One of the most important functions of critical race theory is that it exposes the doctrine of colorblindness—that if one does not "see" race in our allegedly postracial era, the problem of racism will remain in the past—for the myth that it is. As an alternative perspective to understanding race in the United States, critical race theory shifts our conceptualization of racism toward more conditional, material, and power-based factors. In other words, racism is not simply a matter of individual disposition but a matter of the material conditions of disproportionate power in which people live—the material supremacy of whiteness and the material inferiority of blackness.

It is the institution of slavery in the first place, Harris argues, that melded whiteness and property:

> Slavery as a system of property facilitated the merger of white identity and property. Because the system of slavery was contingent on and conflated with racial identity, it became crucial to be "white," to be identified as white, to have the property of being white. Whiteness was the characteristic, the attribute, the property of free human beings.[8]

In other words, due to an economic system based on material profits grounded in property and the construction of whiteness as superiority and blackness as inferiority, whiteness became tied to property both in the sense of land and in the very capacity to possess it. As Harris also points out, making whiteness a kind of property "reproduces black subordination" by default, because the construction of whiteness as superior and as the way to access wealth and property is not possible apart from the dehumanization of blackness.[9] In Harris's words, "the fundamental precept of whiteness, the core of its value, is its exclusivity; but exclusivity is predicated not on any intrinsic characteristic, but on the existence of the symbolic Other, which functions to 'create an illusion of unity' among whites."[10] Here, valorized whiteness needs dehumanized blackness in order to be materially and conceptually powerful. If whiteness is property, then blackness is trespass.

The notion of whiteness as property has its conceptual roots largely in the thought of John Locke, who developed the notion of "possessive individualism," in which private property manifests wherever a (European male) person takes possession of the belonging or territory. It is this theory that leads to the articulation of private ownership of property in the West.[11] This doctrine of possessive individualism depends upon theological doctrines of the creation of the earth and humans, and humans' role within creation. Specifically, Locke and others are working in conversation with passages like Genesis 1:28, which invites humans to "subdue" and "have dominion" over the earth. It is from these passages that Locke and other thinkers develop a doctrine of creation with two valences: one, that God's creation is for humans to subdue and rule over, and two, that in subduing the earth, plots of earth become ontologically the possession of private persons or groups of people. According to this doctrine of creation, the earth is not properly understood as *privately owned* until a (white, European) person acquires and possesses it. In this way, whiteness creates *and* embodies property, wherever it wants to.

From this we can see that Locke's political theory of possessive individualism helps the West, and particularly the United States, to fuse ontology, property, race, and the doctrine of creation together into one entity with multiple dimensions. Put another way, Locke's theory develops the West's understanding of property in such a way that property is possessed not only in the form of land but in the form of white personhood, which alone is given the powers of creative possession. White personhood is a godlike power that manifests materially in property ownership, immunity from legal harm, and subordination of nonwhiteness. As Native American theologian George Tinker shows, Locke's personal investments in colonial enterprises combined with his philosophical and political acumen allowed for the legal justification of both the theft of land from Indigenous persons and the making of "property" of persons of African descent.[12]

LEGENDS ARE LARGER THAN LIFE The notion of whiteness embodied in heteropatriarchy makes legends out of white, propertied men and imagines wealth as a phenomenon to articulate and act out the forbidden in American culture. The examination of this tendency has been a necessarily fearless one. As Toni Morrison says, in "an effort to avert the critical gaze from the racial object to the racial subject,"[13] evil offered up as white lies gets transmuted as truth without question, often promoting the kind of cowardly criticism that fails to address the Africanist presence in American literature.

Whiteness as wealth assumes that the racial disparity found within America's wealth gap is due to lack of incentive, absence of ingenuity, outright laziness, and inadvisable financial choices on the part of people of color. Nothing could be further from the truth. This equation has come into existence neither by divine providence nor by chance. Rather, it is the product of a long history in the United States of legal, legislative, institutional, and economic policies specifically designed to prop up and privilege the economic and social advancement of white Americans at the expense of the very same opportunities for Americans of color.

Legends of exploitation depend heavily on inverting reality and truth to champion the cause of white patriarchal power and property. Hence the white myths talk about discovering a new world rather than stealing land, civilizing a heathen people rather than savagely enslaving civilizations, patrolling borders to keep out illegal aliens rather than moving borders to annex land, containing resident enemies rather than imprisoning forced cheap labor, providing safe haven or a promised land to an otherwise despised or disposable people rather than micromanaging and compelling cultural accommodation and ethnic assimilation, and protecting and elevating the so-called weaker sex rather than enforcing biological determinism through childbirth and marriage as a way to hold women hostage via domesticity and second-class status.

The mythic construct of race becomes a guiding episteme in

knowing how the world works in racially meaningful ways, but avoiding naming it in these terms. Whites know how to talk about race without actually mentioning the word, opting instead for terms such as "ethnicity," "nationality," and "background," asking questions like "What are you?" or that the most veiled of all euphemisms, "Where are you from?" When a person of color names a state (e.g., New York), the question is restated as, "No, where are you *really* from?" Moreover, knowing how to invoke the concept of racism without having to utter the word is a trademark of even the liberal White discourse. Manning Marable found common substitutions, such as "'the country's racial picture,' 'the overall racial climate,' 'relations between Americans of different races and ethnic background,' 'racial matters,' 'the race theme,' 'an incendiary topic,' 'this most delicate and politically dangerous of subjects.' . . . 'the state of race relations,' 'the racial front,' 'Black-white relations.'"[14]

These terms were and are employed to mollify white fragility rather than clarify the stakes or be upfront about racist activity. Instead of explicitly acknowledging the socially and politically charged nature of the topic, whites often use racially neutral or "colorblind" terms when talking about race. Through surveys of Black and white racial attitudes in the Detroit area, Eduardo Bonilla-Silva concludes that "whites avoid using direct racial references and traditionally 'racist' language and rely on covert, indirect, and apparently nonracial language to state their racial views."[15] Moreover, his research team found that "only a handful of white respondents did not say something that was [racially] problematic at some point in their interview."[16] Even more, as legal scholar Ian Hany-Lopez has illustrated, much of contemporary American racial discourse is pervaded by racist rhetoric, a rhetoric commonly known as "dog whistle politics," to activate deep-seated racial animus among whites and at the same time to provide plausible deniability if accused of bias and discrimination. In *The Wages of Whiteness*, David Roediger writes:

> Even in an all-white town, race was never absent. I learned absolutely no lore of my German ancestry and no more than a few meaningless snatches of Irish songs, but missed little of racist folklore. Kids came to know the exigencies of chance by chanting, "Eeny, meany, money, mo / Catch a nigger by the toe" to decide teams and first batter in sport. We learned that life—and fights—were not always fair: "Two against one, nigger's fun." We learned not to loaf: "Last one is a nigger baby." We learned to save, for to buy ostentatiously or too quickly was to be "nigger rich." We

learned not to buy clothes that were a bright "nigger green." Sexuality and blackness were of course thoroughly confused.[17]

Legacy: Stereotypes, Blind Faith, and Inheritance of White Blessings

Myths have a life of their own and legends never die. Legends inevitably give way to legacy, which makes them larger than life. Even though lies and disingenuity are the lifeblood of cultural myths, that does not make them unreal or impotent. Their existence in itself gives them potency, a power that is taken up, used, and sustained by those within society for whom they are beneficial. However, others fall prey and victim to these myths as they endure and are passed along from generation to generation—which is to say that cultural myths endure in a self-generating manner. Much like a virus perpetuates itself while also shape-shifting to live off the host to which it attaches, myths perpetuate the shared reality of all within a culture, invading and altering their perspectives and understandings of themselves and each other.

I recall my grandmother's saying, "There are the lies that have short legs and the lies that have a long nose." Some lies have short legs and a short run, because the truth catches up quickly with them. Others have long noses—those that are obvious to everyone . . . except the person who tells them. These lies make the liar look ridiculous.

While the truth catches up quickly to some lies and other lies that are obvious to everyone except the person who tells them end up making the liar look ridiculous, there are some lies that are epic: deep-seated cultural myths that become legendary and have legacies that endure well beyond the people who launch them. These lies become the poisonous lifeblood of a society. They multiply and become legion because, as the biblical adage goes, they are many and take hold of all who encounter them. If there is no concern for the demonstrable difference between truth and fiction, then what people believe becomes more important than what is true. The evangelical mantra "God said it, I believe it, that settles it" takes on an entirely different meaning when our cultural legends are bestowed with divine authority. This surrender to myth as truth has atrophied the muscle memory of the American body politic to such an extent that false projections of reality prop up the power of the most slothful in society.

In America, the legendary myth of wealth being the outcome or product of hard work of a few good white men props up the American white lie and legacy of sloth. Whereas the accumulated wealth of current generations is alleged and assumed to be the outcome of the pioneering efforts and laudable work ethic of their forebears, it is actually often an inheritance of unearned benefits that were initially gained and subsequently maintained at the expense of the exploitation of others. The result has been a seeping, stealthy, viral attachment of an almost exclusively white supremacist and toxic masculine America to a generational inheritance of sloth, one supported by a legacy of white lies that have determined which bodies are the beneficiaries and which are the victims of American unearned economic privilege. Sloth is highly contagious, spreading from generation to generation. With each new generation, lies perpetuate lethargy, laxity perpetuates loucheness, and indolence perpetuates insolence.

As white antiracist allies Jane Elliot, Peggy McIntosh, Tim Wise, Robin DiAngelo, and many others have reminded us, white supremacy and racism come easily to their inheritors. Like a windfall, succeeding generations of whites believe that the world is their oyster, and theirs alone. This notion of inheritance without labor is white privilege—an invisible, potent social reality upon which many white people depend, yet are unwilling to recognize. It is evident in small and large ways. Thus, a white person always will find white-appropriate hair products and white flesh-toned Band-Aids in a store, signaling that their hair and skin are the norm. They can take for granted that their embodiment and likenesses will be affirmed and celebrated in every advertisement, television program, big screen film, and any form of popular culture. Even God will bear their likeness. White privilege ensures that white people will be forever normalized, yet never marginalized.

This legacy of white privilege is a legitimation of lethargy, bad faith in unmerited advantages that have become a signature feature of America at home and abroad. Most white Americans exempt and declare themselves innocent of their forebears' actions of enslavement and oppression, failing to recount or account for the violent, exploitative origins that created and put into perpetual practice their unique freedoms and systems of privilege. They are incensed by the suggestion that their privilege is unmerited, and insensitive to and ignorant of the very existence of this privilege, a privilege that is not simply the origin of, but also their legacy and role in, much that ails this country and the world. This privilege of inertia is their cultural legacy and inheritance—the natural resistance or sloth toward changing this state of affairs or being moved by anything that wrests them from their comfort zone. This enables an implicit bias that ignores or renders invisible the suffering and opposition that many women and people of color have for centuries recognized as the staying power of white male privilege. And so whites claim that those who do the most laborious work without just compensation are rightfully disinherited, because they are, in fact, inferior.

Legacy, then, is no longer the original sin of the first lie. It is no longer the overt oppression inflicted by founding or preceding generations. Rather, white legacy has become the faith and assurance in those lies as inherent, blessed assurances and merited privileges, the faith and the assurance that dares not ask who was exploited, enslaved, or exterminated for one's everyday enjoyment. Succeeding generations believe the lies they have inherited as a form of blind faith, in which their privilege is in fact "the evidence of things not seen and the substance of things hoped for."[18] Their status confers upon them not what they have earned but what they have been bequeathed in the form of a legacy of assumed values that secure valuables and material wealth. The American myth, therefore, is a cultural heritage and performance in which white supremacy and patriarchy determine how everyone lives out their destiny. This heritage is a shared experience that is informed by attitudes, beliefs, ideas, and ideals that shape how people see themselves and others, along with what they believe to be good, virtuous, and the norm.

To the extent that myths become belief systems that are assumed to be inerrant while universal, no one is untouched by them. They bring into false focus a normative gaze that literally produces stereotypes as typologies. In so doing, the American myth is not representative of a factual reality but of an artificially created and socially normalized material and cultural reality that defines those who are and are not made in the image of whiteness, perceived as the image of the divine. This normalization process is caught in the intersectional grips of American notions of race, class, and gender. Via this process, each and every person is perceived as inhabiting a place on the racial-ethnic continuum that ranges from honorary whiteness to dishonorable blackness, from male ingenuity to feminine sensuality, and from propertied to dispossessed. Through the American normative gaze, such myths produce, prohibit, develop, and delimit specific idealized cultural conceptions of truth, knowledge, beauty, and character. The privileged needs and expectations of the dominant white racial group define who and what is American in all respects, of course assuming the white male to be at the top of this pyramid of worth. Ultimately, a white supremacist myth of beauty, culture, and intelligence embodied and exemplified by white people alone controls what it means to be not only American but human.

This notion of normalcy establishes both what belongs to certain bodies and where those bodies belong. Inherited legacies demarcate memberships with fixed privileges. Any efforts to extend access to wealth to those who have worked for it as a way to make reparations for historic wrongs against Black or Brown people are instantly equated with what are considered the most virulent forms of liberalism. This simultaneously protects and hides the actual functioning of white supremacy in US society that would be threatened by reparations. As legal scholar and critical race theorist Patricia J. Williams explains:

> In the charged context of dismantling a system of favoritism that "favored" whites and "disfavored" blacks, the majority glibly reversed the vocabulary of preference so that it was blacks who were favored and whites automatically disfavored. The casual ahistoricism of this reversal implies a causal link between the inclusion of blacks and the oppression of whites. To give an example that would be extreme were it not asked so often, a student recently demanded of me, "Don't you think affirmative action is what creates a David Duke?" Blacks are positioned in this query as responsible for the bitterest backlash against them, an eerie repeat of the responses (one being the founding of the Ku Klux Klan) to black gains, having nothing to do with affirmative action, during Reconstruction.
>
> In fact, affirmative action and minority set-aside programs are vastly more complicated than this "you're in, I'm out" conception suggests. Nothing in this rigid win/lose dichotomy permits the notion that everyone could end up a beneficiary, that expansion rather than substitution might be possible, and that the favoring of multiple cultures is an enhancement of the total rather than a sweepingly reflexive act of favoritism for anything other than the monolithic purity of an all-white nation.[19]

Every effort to right the wrongs of previous generations by means of solutions that approximate restorative justice, such as affirmative action efforts brought about by civil rights protest and legislation, has been met with white reactionary resistance insisting that such efforts are, in fact, reverse racism. Consider the meritless claims about the purported racial scheming of minorities who supposedly play the "race card" to give themselves an unfair advantage in processes such as employment hires and college enrollment at the "discriminatory expense" of whites. Every addition of a person of color is seen as a massive attack against whiteness—a veritable theft of a white person's birthright and inheritance and a trespass onto a space that is reserved exclusively as their own.

Legacy admissions into institutions of higher learning bear this out. According to *The Atlantic*:

> Applying to college as a legacy is like having a superpower. It has been estimated to double or quadruple one's chances of getting into a highly selective school, and has been found to be roughly equivalent to a 160-

point boost on the SAT. At the most selective institutions in the United States, it's typical for 10 to 15 percent of students to have a parent who also attended.[20]

This privileged legacy status is an example of reserved white space. It is an unearned benefit to the children of alumni, a benefit for those regarded as rightful heirs to these institutions. Most people of color did not find their way into higher education in significant numbers until the late twentieth century, and even today the majority of students of color are first generation college/university attendees. This system of legacy admission is largely unique to the United States and is a practice and policy that protects and promotes primarily white and rich applicants with an automatic advantage solely on the basis of their privileged academic lineage. Legacy admission, as a form and manifestation of white sloth, affords some the ability to fail and fall upward, so to speak. As one famous example, former President George W. Bush was denied admittance to the University of Texas because of his noncompetitive academic portfolio, but nonetheless was accepted into Yale because of his legacy connection to the institution. Likewise, former President John F. Kennedy's high school academic performance was distinctly unremarkable, but he managed to gain admission to Harvard University by virtue of his father's status as an alumnus of the institution.

More recently, in 2019, one of the most extensive college admissions schemes in history was exposed. Numerous rich, wealthy, celebrity parents, and college preparatory athletic coaches were accused and charged of not only paying a total of $6.5 million in bribes, but also of knowingly participating with college officials and recruiters in a coordinated process of misrepresentation, bribery, and standardized test cheating, in order to gain college admission for their children who lacked competitive credentials. As startling, shocking, and devious as this might seem, it was neither an exceptional nor a new phenomenon for those familiar with the biased college admissions system that extends from elite, private college preparatory secondary schools to state universities and colleges all the way up to the most rarefied Ivy League institutions. Wealthy and privileged white students have always benefited from a stacked deck and had the upper hand in a system of admission into prestigious universities. Likewise, even as female applicants have started to outperform men academically and on college standardized tests, there has been little discussion as to why the gender tipping point has exceptionally if not exclusively favored men but has yet to include equality, equity, and excellence in a way that would engender the academic ability and presence of women in greater measure. Of course, the inferred rationale would be that a tipping point that favors men is a "healthy norm." Cries of "healthy norms" and "reverse racism" are obstructionist reactions against legalized and restorative affirmative action college admission initiatives. They are attempts to problematize the nonwealthy and the most vulnerable people of color by those who are well aware of and benefit the most from the unarticulated but very real "affirmative actions" that privilege those who simultaneously design legacy preferences and then target them specifically for themselves.

CULTURAL APPROPRIATIONS Whereas previous generations stole land and enslaved people, their heirs apparent have continued this tradition by also ripping off the culture of Black people and other underrepresented groups. Like systemic racism, white cultural appropriation is ubiquitous and normalized to such an extent that most white people can actively engage in it while never being forced to confront that fact. This trend is an enduring feature of sloth: the arrogance of ignorance and apathy. Those who are seemingly cognizant of their white appetite for cultural consumption often delude themselves by regarding this as appreciation and proof that they are not racist but are celebrating the "spice" and "flavor" that people of color offer to their otherwise bland lives. What Black cuisine did for antebellum white families is akin to what the blues did for country music in the early part of the twentieth century, to the melding of the inspiration of gospel music with the bending of blues notes and the embodied rhythm and sensuality of Black dance that gave birth in the 1960s to the new art form of rock 'n' roll, and to what hip-hop and rap did for white suburban youth in the 1980s. This type of cultural theft generates cultural capital for whiteness while leaving mere pennies on the floor for the very people who produced it.

The enduring influence of white people's exploitation of Black culture in America alone, least of all worldwide, was not only a matter of taste but also a matter of money. Cultural appropriation and stealing from Black culture has proven to be equally, if not more, lucrative than the forms of economic exploitation of previous generations. From Bo Derek to Kim Kardashian to Fergie to Iggy Azalea, white female celebrities and the generations that they influenced actively have tried to take on Black physical attributes (e.g., injecting potentially poisonous fillers into their lips and hips and risking cancer by tanning to darken their skin) not simply for their benefit but at the cost and risk to their own lives. As they do so, however, they neither celebrate nor compensate the Black people who created the styles they strive to emulate. White slothful trendsetters and influencers literally hijack the aesthetics of a group's culture and leave its originating creators behind. While whites dissect, disseminate, and disburse Black culture to satisfy their white cultural appetites, they regard these very same cultural attributes as the stereotypically denigrating and dehumanizing attributes of the Black people from whom they were taken. All this is to say that white appreciation is inextricably linked to Black depreciation.

The sloth of white individuals who lacked inventiveness resulted in empires of greed built on the creativity and culture of minoritized groups. Record companies stole publishing rights and the subsequent royalties from musicians.[21] Sports agents, team franchises, and talent scouts received huge financial windfalls from the literal sweat equity of countless athletes.[22] White female celebrities of domesticity engineered their fortunes by stealing the recipes and culinary inventions of women of color. Numerous white artists have unabashedly appropriated Black musical ingenuity and innovation to fuel their own mainstream successes. White stylists made curly or braided hair, dark skin, big hips, and full lips beautiful—but only when attached to white skin. As with previous generations before them, they make money off the work and ingenuity of underrepresented others to serve and privilege their own.[23]

Thus, the racial identity crisis of American culture is based on the fetishization and demonization of people of color for the idolatrous purpose and the continued elevation of whiteness. In her essay "Eating the Other: Desire and Resistance," bell hooks likens this to the conspicuous, capitalist consumption of white patriarchy, whereby people of color are metaphorically consumed:

> Within current debates about race and difference, mass culture is the contemporary location that both publicly declares and perpetuates the idea that there is pleasure to be found in the acknowledgment and enjoyment of racial difference. The commodification of Otherness has been so successful because it is offered as a new delight, more intense, more satisfying than normal ways of doing and feeling. Within commodity culture, ethnicity becomes spice, seasoning that can liven up the dull dish that is mainstream white culture.[24]

Scholars such as hooks and others have shown that what whites tout as cultural appreciation is in fact cultural appropriation. There are numerous examples, from white appropriation of music, to the fashion world's appropriation of Black aesthetics, to white sexual appetites and exotic affectations of the Other, to gorging on the ethnic food of otherwise underrepresented groups for which white appetites are insatiable. Unable to reflect upon how their actions stem from such exploitative origins, the heirs of the most rabidly racist predecessors continue to partake in the **feast** of such forms of cultural consumption—via **f**ood, **e**ntertainment, **a**thletics, **s**ervice, and titillation—all the while deluding themselves that doing so represents a fulfillment of the telos of white supremacist culture. Whereas the actual lives and welfare of people of color rarely matter on their own terms in mainstream society, such cultural appropriations of their life's labor afford white culture a self-congratulatory but artificial closeness with and concern for the racial/ethnic Other.

Thus, to say that the legacy of American wealth is whiteness is a blasphemous, supersecessionist myth. It is a table prepared in the presence of one's enemies that offers up for consumption the most victimized, rather than the most villainous. This banquet of white cultural appropriation represents a form of salvific sacrament that transforms white American consumption of the embodiment and lifeblood of people of color into the eternal livelihood of white supremacy. It guts the lives of people of color to provide spice to the legend and legacy of white slothfulness for succeeding generations of supremacist disciples who sit at this table and partake insatiably of its buffet of power and privilege. The vapid defense that to appropriate is to celebrate the lives and productions of others only shores up the slothful posture of those who feel responsible for neither the legacy of sins of their ancestors nor the sufferings of those to whom their privilege has denied access. As such, they do not feel led or stirred to respond to how they can and should repair that which has been broken for their benefit.

Leisure Class: Lifestyles of the Rich and Shameless

Cultural legacies and their enduring mythologies are so ubiquitous that they leave indelible impressions and powerfully shape the fabric of social life. While their impact may appear to be merely symbolic, in actuality they reveal the strong appeal and lure of the notion of wealth without work, an enticement that is grounded in empty rhetoric, facile popular culture, and misguided opinion. The uniquely American notion of easy money is one that casts a shadow that is in many respects more potent than the reality itself. The myth of the American good life promotes the self-assured confidence and belief that *being* American and/or simply *living* in the United States gives one the inalienable right to the pursuit of happiness by means of guaranteed wealth and prosperity. To make it in America is, at the very least, to enjoy a semblance of identification with the legacy of privilege, in order to capitalize on one's proximity to it. This myth of "having it made" in America not only promulgates the belief that every person is afforded a clean slate of opportunity, it also motivates each generation to remake itself by refashioning exploitation and appropriation as a way to manifest their own American dream.

As geographer Yi-Fu Tuan explains, any given "place" or "space" is more than a fixed location or expanse of land. It has extended significance in that it represents a social marker and personal location that maps one's path to a desired destination.[25] The people who inhabit that place embody the myth that marks their needs, desires, authority, and destinies as reserved for them and them alone. When a myth takes on meaning such that it inhabits spaces, marks places, and possesses people, it becomes an enduring affliction that attaches itself to every person. Such is the myth of the American success story, in that it bends the wills of the people of each generation, controlling their destinies and framing their understanding of success and social standing to be synonymous with moral virtue and social worth. As a result, mythmaking means making your money work for you rather than working for your money. This is often the success story of some of America's greatest self-made men, from Andrew Carnegie to Mark Zuckerberg to Jeff Bezos. These tycoons are iconic of American culture, and their success stories serve as a guide for living the good life. According to ethicist Johnathan Walton, these success stories

> carry as much meaning as the stars and stripes and are as influential as the Gospel narrative if not more so. The story of the heroic man or woman, though usually a man, who carves out his own path and rises to prominence by his own efforts is well known. Though in actuality such people are rare, they have come to signify the dreams and ambitions of the common person.[26]

But these stories cannot go unexamined, in that they set mythic parameters for what it means to be an American and why some Americans are successful and others are not. These stories are not rational or based in fact; rather, they are idealized, rehearsed, stereotypical cultural narratives that champion the purported work ethic, morality, and ethos of individual examples of success. According to Robert Wuthnow,

> they are the stock of political rhetoric but also of our private understanding of our nation. They vary among different ethnic groups and from one region to another, and yet they provide us with common narratives about our shared existence. . . . They tell us how to worship and how to identify ourselves ethnically and racially. They help us understand our love-hate relationship with material possessions—and keep us from doing much to change this relationship. . . . There are also deeper assumptions implicit in these stories that merit closer examination. For better or worse, these assumptions keep us from changing quite as much as we wish. They keep us from realizing our ideas as a nation and as a people.[27]

In fact, the myth that gives meaning and makes money within society for the prosperous patriarchs often translates into the public perception and pain of the most oppressed, as it sparks class war and real conflagrations among the marginalized masses themselves, rather than among those who lord over them. According to Toni Morrison in her classic interview in 1989 with *Time* magazine, the United States' class war is a race war launched by white lies that exploit public perception. These lies presume not only a level playing field for all but also the inability of the underprivileged to distinguish clearly between oppressor and ally:

> If there were no black people here in this country, it would have been Balkanized. The immigrants would have torn each other's throats out, as they have done everywhere else. But in becoming an American, from Europe, what one has in common with that other immigrant is contempt for me—it is nothing else but color. Wherever they were from, they would stand together. They could all say, "I am not that." In that sense, becoming an American is based on an attitude: an exclusion of me.
>
> It was not negative to them—it was unifying. When they got off the boat, the second word they learned was "nigger." Ask them—I grew up with them. I remember in the fifth grade a smart little boy who had just arrived and didn't speak any English. He sat next to me. I read well, and I taught him to read just by doing it. I remember the moment he found out that I was black—a nigger. It took him six months; he was told. And that's the moment when he belonged, that was his entrance. Every immigrant knew he would not come as the very bottom. He had to come above at least one group—and that was us.[28]

This is not a novel phenomenon or a cultural narrative exclusive to the American immigrant. It is a perennial and permanent part of the American class system that plays out interpersonally, often along racial/ethnic lines. Whether it is the Korean owner of a beauty supply store in a Black urban neighborhood who has contempt for the clientele from whom he exclusively makes his living; or George Zimmerman, a Latino, who shot and killed the Black teenager Trayvon Martin as he walked home from a convenience store with soda and candy in his hand; or the armed father and son Travis and Gregory McMichael getting into their pickup truck to hunt down and kill twenty-five-year-old Ahmaud Arbery as he jogged in his neighborhood—all these persons exhibit the racial animus fed by class anxiety. As preeminent sociologist and urban policy scholar William Julius Wilson notes, racial, ethnic, and class tensions exert significant influence on the spaces we take up and the neighborhoods in which we choose to live. They all have great meaning and value for each citizen's understanding of what it means to live well in America.[29] Ask Americans about the racial demographics of the places where they live and have lived and you will assuredly receive salient, first-person narrative accounts that both prove Wilson's thesis and reveal the ways in which the elusive American goal of integration is in direct tension with, if not outright opposition to, the standard of exclusivity necessitated by the mythic dream of the American good life. Both aspirations—neighborhood integration and exclusivity—*in fact* reflect far more accurately the power and meaning exerted by American cultural and class myths than they do the actual existence of such demographic and residential realities.

The people who inhabit a space establish and reflect the value of both the space itself and the people with whom they coinhabit it. Zip codes in any given city are encoded signifiers of such meaning and value. Based on various modes of environmental racism, public policy scholar Robert Bullard also notes that zip codes can be an indicator or predictor of people's mortality, with residence in one area predictably extending a person's life over that in another area by as much as a decade.[30] The people who inhabit a place can shift or affect one's personal worth and social value. One's proximity to immigrants and people of color can move one further to the right or wrong side of class. Race, class, and gender feed each other in relation and with regard to place and space, perception and regard. For example, literal proximity to blackness lowers one's personal value, whereas one's proximity to whiteness increases value and can situate one above the fray. However, rather than recognize the myths for the lies they are, people tend to turn the menacing gaze inward on themselves and outward on others in an effort to outclass their peers and arrange themselves accordingly.

Consider the recent phenomenological rise of the social media meme and caricature of the "Karen"—a moniker and signifier of privileged white women who actively police various settings, spaces, and scenarios as reserved for or exclusive to white people. Ever ready and zealously eager to go angrily straight to the punitive top whenever things both large and small fail to go their way, Karens represent recent manifestations of the racial violence that white women have been able to foment for centuries against Black people in general, but particularly against Black men. White women as "Karens" have a long history in the United States of weaponizing their perceived "victimhood" at the hands of people of color in general and Black men in particular, as an indirect effort to protect their privilege and to police white spaces within which such presence is deemed out of place when it is not in service to whiteness. The vilification of Black people in the face of white female victimhood and vehemence originated in the period of American slavery. This pattern began as a deflection away from the reality that white slave masters were routinely raping enslaved Black women by projecting and directing attention to the concocted accusations that enslaved Black men were raping their innocent, virtuous white wives and daughters. Over time, this notion came to justify unmerited suspicion of and violence against Black men by fostering both consciously and unconsciously the biased notion that white women require vigilant protection from the threat of Black men's unchecked impulses, misbehavior, and desires.

As a modern extension of this myth of inherent Black compulsion, Karens routinely weaponize their reactionary surveillance of Black people and presence, most often by contacting authorities of all types—store owners and managers, police and government authorities—to accuse people of color of crimes as they simply go about their day in public. Indeed, there is no paucity of video witness of such Karen behavior, such convergence of gender, unmerited privilege, racial prejudice, and class anxiety. Think of the example of (white) Amy Cooper walking her dog in Central Park who crossed paths with Christian Cooper (no relation), a Black man who was birdwatching with his pricey Swarovski binoculars in the Ramble, an area designated for birdwatching where the rules stipulate dogs are to be leashed. Mr. Cooper's quiet scouting for songbirds was disrupted by Ms. Cooper shouting at her unleashed dog. When Mr. Cooper asked that she follow the rules by leashing her dog, Ms. Cooper not only refused but threatened to call the police to falsely claim that "an African-American man is threatening my life." Mr. Cooper's phone video camera revealed Ms. Cooper spitefully calling the cops in false, accusatory fashion to protest his legitimate and peaceful presence in the park.

Mr. Cooper's mere physicality and presence as a Black man triggered Ms. Cooper's underlying class insecurities and racial anxieties. Having internalized racist stereotypes and norms, she reactively, without thought, projected them upon Mr. Cooper, who was her equal in terms of education, professional background, and economic means. What is obviously implicit from this wrenching encounter is how Ms. Cooper assumed that her white, cultural capital should allow her to accuse Mr. Cooper's blackness with any claim, however false, so as to hide her misbehavior and turn the tables to her advantage. Understanding how race and gender are classed, Mr. Cooper responded after the incident by doing what is often expected of Black men in a situation such as this: He came to the rescue of the dog whistle politics of the white "damsel in distress" by saying, "I'm not excusing the racism, but I don't know if her life needed to be torn apart." Knowing full well what would likely prevail in the end, he went on to say, "She went racial. There are certain dark societal impulses that she, as a white woman, facing a conflict with a Black man, . . . thought she could marshal to her advantage.

She went there."[31] Due solely to the fact that it was videoed and occurred at the same time as the highly charged Black Lives Matter protests, the event resulted in Amy Cooper losing her job and consideration of charges against her for falsifying a police report.

To create class, and its social ill, classism, is to organize space and to place people in relation to socially constructed ranking systems. To create class is to project second-class citizenship onto those who are not legends and/or legacies of wealth. Elites' slothful ability to be at ease in their abundance thanks to their exploitation and appropriation of others leads to class anxiety in those others, who must then work even harder to climb a ladder that never reaches a level playing field. People are categorized by and cast into groups that share the same perceived status or social esteem. What is important to note is that class is not merely about economic wealth; there are many other influential indicators: ancestry/pedigree, familial expectations, lifestyle, social networks, political stance, religious affiliations, language, portfolio, education, employment, family lineage, leisure, aesthetics, and etiquette. Taken together, these indicators situate people into social groupings by which they will be subject to anything from esteem to exploitation to annihilation. For many, it is seemingly impossible to be living the good life in America without attaining social acceptance within what is regarded as an elite or aspiring class; one does not want to be outclassed. As such, classism creates an infrastructure that builds and supports one's social worth or personal value. Simultaneously, it fosters class anxieties for subordinated groups of second-class citizens, who feel the imperative, day in and day out, to strategize how best to negotiate or camouflage the systematic assignment of their space, place, and status within society.

Class anxiety informs the individual attitudes and behavior of most Americans. This is apparent in the misconceived notion and myth surrounding the reality of a "middle-class America," the nation's most paraded—and pandered to—demographic, which most Americans claim as their own, but which in fact is no more real or economically equalizing than the elusive pot of gold purportedly found at the end of a rainbow. This permanently entrenched cultural and political myth promotes the United States as a "land of opportunity" for attaining one's place within "middle-class society" by means of free enterprise. Anyone who works hard and pulls themselves up by their bootstraps is allegedly afforded the opportunity to be successful and achieve the middle-class standard of living as a self-made person. This myth, however, is simply another white lie, belied by the fact that US capitalism (corporately) and American classism (interpersonally) necessitate the ongoing creation and existence of a sizable class of permanently poor people.

There exists an infrastructure secured by policies, politics, and practices that solidifies and secures the perpetual wealth of the ultra-elite minority at the expense of those who actually do the work for their benefit, making permanent the wealth inequality gap of the masses. The creation of class standing creates anxiety for the majority of people who ascribe and value themselves accordingly along these socially curated economic lines. To be situated amid the minority and dominant group of the ruling-class elite is to be deemed valuable and virtuous as smarter, sophisticated, and significant, and thereby worthy of its power and prowess, whereas working-class people are regarded as simple, subpar, and necessarily subordinate in character and standing. But given the solid economic barrier of opportunity that demarcates the ultra-elite from all others, coupled with the artificiality of the mythic "middle class," the only option for those who seek greater class status and standing is to participate as charlatans. In this way, the system works for the rich while the only ones actually laboring and working are the masses in the class hierarchy through their quest to be esteemed.

Not surprisingly, the internalization of self-worth grounded in being measured by one's class cultivates insecurity and a sense of unrequited toil. The working masses, ignorant of or impressed by the economic ploys of the wealthy, either assume that their lot in life is to be second-class citizens or to succumb to the game of trying to outclass those with whom they hold community and common rank. Attempting to climb the class ladder has significant consequences, for it can include denial of one's familial heritage, shame about one's racial-ethnic background, disdain for those who are working class, and even elective plastic surgery, all in an attempt to be deemed desirable by the wealthiest. Conversely, the loss of middle-class status, as fundamental as it is to one's American identity and sense of belonging, renders one vulnerable to social ambiguity and capitalized chaos. Efforts toward diversifying class and fostering class mobility have not altered the ideological and hegemonic mandates of the dominant master class. Second-class citizens who work for a living exist under the duress of compulsory consumption and class anxiety, which stems from a false patriotic imperative that their labor is mandated to keep the economy healthy. They become convinced that spending their hard-earned money is crucial for the social welfare of an economy that routinely bails out big banks, provides tax cuts for the rich, and is bound and determined to enlarge the power and property of the "master" class.

The myth of meritocracy presents a worldview wherein all are free to rise to the highest level that their talents and work ethic permit, suggesting that there are no obstacles (even such as the enormous ones of a genocidal and feudal past, a history of enslavement, patriarchy, globalization, etc.) that stand in the way of autonomy, creative opportunity, security in work, and access to adequate food, health care, and quality education. Thus, the hidden injuries of class are many: the habitual hoarding of possessions conspicuously consumed to cover up for personal powerlessness; Darwinian distortions of economic evolutionary justifications that the fittest are those who survive to escape into and maintain their status in a higher class; and a culture of inequality that results in horizontal violence among minoritized groups. This final injury is particularly damaging, in that far too often socially marginalized individuals or groups will either direct their frustration and anger at those in similar or parallel social groupings (e.g., whether racially, ethnically, or gender based, etc.) by accusing them of taking away opportunity, or claim that they themselves represent model minority status, as opposed to holding accountable the actual infrastructures and institutions that withhold recognition and opportunity from them.

The cumulative effect of these class crises is a lack of sense of self, making it far less painful to think of oneself and one's status in life because one is now merely a cog in a machine. One can then easily believe that those who are wealthy are predetermined to be so because of their special status in God's plan, and that those who are poor are so because of curses placed on them and people like them. The only mechanism one can then imagine to achieve upward mobility is to work even harder at being engagingly exploitable, whether that is by being the most employable, entertaining, or enticing, in order to be accepted by those who do no labor while controlling all that is of value.

Class camouflage is a primary means by which many people find meaning. Whether trying to imitate celebrities by wearing particular brands of clothing, buying expensive cars but renting a tiny apartment, or leveraging bank loans to buy a house in a neighborhood outside of their income level, many Americans imagine themselves to be living the good life. This social practice is particularly common among the leisure class. As people strive to lay claim to an elusive, if not unattainable, American dream and accompanying sense of self and success, class camouflage maps a mythic, imaginary landscape onto a lie of putative social standing for those who otherwise feel socially and economically out of place. Ninian Smart reminds us that

> myth is told or enacted through a ritual like a kind of drama and exists in an unquestioned atmosphere. It is uttered with the implicit idea "This is how things are and this is how things have been." Unlike history . . . myth can tell about the future—what the end of the world will be like.

> . . . Not only are myths "given," that is, they are told with authority—a breathless air of unquestionable truth—but they also often play strange tricks with things and people.[32]

When there is no substantive hope for a better future, people nevertheless hold fast to the myth of their social standing within a system of class symbolism that inscribes vice onto its victims and laziness onto its laborers. Camouflaging is a survival strategy profitable only in that it enables one to experience a fleeting sense of belonging and of rising above the masses. However, being held captive to a capitalist myth is not only to experience objectification, but also to be held prisoner to symbolism that is of little substance. One becomes grounded in metaphors that purport a sense of meaning but lack value. Substance, symbols, and subterfuge are basically indistinguishable, if not irrelevant, for those who have adopted myths as truths and objectification as liberation. As such, the chaos and frustration caused by the desire for upward mobility often renders life aspirations futile, if not fatal, akin to the tragic fate described in ancient myths such as the Tower of Babel or Sisyphus's climb.

The competition to claim a throne that one can never have is well depicted in the popular HBO television series *Game of Thrones.* Petyr Baelish, the Master of Coin better known as "Little Finger," states, "Chaos isn't a pit. Chaos is a ladder. Many who try to climb it fail, and never get to try again—the fall breaks them. And some are given a chance to climb, but they refuse. They cling to the realm, or the gods, or love . . . illusions. Only the ladder is real, the climb is all there is."[33]

This climb is depicted again and again on the silver screen in American classic films such as *The Great Gatsby*, *Guess Who's Coming to Dinner*, and *The Talented Mr. Ripley*, films that depict characters who are devastated and destroyed by the vapid core of class structure and the tragic outcomes of class aspirations. The popularity, hysteria, and illusory influence that were the main attraction of the soap-opera dramas of the Lost Generation through the Baby Boomers have now evolved into the oversaturated, 24/7 appeal of mythic "reality" television programs such as *The Kardashians* or *The Real Housewives* franchise (whose casts, ironically, mostly include women who are neither married nor housewives). Part of the climb is the inevitable indebtedness that comes from rolling the dice, taking a chance, trying to hit the number or win the lottery—gambling away resources that could otherwise be used for necessities or be saved for the rainy day that will surely come, or the idleness brought on by vicarious fantasies of striking it rich and winning big on *Wheel of Fortune*, *The Price Is Right*, *Who Wants to Be a Millionaire?*, *Jeopardy*, or *Family Feud.*

When one's class aspirations cannot be concretely realized, they become virtual, suspending one's stature in the liminal space where their aspirations and/or self-worth hang in the balance of a class system that curates human value and social arrangements. Like all legends, the myth of accessible upward mobility consists of traditional tropes (e.g., "Get Rich Quick!," "Work Smarter, Not Harder!," "Fake It 'til You Make It!") that are commonly remade, revised, and repackaged from generation to generation. They are popularly regarded as historical and true, even as they lack authenticity, in that the "happily ever after" rarely, if ever, arrives for most people. Overnight sensations and successes are empty promises and vapid metonyms in an economic systemic reality in which the wealthy are slothful because they live off the work of the masses who toil to acquire unattainable wealth or at least the appearance of a life of leisure that is represented as lying just beyond one's reach.

Like all legends, the myth of the leisure class trickles down to the working class in every dream and painstaking effort to become the "self-made success story" so as to "keep up with the Joneses." In fact, America's fictions actually cost people their livelihoods, if not their lives. As Hortense Spillers reminds us, Americans don't like talking about the truth, which is simply too embarrassing and uninteresting: "Neither the shameface of the embarrassed, nor the not-looking-back of the self-assured is of much interest to us, and will not help at all if rigor is our dream."[34]

This temptation for "wealth without work" particularly afflicts the white working poor, who have bought deeply into the American myth that any person in the United States (especially a "good, decent white person") can achieve economic success through the merit of hard work alone. Operating from sociologist Pierre Bourdieu's notion of cultural capital, this expectation of thinking they should achieve success through hard work, but ultimately being unable to do so, results in dissonance and contradictions in the subjective realities of the white working poor.[35] The more immersed they are in the American mythos, the more the disappointment of both failing to realize it and the accompanying external social judgment become integrated into their fundamental self-identification. This is a direct result of a preoccupation with seeing one's worth through the eyes of the white privileged world—the normative, judgmental gaze that penetrates every facet of American life.

One of the most fundamental effects of the white normative gaze is its constant assault on one's dignity in terms of what it means to be a "first class American." Philosopher Charles Taylor asserts that personal dignity is essential to the formation of the modern self, in that it reflects "our power, our sense of dominating public space; or our invulnerability to power; or our self-sufficiency, our life having its own center, or our being liked and looked to by others, a center of attention."[36]

The problem with Taylor's assessment is that, while he offers universalizing principles with lofty standards and claims, the moral sources of dignity invariably presuppose that the person in question is white, Western, privileged, and male. For Taylor, selfhood and dignity is informed by what feminist critics call "the male gaze." Feminist Laura Mulvey would contend that Taylor's projection of his own specific "subject position" onto all members of society assumes that others conform to his image of himself or that everyone else is an imagined extension of himself.[37] Thus, being the "center of attention" as Taylor suggests has distinctly different connotations for most people, especially those who do not embody the American mythic norm when examining their subjectivity in classed, racialized, and gendered terms.

As a result, for many people cultural capital becomes the only way to camouflage class. White and nonwhite, male and female, educated and uneducated—all are forced to work ever more not in pursuit of real wealth that materializes in better life options, but rather for the nonmaterial possessions that the dominant deem to be valuable—like the zip code where they live, the way they dress, how they speak, what they believe, whom they love, how they look, and what they do for sport and play. Meanwhile those who have curated this scenario not only monopolize but operate by an entirely different system.

Even when there is little or no actual financial inheritance, this sense of entitlement is inherent in the way white privilege can not only capitalize on honorary whiteness, but also weaponize it to devalue and dispose of others as dishonorable, unmerited, and undeserving when they are felt to be equal to, alongside, yet still out of place, as we saw in the Central Park incident described above.[38] Critical theorist and antiracism activist Robin DiAngelo states that this privilege is driven by a "white fragility" stemming from the fact that when white people have lived with privilege for extended periods of time, any change in that privilege feels like loss or even oppression.[39] For those who are marginalized, the confluence of race, class, and gender creates a sphere of domination and control as they aspire to be legendary and legacies in their own right. In cases like that of Amy Cooper from the Central Park incident, the equation of people formulating their identity with honorable whiteness also includes factors—sometimes hidden, sometimes explicit—affixed to dishonorable blackness.

An example of this negative view of blackness was made evident during the looting activities that accompanied the protests during the Black Lives Matter movement. In a short video that went viral on social media at the time, activist Kimberly Jones offers a street lesson in the economics of racism and rioting by analyzing the taxonomy of people who take to the streets, such as those who did after George Floyd was brutally murdered by the police. Jones describes the three categories of people as protesters, anarchists, and looters. While the news media often highlight looters as exclusively Black, and play the blame game with the refrain "Why loot?," Jones notes that the frustrated, dejected, working poor often "just want to get stuff." For Jones, these are people who "feel like their only hope and only opportunity to get some of the things that we flaunt and flash in front of their faces all the time is to walk through a broken glass window and get it. . . . They feel like it's their only shot. They are shooting their shot, by walking through that broken window."[40] Jones argues that rather than jump quickly to denigrating looters for those actions, it might be more useful to ask *how* and *why* it is happening. In Jones's words:

> If I right now decided that I wanted to play Monopoly with you, and for 400 rounds of playing Monopoly, I didn't allow you to have any money, I didn't allow you to have anything on the board, I didn't allow for you to have anything, and then we played another 50 rounds of Monopoly and everything that you gained and you earned while you were playing that round of Monopoly was taken from you, that was Tulsa. That was Rosewood. Those are places where we built black economic wealth, where we were self-sufficient, where we owned our stores, where we owned our property, and they burned them to the ground.
>
> So that's 450 years. So for 400 rounds of Monopoly, you don't get to play at all. Not only do you not get to play, you have to play on the behalf of the person that you're playing against. You have to play and make money and earn wealth for them, and then you have to turn it over to them. So then for 50 years you finally get a little bit and you're allowed to play. And every time that they don't like the way that you're playing, or that you're catching up, or that you're doing something to be self-sufficient, they burn your game. They burn your cards. They burn your Monopoly money. And then finally at the release and the onset of that, they allow you to play, and they say, "Okay, now you catch up."
>
> Now, at this point, the only way you're going to catch up in the game is if the person shares the wealth, correct? But what if every time you shared the wealth, then there's psychological warfare against you to say, "Oh, you're an equal opportunity hire." How can you win? You can't win. The game is fixed. So when they say, "Why do you burn down the community? Why do you burn down your own neighborhood?" It's not

ours. We don't own anything. We don't own anything. . . . They are lucky that what black people are looking for is equality and not revenge.[41]

Conclusion

Now clearly the cost of the American myth of self-made success and the sloth it privileges and protects is not an issue of tall tales and board games; it is made up of legends, legacy, and the ruling class's leisure to exploit people, often to death. Even as his brother watched, George Floyd was brutally killed by a white police officer while other officers further restrained Floyd and prevented onlookers from intervening. Why? Because unbeknownst to Floyd, he was passing off a counterfeit $20 bill at a convenience store: "What is a Black man's life worth? Twenty dollars?" As cultural studies scholar Debarati Sanyal reminds us, "The cynical calculus of disposable life is entrenched in our nation, built on the extraction of Black labor and Black death" and the "necropolitical factories and fields still haunt the fiction of a seat at the table, the fake money and plastic houses on the playing board of our economy. The game does not need to be rigged; it was always already 'fixed' beyond repair."[42]

During his interview of Jones on the satirical television program *The Daily Show*, host Trevor Noah advances Jones's rejoinder to the problematizing, reactionary question "Why loot?" with a profound "Why not loot? Police in America are looting Black bodies."[43] By taking Jones's analysis a step further, Noah joins her refrain of breaking the silence. He changes the narrative of the hunter and the lion by providing an opportunity for the hunted to speak and be heard. Here the lion reverses the gaze and uncovers the lies that have vilified the victims and rendered the actual villains victorious. Jones and Noah go beyond exposing the myth and legend of looting as the stereotypical, savage behavior of Black people poised and prone to steal. By illustrating how white patriarchal supremacy, capitalism, and the formulation of American racial economics have looted the labor and stockpiled the bodies of poor, largely Black, communities, they also illustrate how looting is a hopeless, frustrated response of poor people when their backs are against the wall as they rail against a system that exploits them.

It is in this respect that the telling of the counternarrative—the disarming of a myth—is most crucial, because, as anthropologist and folklorist Zora Neale Hurston reminds us, "If you are silent about your pain, they'll kill you and say you enjoyed it."[44] The bitter irony is that the truth of the matter often fails to change the harsh reality of the truth. Myths allow lies to become stubborn truths, in spite of corrective counternarratives. They are not only simply stories we are told, but ones that endure because we come to believe them ourselves and then pass them along. No matter how effectively counternarratives might reverse the gaze and highlight that the hunted are victims who are slaughtered on their own ground, it does not change the fact that the hunter wins. The victor takes the spoils, while the victims are killed or remain with only vices to which to lay claim. The cycle of poverty exists not because those who are poor are lazy freeloaders who do nothing while demanding handouts from those who have worked for their wealth; rather, it exists because the slothful have become rich by manipulating, taking advantage of, and routinely stealing from those workers who actually built America and whose labor they capitalize upon and monopolize. This has had the effect of creating generations of working poor who are denied any substantive means by which to escape dire, inherited economic circumstances not of their own making.

This is a piercing irony and turn of fate for the Protestant work ethic. Indeed, as the Gospel of Mark 8:36 asks, "What will it profit them to gain the whole world and forfeit their life?" In America, it seems it will profit them everything! Ethicist and public commentator Eddie Glaude suggests that America's core problem is not the wealth or achievement gap but—recalling the COVID-19 pandemic inequities with which this chapter started—rather something much more fundamental: what he calls the "value gap."[45] For Glaude, the value gap indicates that white lies and the white lives that told them are inherently more valuable than the Indigenous, the enslaved, the indentured, and the exploited people of color by whose hands and on whose backs America has been made. For the underprivileged, to be valued in America costs everything, and the myth about the correlation between work and worth continues to function at epic proportions.

CHAPTER 4

Doctrine of the Good Life

Pride as Knowledge Without Character

The minds of many Americans have been indoctrinated by the guardians of the status quo at the gates of education and learning. As myths and legends become truths unto themselves, they preserve the way things are and put into place systems of knowledge-persuasion that preserve status for some and bar entry for others. In terms of its religious utility, when it is in service to our reality,[1] a "myth" is not regarded as a "lie" but rather as a revered narrative and perspective that reflects what many people believe wholeheartedly. The enduring power of myths and their accompanying symbols is predicated upon an inability to discern the fine line between belief and truth. When throngs of people share pride in myths disconnected from historical truth (the history that is true, rather than the story that is perennially retold), the power of these myths is magnified exponentially in spite of their lack of any meaningful connection to truth. When myths are *taught*, which is to say undergirded by academic, scholarly, and intellectual power, they not only are given permanence but are also esteemed as objective truth. Nowhere is this clearer than with the right-wing backlash to critical race theory (CRT), fueled by far-right cable news media like Fox News and taken up by far-right politicians like Republican Governor Ron DeSantis of Florida.

It is unsurprising that critical race theory, which arose as a corrective to the indoctrination of white supremacist patriarchal logic within the law and legal studies, is facing what amounts to a DARVO-like (deny, attack, reverse victim and offender) campaign by those committed to maintaining the country's foundational myths. As defined by psychologist Jennifer J. Freyd, this acronym refers to a reaction perpetrators of wrongdoing, particularly sexual offenders, may display in response to being held accountable for their behavior. DARVO stands for "Deny, Attack, and Reverse Victim and Offender." The perpetrator or offender may Deny the behavior, Attack the individual doing the confronting, and Reverse the roles of Victim and Offender such that the perpetrator assumes the victim role and turns the true victim—or whistle blower—into an alleged offender.[2]

Right-wing media and politicians like DeSantis have ramped up the use of this tactic, denying the harms perpetuated and maintained by white supremacy and any responsibility they might have to right them, as well as restricting or outright banning education that includes critical approaches to race, gender, and sexuality studies at all levels by calling it racism and indoctrination with white Americans as its victims.[3] The media uses CRT not to describe it accurately as a legal framework taught only in law schools and universities but as shorthand for any attempt to demythologize dominant assumptions around race, gender, and sexuality.

Under the DeSantis administration, the Florida Department of Education (FDOE) announced in January of 2023 its intent to block an AP African American studies course piloted by the College Board, a nonprofit organization dedicated to preparing students for postsecondary education. According to the FDOE, the course ran afoul of Florida guidelines not only because of its (supposed) historical inaccuracies but also because it violated Florida law, an allusion to the "Stop WOKE Act," which among other things prohibits the teaching of the existence of white privilege and unconscious bias in a way that is not "given in an objective manner without endorsement of the concepts."[4] DeSantis had signed the bill into law in April of 2022, justifying it as an effort to curtail politics in the classroom. "We believe in education," he declared, "not indoctrination."[5]

Despite the governor's professed commitment to education, when you consider DeSantis's assertion that "we will not let the far-left woke agenda take over our schools and workplaces," it seems clear that his real disagreement is with any form of education whose politics he dislikes.[6] DeSantis's complaint about a "political agenda" ignores the fact that all education is political (though not all education is indoctrination), insofar as education is directed at effecting certain values, worldviews, habits, etc., and those effects align with political outcomes. An education that reinforces faith in the rightness of capitalism is just as political as an education that criticizes capitalism as antagonistic to standards of fairness, justice, and equity. What DeSantis will not say but is no less true is that he endorses any form of education when it serves his far-right politics, just not when it serves his political opponents. The fight between Florida and the College Board is not a fight over whether or not education is political. It is a fight over what kind of values, worldviews, and habits we wish for education to effect, what kind of citizens we wish for education to cultivate.

Until recently, it seemed that DeSantis was winning that fight. After Florida's public announcement of opposition, the College Board unveiled the course on February 1, 2023. The symbolic coincidence of revealing an African American studies course at the National Museum of African American History and Culture during Black History Month was undermined, however, when it soon became clear that the course had been gutted. An open letter by the African American Policy Forum stated:

> Contemporary issues such as structural racism, Black Lives Matter, reparations, and prison abolition . . . were reduced or eliminated. Lessons and course goals pertaining to intersectionality, Black queer studies, and Black feminism had been removed entirely or downgraded to untested optional material, subject to state and local censors. . . . The arc of history bends backwards if we allow our conceptual assets to be stripped away. Every time we relinquish valuable insights from those who have come before, we pass on to future generations the burden of reimagining and rebuilding livable futures without the tools that have been fashioned to do that work.[7]

In response to criticism, the College Board pledged to revisit the course once more. But the struggle between DeSantis and the College Board was not simply a contest over one African American studies course. It must be placed in context with a yearslong fight over critical race theory in America. Resistance to education that offers sharp criticism of cherished ideas has long been a part of our nation's history. That resistance entered the spotlight because of actions taken by the DeSantis administration, but there has long been a struggle over what is desirable in education. CRT has become a scapegoat for those who are against progressive values in education.

Contrary to what their detractors say, critical race theorists have used their insights to focus on how we have used the Constitution and the legal system to perpetuate inequality and injustice throughout the history of the US Supreme Court. In this fashion, CRT has been a helpful framework for examining, explaining, and exposing how oppressive social dynamics have undermined our laws and societal institutions. Nearly thirty years ago, in his essay "Who's Afraid of Critical Race Theory?," Derrick Bell was already fighting a battle to defend the legitimacy of this emerging scholarly discourse in some of the nation's most elite law schools. In the process of taking on CRT haters and naysayers, Bell asks: "First, what is critical race theory? And second, what ought critical race theory to be? The distinction is useful even though the dividing line between the descriptive (what is) and the prescriptive (what it ought to be) can be quite fine." He describes

> critical race theory writing and lecturing [as] characterized by frequent use of the first person, storytelling, narrative, allegory, interdisciplinary treatment of law, and the unapologetic use of creativity. The work is often disruptive because its commitment to antiracism goes well beyond civil rights, integration, affirmative action, and other liberal measures. This is not to say that critical race theory adherents automatically or uniformly "trash" liberal ideology and method (as many adherents of critical legal studies do). Rather, they are highly suspicious of the liberal agenda, distrust its method, and want to retain what they see as a valuable strain of egalitarianism which may exist despite, and not because of, liberalism.[8]

Conversely, Bell asserts that what defines the prescriptive element of CRT is that "critical race theorists strive for a specific, more egalitarian, state of affairs. We seek to empower and include traditionally excluded views and see all-inclusiveness as the ideal because of our belief in collective wisdom."[9]

The attack on critical race theory is part of a much larger attack on public education, thought, and critical thinking in general. People are much easier to exploit when they are uninformed, undereducated, and underresourced. That attack is also part of a backlash and retrenchment in response to the gains of the civil rights movement as well as the salient Black Lives Matter protests after the murders of Ahmaud Arbery, George Floyd, and Breonna Taylor in 2020. As Bell argues, social justice is dialectical. For every move forward there are several more moves backward, and this has been the case throughout history. Emancipation and Reconstruction were met with Jim and Jane Crow segregation, while the civil rights movement was met with the school to prison pipeline, a backlash that we are still experiencing today. Meanwhile, people who are invested in white supremacy experience equality as trespass. Let me say that again: People who are invested in supremacy and have the power to exclude—whether it is white supremacy, class supremacy, or gender supremacy—experience equality as trespass, a vile transgression, an affront to everything they know and love.

The impact of white patriarchal power can be seen in writings of some of the most influential white, male European minds as well as early American social and political leaders. When the greatest pioneers, statesmen, and architects of the guiding principles of the Enlightenment espouse white supremacy and yet remain uncritically as our standard bearers, America has a crisis of knowledge production that lacks moral clarity and integral character.

Understanding pride as the *doctrinal* dimension of the American good life is essential for distinguishing between the projections and shadows that myths cast. The American discipline of education and schooling produces knowledge that shapes what Americans consider to be good. In short, American education has long indoctrinated Americans to accept social and cultural norms (aka assumptions and lies) about themselves and others as fact. Pride or "knowledge without character" is the process by which Americans presume and impose the supremacy of their worldview to the exclusion of all others. Through an analysis of knowledge production and dissemination, this chapter explores the ways in which the privileged perspectives of some become the normalizing process by which the general public comes to believe in these death-dealing ideologies as they order our world.

In Christocentric terms, pride is the pinnacle of human hubris, whereby we focus on our own ability, an ability often rooted in delusions of grandeur. Where Hebrews 11:1 articulates that Christian faith is trusting in the divine, pride substitutes our own self-aggrandizing feats and self-serving facts as the source of the "assurance of things hoped for and the conviction of things not seen."[10] Philosopher David Hume assesses pride as a pleasant sensation and humility as a painful one.[11] Many wise people have deemed pride to be the greatest of sins. Specifically, American pride emanates from American nationalism and the alleged magnanimity of the United States as a first world power. Many in the world regard the United States as a country proud in the extreme and profoundly lacking in national self-awareness. Take, for example, "Make America Great Again" as a political motto whose adherents exhibit their reluctance or inability to learn moral lessons from past great empires and to gauge its historical significance relative to them. American pride is founded upon Gandhi's blunder of "knowledge without character."

Rather than doing the hard work of gaining an enlightened, historically informed understanding of their nation, Americans have been indoctrinated to believe that self-knowledge is more about trusting their feelings of superiority, whether based on nationality, race, gender, sexuality, class, or ability. As a result, the goal of establishing and advancing common ideals such as fellowship, freedom, and flourishing is ignored. In short, America's system of knowledge production privileges the national *functionality* of its citizens to the detriment of their national character and moral formation. The rising intolerance in the United States for critical reflection and analysis has coddled the American mind and compromised its ability to search for wisdom and to question untruths.

In the first year of my graduate studies in the early 1990s, I recall that several of my white, supposedly liberal, professors—some historians, ethicists, and theologians but all white males—had David Irving's *War Path* (1978), Allan Bloom's *The Closing of the American Mind* (1987), and Richard Herrnstein and Charles Murray's *The Bell Curve* (1994) on their office bookshelves. This bibliographic trend was as common a feature of my professors' office furnishings as was a leather satchel bag and a bottle of bourbon or vodka in their desk drawers. I often wondered, "Why does Professor so-and-so not only own some of the most heinous forms of human horror-turned-scholarly-conspiracy theory but also shelve and showcase them as displayed knowledge?" One day, I got up the nerve to ask that question of one such professor, whom I assumed to be a moral exemplar among our faculty. His response? "Having an open mind means that we contend and consume ideas that are not our own, even when we stand in opposition to them." To which I replied, "That's what I thought at first. But where are books such as Cornel West's *Race Matters* (1993), George Fredrickson's *Black Liberation* (1995), or bell hooks's *Black Looks* (1992), works that offer the truth about America—the truth about which Irving, Bloom, Herrnstein, and Murray are denying through lies disguised as historical revision?" His response: "What are lies to some are merely opinions to others. Our job is to attend to both." As with most concepts that have social, political, and economic consequences, how we "attend" to these distinctions can make all the difference for some individuals and groups—even life and death.

At its best, scholarship does more than merely describe some physical or social phenomenon: It also provides the evaluative tools to determine the relative veracity of the alternatives available. Scholarship should not only be able to distinguish between facts, lies, and opinions, but also provide sound reasoning for doing so. As part of the larger framework of education, scholarship serves as the systemic enterprise of advancing rigorous thought, intentional pedagogy, the capacity of critical thought, the cultivation of character, and the celebration of culture. In other words, the role of scholarship is not limited to the library, classroom, or research facility but extends into society as a whole. The process and substance of scholarly research must inform both the production of knowledge that academics, professors, and teachers transmit to our children and the information our policymakers use to govern our society. As it functions within society, scholarship is typically assumed valid and generally trusted because it has gone through a vetting process by academic peers who themselves possess verifiable expertise.

Though commonly understood as a primarily cognitive endeavor, the actual scholarly enterprise is much more than that because it also shapes various forms of understanding, including the social, political, psychological, religious, and cultural. It encompasses both head and heart on a thinking-being-doing continuum, one that informs the *logos* (how we know), *ethos* (what we value), *pathos* (how we feel), and *theos* (what we deem to be sacred). As such, scholarship is bestowed with social power to be freethinking and far-reaching. It creates worlds of knowledge that are assumed to be undergirded with research and documentation capable of serving as the foundation of their reliability, trustworthiness, and suitability. Yet the scholarly profession's practice is limited in its engagement in that it does not attempt to explain what is already commonly understood (among the dominant culture) and it usually refrains from engaging that which is unfounded and undeserving of research (as perceived by the dominant culture). This is especially the case in the face of false premises where there is an abundance of evidence that can bear clear witness to their unfounded, invalid nature. Without question, bearing false witness wastes the resources of research and risks the reputation of both scholars and the scholarly endeavor.

As noted within womanist epistemology, the arduous work of those scholars who do not embody the personas of dead white men is that they are compelled to "undertake praxis that liberates theory from its captivity to the intellectual frames and cultural values of those which cause and perpetuate the marginalization of [others]."[12] Both obvious truths *and* objectified scholars are continuously placed on trial, burdening women and racial-ethnic minoritized scholars with the imperative not only to know their field, but also to defend and arm themselves from the predictable and unavoidable reality of hate masquerading as history and terror projected onto theory. In so doing, Katie Cannon claims that knowledge is legitimized only when vetted by and interpreted in light of "the gaze of misogynistic subjectivities that masquerade as human normativity."[13]

When underrepresented scholars and perspectives refuse to pay homage or give deference to these theories of terror, they are compelled not only to be doubly informed scholarly experts, but also to be armed revolutionaries, because the truth will not always win out. There are many people who have profited from the "lost cause" of counterfactual research, a scholarly pursuit that promotes fiction as fact, typically without suffering professional or personal consequences. They are the harbingers of history who aim to preserve the aforementioned lies that have assumed the status of myths establishing birthright to the legacies. They provide gravitas to these myths that have not only menacingly mocked the horrors of the past but have also muzzled scholarship in order to accelerate the decline of the pursuit of truth and greater knowledge. The underrepresented scholar often finds herself under the gun and compelled to respond to and disprove controversial counterclaims recognized as worthy of scholarly attention. Yet at the same time, she lacks the agency to do so, in that misinformation rather than scholarly expertise is used to indoctrinate and inform social power.

Dead White Men/Great Books Debate

In his classic writings on world history, German philosopher G. W. F. Hegel argued, "[Africa] is no historical part of the World; it has no movement or development to exhibit. . . . What we properly understand by Africa, is the Unhistorical, Undeveloped Spirit, still involved in the conditions of mere nature."[14] What can one learn from such false accounts that pass as accepted knowledge or conventional wisdom? Such ideas are not merely innocent opinions, but ideologies that annihilate individuals and entire communities while simultaneously building and buttressing institutions of false white pride that some esteem as superior knowledge. What happens when these shameful, destructive cannons become canonical? They take us out. The long tradition of denial and dehumanization has cloaked itself with the power of white pens held by white patriarchs turned philosophers and professors. There is a historic avalanche of scholarly projects and philosophies that served as platforms of publicity and the basis of intellectual policymaking that assigned inferiority to the intelligence of entire races and civilizations of people. The goal and results were not only to deny those peoples' intellect but also to create the impression, first, that this rhetoric was earthshaking discovery and, second, that this was considered knowledge production. The loathsome and age-old thesis—that whiteness was enlightened and blackness was inferior, making explicit that race denoted intelligence and virtue—was embedded yet edited out (e-raced as portmanteau for "erasing race") of our educational project's greatest architects.

These architects of culture, politics, and education were anything but "great" when it came to racial beliefs. Even during the Enlightenment as the alleged peak of human intellectualism in Western society, history reveals a litany of racist insults:

- in 1748, Scottish philosopher David Hume deemed Blacks "to be naturally inferior to the whites" and without "any symptoms of ingenuity";
- in 1756, French philosopher and historian Voltaire described Blacks as "not capable of any great application or association of ideas";
- in 1764, German philosopher Immanuel Kant posited a person's blackness as "clear proof that what he said was stupid";
- in 1787, Thomas Jefferson, Founding Father and third president of the United States, described Blacks as having a "strong and disagreeable odor," an "inferior" intelligence, and an "imagination . . . dull, tasteless, and anomalous";

- in 1846, Swiss-born American biologist Louis Agassiz found it "impossible . . . to repress the feeling that they [Blacks] are not of the same blood as us";
- in 1857, Roger Taney, Chief Justice of the US Supreme Court, opined that Blacks "had no rights which the white man was bound to respect";
- in 1858, the sixteenth president of the United States, Abraham Lincoln, said, "There is a physical difference between the white and black race which I believe will forever forbid the two races living together on terms of social or political equality";
- in 1870, Edward Drinker Cope, University of Pennsylvania zoologist, warned that "the greatest danger which flows from the presence of the Negro in this country is the contamination of the race";
- in 1881, E. A. Freeman, Regius Professor of Modern History at Oxford University, said, "America would be grand if only every Irishman would kill a Negro and be hanged for it";
- and, in 1903, Theodore Roosevelt, twenty-sixth president of the United States, dismissed Blacks as "a perfectly stupid race."[15]

Since the time of these canonical thinkers, classical philosophers, and Enlightenment architects and statesmen, problematic knowledge production and method have aligned prejudice with truth, which in turn has proffered such theories as rational thought. As a result, whatever is worthy of knowledge production or worth knowing supports this explicit bias as the implicit bias of the intellectual project of modern history to conform to the ontological affirmations and epistemological privilege of those who literally embody their norm. In his essay "The Imperial Scholar," legal scholar Richard Delgado states, "It does not matter where one enters this universe; one comes to the same result: an inner circle of about a dozen white, male writers who comment on, take polite issue with, extol, criticize, and expand on each other's ideas. It is something like an elaborate minuet."[16] And yet, while most scholars would claim that prejudice has vacated knowledge production (at least since the 1960s), the fact remains that any counterpoint in intellectual deed or person serves ultimately as the negation of the "ideal" of scholar-thinker either in theoretical praxis or in the person as theorist. The reckoning and dissonance caused by these contradictions between logic and embodiment becomes the ultimate criteria for what it means to be a rational being.

A clear indication of pride is self-praise, the power of which rests in its ability to dehumanize others and to reinforce itself even as it inverts common sense and social realities. The formation and undergirded canon of the great books of white men not only is racist and patriarchal, but also actually exists to blow away the competition so that competing ideologies that expose bolstered sentiments on white racial superiority and patriarchal posturing are considered heretical rather than appreciated for the factual histories they reveal.[17] This juggernaut force of a white male canon virtually blows away and obliterates the majority of US citizens—people of color, all women, working-class people, any group outside of that which does not immediately resonate with the white, Anglo-Saxon, Protestant man. This intellectually designed project manipulated the humanities, social sciences, philosophy, sociology, history, the arts, and even the "hard" sciences. The institutions of education, research, and journalism are also indebted to that project. Literary scholar Paul Lauter invites us to critically reflect upon this highly selective process:

> [Why] is the literary canon of importance and what precisely was the history of its development in the twenties? I mean by the "American literary canon" that set of authors and works generally included in basic American literature college courses and textbooks, and those ordinarily discussed in standard volumes of literary history, bibliography, or criticism. Many such books are also available in widely marketed paperback series of "classics." Obviously, no conclave of cultural cardinals establishes a literary canon, but for all that it exercises substantial influence. For it encodes a set of social norms and values; and these, by virtue of its cultural standing, it helps endow with force and continuity. Thus, although we cannot ascribe to a literary canon the decline in attention to the concerns of women in the 1920s, the progressive exclusion of literary works by women from the canon suggested that such concerns were of lesser value than those inscribed in canonical books and authors. The literary canon is, in short, a means by which culture validates social power.[18]

The design, thought, and purported goals of the Enlightenment are to foster and advance the formation of an open society in general, and education in particular, so as to make reliable information, facts, and knowledge accessible to better understand the world. No small part of the Enlightenment endeavor involves cultivating a deeper understanding of cultures, communities, and character, and drawing from a diverse range of knowledge that affects and informs the diversity of issues that help sustain a better world. Toxic perspectives and theoretical prejudices that are *extolled* rather than *interrogated* for their implicit biases create a heavy burden for the employment of knowledge toward the formation of competence and character. Those who are given privilege and power to perpetrate this type of empowered knowledge-disinformation make it infinitely harder to reverse and overturn false evidence appearing to be real by those who stand on the margins or are in alliance with them for fear of professional or personal reprisal.

Teaching and Learning Pridefully

Pride is a motivational force in teaching and learning. Primary and secondary educators, with both the Pledge of Allegiance as their first order of business and their preoccupation with a "teach to the test" mentality, "school" (read: indoctrinate) young children into a reward system of belief that to follow such a regime is to be meritorious, and thus extolled.[19] Parents take "pride" in their children's performance, wearing their grades, and even their school pride, on varsity jerseys and car stickers, credentials that promote and elicit pride that connotes high regard and social esteem. These public displays of academics (and athleticism, when all else fails) eschew any value of humility or collective sense of educational equality. Within a society and culture steeped in Eurocentric norms versus Afrocentrism, Cartesian logic of "I think therefore I am" outperforms and overshadows Ubuntu philosophy of "I am because we are," except in the case of the many male student-athletes of color who are expected to forgo their educational cultivation at their own physical and intellectual expense for the good of the whole and the championing of collegial coffers and school spirit.

Consequently, cultural norms have reified these modes of pride to be celebrated as the veritable pep rally of education. As ethicist Michael Eric Dyson notes, pride does play a critical role in cultivating confidence, determination, and the execution of the seemingly impossible.[20] Without some sense of pride, what else would engage and motivate excellence in the scholastic endeavors of students and the scholarly production for academics? However, pride within institutions of education is not merely one aspect or feature within teaching and learning, but rather is privileged and prioritized over knowledge itself. To be sure, though pride plays a role in education writ large, it is not culturally or universally homogenous on the world stage. The presumed role of knowledge to form character and aid in the construction of solutions for the common good and the benefit of society lends itself to a collective sense of knowledge being inextricable from a greater good beyond the individual. The social value of knowledge, then, should place in perspective, if not in check, the self-conscious emotion of pride and serve as a mediator between self-esteem and social contribution so as to differentiate between competence and conceit.

White Epistemic Solipsism and PWIs

Central to the examination of the Enlightenment and education in America is the understanding that the accommodation of masculinity and the affirmation of whiteness have been a privileged reality. American pride is a signature form of Eurocentric, patriarchal *epistemic solipsism*, an ideology that has remade the world for its own purposes and desires.[21] This epistemic solipsism incarnates itself as a place where the preservation of white and mostly male privilege (and the power associated with both) is ensured by the exclusion of other people's realities. This has come to be the defining characteristic and very being of whiteness in its encounter with nonwhite people, both locally and globally.

Informed by the "willful oblivion" and "fantastic hegemonic imagination" of white supremacy, womanist ethicist Emilie Townes states that this reality has such a hold on academic discourse and theological worlds that it manipulates knowledge production to create cultural caricatures and historical stereotypes. Furthermore, Townes explains that the fantastic hegemonic imagination is indebted to an insurmountable influence on social order.[22] She states:

> In dazzling displays of intellectual hubris . . . discourses ignore the diversities within their (and our) midst in an ill-timed and increasingly irrelevant search for an objective viewpoint that can lead us toward the [T]ruth. Such inquiries have served (and continue) to preserve a moral and social universe that has mean-spiritedness at one end of its ontological pole and sycophancy at the other. A large portion of *noblesse oblige* often acts as filler and buffer for those who seek to maintain or recapture an intellectual and material corpus that reeks of an onerous status quo. This often makes [women and people of color] in the academy and in society the invisible visible.[23]

The social construction of educational institutions converges around issues of power. As veritable knowledge producers, they become a means of social control in which fundamental identity markers, such as cultural heritage, religious beliefs, and communal experiences, become subsumed, dominated, and domesticated. Taken in the aggregate, the works of Michel Foucault, Anthony Giddens, Pierre Bourdieu, and Erving Goffman among others reveal the interiority and scaffolding of Townes's insights by displaying how this phenomenon, under the auspices of race, culture, and power, drives educational formation in a purportedly modern age.[24] In essence, white racial identity as the embodiment of rational thought is socially constructed within the United States and is valorized in what Foucault calls "learning machines," which are most often predominantly white educational institutions (PWIs)—schools, colleges, and universities, both public and private.

Giddens and Goffman demonstrate how this is accomplished by means of a *sequestration experience*,[25] which upsets the general sense of personal well-being and equilibrium held by individuals, particularly women and people of color, who matriculate within these institutions. This sequestration leads to the reconstruction of identities in a world that implies, if not insists, that the color of one's skin overrides the content of one's character. Meanwhile, Bourdieu's concept of *symbolic power* helps us understand the ways in which nonwhite men may aspire to "exceptional" status by recreating themselves as credentialed and cultivated individuals within these male-endorsed, predominantly white contexts. Ironically, through this transformation, women and people of color, once hailed as inferior or aberrations, now come to serve as tokens in the perpetuation of white institutions. In so doing, they (often unwittingly) facilitate and approve the disavowal of the very theories, histories, philosophies, and cultures that would otherwise afford their freedom, flourishing, and further factual pursuits.

This is not a blanket indictment accusing all predominantly white educational institutions of perpetrating the myths of white supremacy or male patriarchy in all their glory. Some PWIs have worked to incorporate intentional efforts to improve diversity, equity, and inclusion (DEI) within their institutions. Their moves toward self-correction are most certainly welcome, and some are increasingly effective. However, in spite of such efforts to overcome a legacy of institutional attachments to entrenched American values and practices that have long incorporated white and male supremacy, this is difficult to accomplish in a brief period of time. Institutional characteristics and systemic practices developed within PWIs possessing long histories and employing professors and administrators themselves influenced over their lifetimes by pervasive American practices prioritizing certain racial and gender realities make even intentional and willful self-correction a project for the long haul. These efforts are even more complicated in a context where most conservative-leaning states have outlawed funding DEI programs in state university settings during Trump's second term.

The Construction of Institutions

Education professes to provide a road to success within a nation that purportedly promises social mobility rather than social hierarchy. For the working class, it offers a pathway out of poverty. For the privileged class, it secures a dedicated fast lane, bypassing what others must endure. As a result, public schools are filled with underserved students who are vulnerable to manipulation and exploitation that stems from overcrowded classrooms, underpaid teachers, and inadequate resources and services. Meanwhile, exorbitantly expensive, elitist, and exclusive private schools chart their students' paths to the winner's circle. The determination by the US Supreme Court in the 1954 decision *Brown v. Board of Education of Topeka* that "separate is inherently unequal" remains true to this day, as long as the Supreme Court continues to uphold it through *stare decisis* (unlike its recent overruling of *Roe v. Wade*). Which is to say that "many schools for the richest American kids have gates and security guards; the message is you are precious to us. Many schools for the poorest kids have metal detectors and police officers; the message is you are a threat to us."[26]

Following this path, the entire realm of private education, including American charter schools, private schools, parochial schools, boarding schools, and elite colleges and universities, serve as valorized institutions that provide the most assured means of achieving ultimate success, albeit at no small cost in terms of personal character formation. In her 2021 exposé in *The Atlantic*, "Private Schools Have Become Truly Obscene," Caitlan Flanagan describes how

> elite schools breed entitlement, entrench inequality—and then pretend to be engines of social change. . . . These schools pass on the values of our ruling class—chiefly, that a certain cutthroat approach to life is rewarded. True, they salve their consciences with generous financial aid. Like Lord and Lady Bountiful, the administrators page through the applications of the nonwealthy, deciding whom to favor with an opportunity to slip through the golden doors and have their life change forever.[27]

Within these institutions, character is mainly determined by skin color and rationality is automatically equated with masculinity. During the course of one's schooling, many come to realize that such a skewed worldview is diametrically opposed to, or at least in tension with, their own worldview that once might have been formed by such factors as cultural heritage, religion, and family. In short, marginalized peoples' educational experiences within these solipsistic institutions are governed by an ontology that is antithetical to their own. These institutions masterfully disengage individuals from their unique modes of communal formation. By means of the experience of sequestration, they undermine empowering, effective, and nurturing expressions of familial, cultural, and/or religious group identity, such as common sense, intuitive reasoning, and hermeneutics of suspicion. As Flanagan contends:

> What makes these schools truly ludicrous is their recent insistence that they are engines of equity and even "inclusivity." A $50,000-a-year school can't be anything but a very expensive consumer product for the rich. If these schools really care about equity, all they need to do is get a chain and a padlock and close up shop.[28]

Even educational institutions that hold fast to tradition and heritage (e.g., girl's/women's schools, HBCUs, Jewish schools, Catholic schools, Freedom Schools, etc.), however socially necessary they might be, still in some ways take pride in their particular elitism, exclusivity, power, and prestige. To distance oneself from public school is to distance oneself from the public itself, with its diversity of race, class, and ethnicity, and from aspirations that education should be regarded and treated as a common good. There's an argument to be made that Milton Friedman's case for charter school vouchers in *Capitalism and Freedom* sought to impose market-driven values upon a rightward retrenchment of social conservatives deeply troubled by a post-*Brown* and post-Title IX cultural shift. So much of this debate is clogged up with "more money makes things better," as opposed to focusing on "much more money + much less white supremacy and elitist paternalism" as a truly winning combination.

Today, the privatization of secondary education is an attractive option for those threatened by the developing diversity of American demographics. Liberty University provides an illuminating example. Created in 1971 by evangelical pastor Jerry Falwell Sr., Liberty is one of many private Christian higher education institutions in America. Together, these spaces offer tens of thousands of students the promise of refuge from a society deemed corrupt by conservative opponents of progressive stances toward issues like race and gender. Institutions like Liberty justify their existence with a commitment to advancing conservative values, but history reveals that their roots are in segregation and resistance to a changing America. Falwell opposed integration, and it was his resistance to the erosion of interracial barriers that drove him into the world of private Christian education, first with Lynchburg Christian Academy and then Liberty University. Falwell's defense of a racist status quo, as Anthea Butler says, "would become the bedrock of evangelical organizing in the 1970s and beyond. While abortion is commonly understood as the issue that began to unite evangelicals in the 1970s, I give that dubious honor to the issue of race."[29] Once a part of the conservative resistance to civil rights, today Liberty remains enlisted in an effort to reverse the waning of evangelical Christian influence, with its present opposition to critical race theory, reproductive rights, gender-affirming policies, etc. The ultimate goal of Liberty University and other private white institutions of that ilk is to wield enough political power to bend society to their vision. "Evangelicals," Butler warns, "are concerned with their political alliance with the Republican Party and with maintaining the cultural and racial whiteness that they have transmitted to the public."[30] Liberty University's private status is juxtaposed alongside its desire to define the public space in which we all live and move.

As private and public education is divided for America's schoolchildren, and public education is increasingly populated by a majority of diverse faces in systems still largely controlled by white money and power structures, and private education is largely white and intentionally separated from the diversity that characterizes developing American communities, the fault lines built into America's future seem clear. Nikole Hannah-Jones assesses the privatization of education as an inherently immoral American phenomenon, one that promotes itself as furthering the ideals of learning and character when, in actuality, it is rigidly entrenched in the hypocrisy of racism and classism, all the while masking it as educational success:

> We have a system where white people control the outcomes, and the outcome that most white Americans want is segregation. . . . If one were to believe that having people who are different from you makes you smarter, that you engage in a higher level of thinking, that you solve problems better, there are higher-level ways that integration is good for white folks. . . . For black children, the benefits of attending integrated schools are much more drastic. It's literally, will you receive a quality education or not? Will you be a full citizen in the country of your birth?[31]

Elite schools foster epistemic solipsism that disrupts character and undermines actual learning processes that ground and form identity outside of its parameters. In that they possess the power and will to make their epistemic solipsism an assumed "reality," these schools are able to impose their particular worldview upon their environs. This imposition has contributed to their historic ability to create a *manmade* world out of disparate yet naturally emerging identities that can be interpreted as education and the formation of character and represented as the tradition of "Americanization."[32] Every effort is made to inscribe these institutionalized values upon those schooled within the learning machine. By discounting as substandard or secondary that which makes people uniquely who they are—for example, their religion, cultural heritage, ethnic identity, and family—and thereby depriving and denying them opportunities to engage and learn from the organic intellectualism that diversity affords, the refining and enlightening processes of "schooling" wield the power to transform peoples' identities and then validate how they interact. This solipsistic schooling strips individuals of their hermeneutical points of reference and imposes upon them a monolithic civic humanism and religiosity. Following this logic, every step toward this assumed pathway to success renders its adherents as desacralized and dehumanized beings. While such an experience is horrific for any person, people of color must soon realize that their hyphenated identity and disconnection from the traditional (and by extension the divine) is not only apostasy but also potential genocide.

This phenomenon specifically circumscribes moral development and the formation of self-identity.[33] The educational institution's objective is to operate as a learning machine that serves as a mechanism for supervising, hierarchizing, and rewarding its subjects. Under the guise of cultivating successful individuals for the greater good of society, PWIs are granted maximal latitude in the formation of the self, the desires, and the vocations of its ranks. In any attempt to become a part of such an institution, the person seeking to be included and ultimately achieve success must often assume as doctrinal the characteristics that are legitimized by their inclusion into this august, credentializing body.[34] This codification of belief requires board members, administrators, faculty, and students to hold fast to false doctrines of success (e.g., matriculation, employment, promotion, and governance within them) as unquestioned truth. Attending, teaching, working, and governing within the richest and whitest private school in one's community, the most elite boarding school, and the rarified Ivy League institution signals success in and of itself, separate and apart from one's actual aptitude, talent, qualifications, and achievements. These institutions continually validate a person's sense of entitlement, privilege, and virtue, as long as the person pledges allegiance to them alone. This institutional practice occurs by creating a space in which privileges are incontestable, in spite of any transgressions. Without institutional recognition, unaccredited persons effectively have no cultural identity of their own. This is, once again, the inevitable result of living an existence informed by the dominant society's epistemic solipsism, together with its conscious dismissal of the rest of the world.

Academic institutions as such lay claim to students' most formative years, the time when not only what they learn, but also who they know themselves to be and aspire to become, is reflexively formed and somewhat finalized. The question of "How shall I live?" becomes the foremost concern in their day-to-day lives. Such an ethical imperative, however, is not self-determined. In one's daily life and interactions with others, intimate expressions of selfhood and engagement with one's environment often prove to be more powerful than one's education, and the more marginalized one is (by gender, race, class, nationality, language, religion—or lack of it—and sexuality, etc.), the more angst-ridden this normalizing process becomes. How to behave, dress, speak, and eat are among the innumerable questions regulated by one's peers, through the media, and within an institutional legacy, questions that have to be answered in day-to-day decisions.[35] In other words, as Giddens explains, "self-identity . . . is not something that is just a given, but something that has to be routinely created and sustained."[36] In this regard the real question is not "Who am I?" but rather "Who am I expected to be?"

Therefore, this reflexive project of the self is particularly evident when observing the lives of marginalized people in PWIs. In choosing to come to these contexts and elite schools, they strive to accommodate the institutional legacy of what an Ivy League graduate or boarding school student should be. However, many are confronted with the realization that they can never embody these visions. Being *other*, they can merely ascribe to the roles that have been cast for them. Needless to say, women, people of color, or students from nonnormative socioeconomic contexts and roles are bereft of the societal worth and influence idealized in the romantic traditions established by these institutions. One of the consequences of this experience is that their lives become fragmented and their realities become inverted as they diverge from the norm defined by the college and the larger society. Another consequence is captured in words often associated with the liberatory educator Paulo Freire: "When education is not liberating, the dream of the oppressed is to become the oppressor."[37]

Taking pride in oneself is based more on membership or affiliation within a given learning machine than on the educational endeavor itself and focuses less on what the student wants or needs to become and more on what the institution and society would have the student become. In the same way that finishing schools were designed specifically to indoctrinate young women into upper-class cultural rites and social graces so as to gain a husband, so, too, the most elite learning institutions supplant knowledge formation with identity formation as a means of being groomed for success and social standing in society. Instead of knowledge, you look for "know how" or "how to work the system." Instead of "how to put knowledge to work," identity and ideation are formed by peer group consensus and social stratification within the purview of the institution's normative gaze. Pridefully playing the part while confronted with being different from that stereotype results in a thoroughly dissociative self that compels the underrepresented to become disembodied in an attempt to be safe.[38] Minoritized students, for instance, in this situation are unimplicated in, though aware of, their bodily desires and dangers. With this disposition, many regard themselves, as Du Bois would note of his own educational experience over a hundred years ago, with the same "amused contempt and pity" with which the dominant society gazes upon them.[39] These institutions are detrimental and death-dealing to the self-reflexivity of educational identity development. Thus, by fixating their own needs on meeting external standards, these students lose sense of their bearings. As Helen Lynd puts it,

> once this happens, "we have become strangers in a world where we thought we were at home. We experience anxiety in becoming aware that we cannot trust our answers to the questions, 'Who am I?' 'Where do I belong?' . . . [W]e become again children unsure of ourselves in an alien world."[40]

The Role of Corporate Media

What educational systems enact, the corporate media produces in excess. As these educational systems teach Eurocentric ideals, they project whiteness as the perspectives of a demographic majority and perpetuate a false, minoritized representation of US demographics. However, these ideals represent only one-third of a global reality that is populated by a two-thirds majority of people of color. The corporate media projects as "public knowledge" commonly held realizations of what it means to "be in the know." Thus, through soundbites or snapshots one can succinctly deduce the truth of the matter rather than a stereotype or skewed statistic. Where whiteness, maleness, or wealth are seen or operative, the assumption is that "all that's fit to print" is all the truth there is and all that's worth knowing. Little doubt or regard comes into play as to what is considered "newsworthy" or how the media moguls, rather than good journalism, report social realities as such, as opposed to socially constructed myths proclaimed as truths.

The omnipresence of corporate media takes hold of the average American. What reading books or testing theories (however slanted) did as a part of the educational process in schooling, the media does by positioning itself as the lifelong learning machine. Newspapers, cable news shows, social media journalists, pundits, and commentators now substitute and override books, classes, and knowledge production. The general public's connection and reliance on the constant news loop often results in people having only a vague understanding of life outside of the media mill. The ability to figure out, research, or discern fact from fiction becomes stultified because people are compromised by the fact that they are never allowed the time, space, or means to discover and cultivate their own distinct identities, separate and apart from stereotypes. The modern media juggernaut derails them from charting a course of self-actualization. It thrusts them blindly into a tumultuous society, one that is devoid of security and full of risk.

Educational institutions erode identity and inculcate students with knowledge of how to game a system in place of systematic critical thought and knowledge. The deleterious results are many, one of them being a steady, gradual decline in the general population's ability to critically process the news as presented on a 24/7 news cycle basis by the various corporate media outlets. There is a circular system of corruption of power at play here: The media are manipulated so as to manipulate the people who both trust and consume their products. Esteemed philosopher and linguist Noam Chomsky discerned and devised an accounting of the various manners and means—often unseen or unacknowledged—by which the population and popular opinion are purposefully molded by means of media manipulation.[41] This process is buttressed by educational systems for the masses that simply lack the resources needed to educate well, or by elite educational institutions that are founded upon the comfort and complacency of privilege, the erosion of communal identities, and a steadfast devotion to teaching students how to work the elite educational system itself. The result is more and more students who are ultimately less prepared to question the effects and resist the temptations of the purposeful misinformation with which they are increasingly bombarded by the media's manipulation.

First and foremost is the corporate media's ability to focus attention away from pertinent issues and challenges by means of an onslaught of meaningless, worthless drivel. Distractions abound, diverting critical thought and questioning away not only from political, economic, and social issues and challenges, but also from the very misdeeds of the powerful who pull the strings that either cause these issues and challenges or that respond poorly to them. On an ever-increasing basis, the corporate media presents the public with shallow feel-good stories, outright misinformation, clickbait, and loud, talking-head opinion pieces presented as fact, in place of sustained scrutiny and factual exposés. Enthralled by the shiny media objects and ever-less equipped to push back, the public is gradually succumbing to these purposefully diversionary tactics.

"Gradually" is the operative word here. The media phenomena that Chomsky identifies grind away over time, chipping away at the public's critical resilience and resistance. Over time, for example, people become accustomed to the corporate media's solutions offered up in response to faux or misinterpreted social problems of their own making. What better way, for example, to implement economic advantages for the wealthy few than by creating the sense or concern that an overreliance on forms of social assistance is fostering economic weakness and disintegration? How better to undergird violent, racist police systems than by presenting minoritized citizens as a constant menace and threat to white welfare and safety? If the corporate media can create crises such as these, then the public will be more inclined not merely to defer to them but to renounce resources and civil rights as "part of the problem."

Take for instance the dog whistle politics of Fox News, particularly coming from former prime-time Fox host Tucker Carlson, whose program *The Tucker Carlson Show* once ranked regularly as the most watched prime-time cable show. A *New York Times* investigation found that in over four hundred of Carlson's shows he promoted the "great replacement" theory, "a racist conspiracy theory, once relegated to the far-right fringe, that Western elites are importing 'obedient' immigrant voters to disempower the native-born. The Anti-Defamation League called for his firing, noting that such thinking had helped fuel a string of terrorist attacks."[42] Carlson regularly courted followers of QAnon, a conspiracy theory that accuses Democrats of engaging in a child-sex trade and elevates Donald Trump as the messianic figure leading the charge to "save the children." In 2016, Edgar Maddison Welch heeded rumors circulating on the internet that Hillary Clinton was abusing children in the basement of Comet Ping Pong, a Washington, D.C. pizza parlor. Armed with an assault rifle, Welch stormed the restaurant—firing once to open a locked door—and vainly searched the premises before being arrested. The incident, remembered by its Twitter hashtag #Pizzagate, exemplifies the danger of a widespread post-truth, alternative-facts culture and the failure of corporate news to combat the rising tide of misinformation.

Indeed, more and more the corporate media infantilizes the public, presenting us with oversimplified, emotionally driven approaches to complex social issues and events. By appealing simplistically to the public's base instincts and arousing unsettling emotions such as fear, anxiety, sadness, and obsession, the media cultivates a mental field within which to plant the seeds of misinformation, distrust of knowledge and fact, and lack of critical thought. Whether using violent images to justify gun rights or images of babies to promote antiabortion agendas, heightened emotions become placated, assuaged, and comforted by the diversionary news stories and simplistic solutions to issues that are either fabricated or misrepresented. The result is a public that finds itself put on constant emotional edge by the corporate news media, only to be led to a false sense of security and serenity by the social salve it offers.

Finally, the extent to which the media come to understand and know the public better than it knows itself cannot be underestimated. In today's data driven world, corporate media outlets and the powerful few behind them both shape and only then come to know our proclivities, our unarticulated emotions, desires, fears, and joys. Much like with education, there emerges a clear system of mass media misinformation at play here. Media manipulation becomes a cycle in and of itself, one to which people become accustomed and unquestioning adherents and, therefore, one by which they become entrapped and beguiled. As a result, the corporate media is increasingly able to exert power and control over a population failed by an educational system that left it ill-prepared to discern and differentiate between true and false news.[43] In fact, a lawyer for Fox News argued in court in a defamation lawsuit that Carlson did not have an obligation to investigate the truthfulness of statements he made on his show and his audience did not assume that he was reporting facts.[44]

While scholarship and education play a critical role in the knowledge formation of US citizens, the media has far more reach and influence in terms of how most Americans are educated about the world in which they live. Thus, for most individuals the teaching, learning, and understanding of "civics" occur to a greater extent from televisions, computers, and smartphone screens than from chalkboards and lecterns. In many ways, educational literacy has been supplanted by media literacy in terms of how everyday citizens, educators, and political leaders are able to keep themselves informed and persuade others. Our conceptualizations of democracy, economy, social standing, and global realities are brokered less by educational discourses and more by media industries. The well-known adage that "the media can't tell you what to think but it can tell you what to think about" suggests that what journalists present as newsworthy is all that is worth knowing—information rendered as soundbites on loop or as frontpage headlines. Whereas the delivery of the morning and evening newspapers and the broadcast of the local news used to demarcate the major time frames of the day, the 24-hour news cycle can now be found on numerous channels and innumerable online newspapers. These media outlets post in real time, taking pride in their omniscience, omnipresence, and ability to indoctrinate the masses with information whose excesses mask its sins of miseducation, factual omissions, framed agendas, profiled publics, foment of public unrest, and undue influence on public opinion, people's life choices, and ways of life. Thus, broadcast and print journalism inform and shape to a disproportionate degree much of US society's self-perception and normative understandings of local and global events as well as the world around them.

A recent and clear example of the power of news to shape or reinforce values Americans already hold is how the numerous criminal indictments of Donald Trump in his first term as president have been treated. CNN and MSNBC continually stressed the evidence laid out in the thirty-seven felony counts spelled out in the indictment stemming from the Justice

Department's investigation into the classified documents held by Trump in various locations. They reached their largely Democratic audiences, who need little persuasion that the former president is likely a crook. Yet, Fox News and other conservative cable and streaming media venues reinforced Trump's DARVO strategy at every point. The problem is not Trump, who only did what presidents have done forever; the problem is the "weaponization of government," or a "rogue Democratically controlled" or "Biden-controlled" Department of Justice seeking to destroy an opponent in order to steal another election from the American people. Such media reinforcement of prevailing biases of Americans enables contemporary voters to feel quite comfortable believing myths completely dissociated from any connection to truth. Seventy-six percent of Republican voters believe the indictment was "politically motivated," and 80 percent of Republicans believe Trump should be able to serve as president even if he were to be convicted in the case.[45]

In response to broadcast journalism's outsized ability to indoctrinate the public, in 1949 the US Federal Communications Commission (FCC) created the fairness doctrine as a guiding policy designed to uphold basic ethical standards and to urge broadcasters not only to allocate airtime to cover controversial matters of public interest but also to air these matters equitably by representing contrasting and well-researched views. As a result, what was framed as news through news segments, public affair shows, or editorials could be understood as that which was essential to know and verifiably true.

However, in 1987, the FCC eliminated the fairness doctrine and in 2011 removed the rule that implemented the policy from the Federal Register, an action that has heightened political polarization, social prejudices, and the manipulation of the economy. Thus, what was once obligatory subsequently became optional, and now is virtually obsolete. By many estimations, this has enabled media empires and moguls to consume and control the civic impact and investigatory integrity of the vital role and character of the press, with less, if any, regard for rooting out corruption, making accessible information about public policies and political matters, and representing the diversity of societal opinion. The smart, sober, persistent, and courageous news professionals become fewer and fewer in number, and gone is the press that turns raw data and factual information into accessible knowledge for public consumption and civic engagement. The bad news is that news outlets and their attentive audiences prefer distraction to dialogue, problems to solutions, coddling to clarifying, emotions to evidence, and assumptions to accuracy, all the while losing character as this muddles our comprehension of reality in the process.

Conclusion

From noteworthy scholarship to normative educational practices to newsworthy reporting, knowledge is now more about being indoctrinated to the belief that privileged and powerful Americans are good and worthy of the public's admiration. This belief is perpetuated by various knowledge sources imposing quintessentially American false ideologies and faulty policies without regard to practical considerations or the possibility of the veracity provided by the insights and real lived experiences of others. The obsession with self-praise and self-worth stymies and thwarts the formation of critical thought and character capable of fostering the resolve and skill to address and rectify real social problems. Maintaining the center of praise and attention of these knowledge sources necessitates that the public be captivated by matters of no real importance. Along the way, American competence and character become compromised caricatures, built upon a flawed foundation and maintained with poor vision—the hallmarks of a civilization whose pride precedes its inevitable fall.

CHAPTER 5

Material of the Good Life

Envy as Science Without Humanity

Without knowledge that cultivates character and the flourishing of humanity, a fierce preoccupation emerges in people to protect their position and power at all costs. Anxiety and aspiration are tied to the maintenance of enviable power and position over others. Science without humanity leads to control over bodies. Science empowers humanity to create amazing technologies, but when we betray the ideals of science and humanity in the process, we also create the illusion and delusion of becoming God or a god. Many people with religious convictions often assume that the achievements of modern science are in contradistinction to religion. However, the actual work of science often tries to extend God's work and the Divine's objective; it becomes a practice of the supernatural. Science turns God into a verb, for it is the practice of doing what people expect God to do. Science is God-ing. This happens when humans can subdue not only bodies and lives, but can also create and fashion them in accordance with their own imagination, if not entirely in their own image. This arouses in them a longing not merely to transcend human limitations, but to play God, making envy natural rather than evil.

The material dimension of envy spawns the development and tangible manifestation of our greatest yearnings, which we attain in no small degree by means of science devoid of humanity. In response to our longings, we deny the fact that there are limits to our longevity and strive to surpass natural, physical limitations in order to superextend our lives or, at least, refashion our lives according to our own image. Scientific achievements that are unchecked by concerns for humanity render palpable a reality in which the sky is the limit and we expect to fulfill our every desire by any means necessary. Unfortunately, these desires are not always altruistic, the means are not always ethical, and the resulting achievements have included atomic bombs dropped from the sky with their destructive radiation and biological warfare gases that contaminate the air we breathe.

Playing God

The materiality of scientific envy enables humanity to "play God"—to assume power beyond our means. Playing God refers to the unchecked, raw human curiosity either to claim or to create power that is out of bounds to us through natural means. To be the best human, for example, is to be superhuman. We recall the story of Prometheus, who defied the gods by stealing divine fire from Mount Olympus and providing it to human beings for the technological "good" of humanity. Prometheus is credited with bringing the spark of creativity to humanity, transforming humans from subordinate beings made of mere ash and dust to sentient creatures freed to some degree from divine control. Though he was a champion of humanity and the progenitor of the human arts and sciences, the other gods cursed Prometheus with eternal torment for his transgression. With Prometheus bound to a rock, Zeus summoned an eagle to eat his liver, the site and symbol of human emotions, which would regenerate nightly, only to be devoured again by the eagle the next day. Prometheus satiated humans' envy by providing them with the means of the gods in the form of divine fire, the very means by which they could make themselves godlike. Human beings felt they needed to explain the origins of fire as divine gift precisely because fire seemed beyond anything they could have known or have controlled themselves. As science expands the categories of human knowledge and creates what previously was unknown or controls something previously uncontrolled, humanity expands its own self-definition and increases its power in ways that would have seemed superhuman to earlier generations. Thus, humanity appears to grow increasingly more godlike. Whereas Prometheus leans into his human qualities to benefit humanity, human beings incline toward the divine by seeking to know and control that which was previously unknown to and uncontrolled by them.

As in religion and mythology, *anthropomorphism* is the perception of a divine being having human qualities, while *theomorphism* is the human (divinity's creation) understood as having divine form fashioned by the deity itself and imbued with divine power. The Abrahamic religions' emphasis on the theomorphic conception of "man" is inextricably linked to the anthropomorphic conception of God in which God is a "man" and men are God. In considering the pride of humanity and mastery of science, the anthropomorphic inclination informs our good life and the theomorphic agency of science gives shape to our ultimate desire to have and hold a life.

A relatively recent version of this Greek myth is Mary Shelley's classic novel *Frankenstein; or, The Modern Prometheus*, one that also depicts the dire consequences that result when men play with fire and fashion themselves as gods. The novel is titled after its protagonist, Dr. Victor Frankenstein, a scientist whose unfettered curiosity arouses within him not merely the desire to create life, but the envious yearning to be worshiped as the very source of life itself. He believes that a "new species would bless me as its creator and source; many happy and excellent natures would owe their being to me. No father could claim the gratitude of his child so completely as I should deserve theirs."[1]

Victor's yearning illuminates the "god envy" that we often disregard or overlook in our assumptions about scientists and the motivations of their pursuits. Victor is not the stereotypical lonely scientist locked in a lab seeking to fill the void of his loneliness. He did not create the monster out of a desire for family or intimacy but for the sake of creation alone. In fact, he rejected the opportunity to marry and father children with his beloved fiancée, Elizabeth. Instead, he "collected the instruments of life around [him] that [he] might infuse a spark of being into the lifeless thing that lay at [his] feet."[2]

The intrinsic evil of science for claiming God's handiwork situates the human being, "Victor," in perpetual conflict with the scientist-creator, "Dr. Frankenstein." A mutually dialogical relationship between scientist and society is replaced with his exclusive desire to realize the eschatology of his expertise. Dr. Frankenstein disavows and severs all human ties in favor of his divine aspirations, which he hopes his expertise as an inventor will make possible. Instead of doing what seems appropriate (being a good human, husband, or father), he pursues only that to which he aspires: to be a god unto whom his creations "would owe their being," in Shelley's words.

What sparks Frankenstein's envious urges is the drive or desire to address and resolve our most primal angst and concerns as human beings: As we strive for a better life, we find ourselves both daunted by the task and our efforts thwarted by natural and happenstance occurrences, including our physical and mental decline. Like the Greek myth of Sisyphus, the human condition is such that we are simultaneously confronted, if not condemned, by a task akin to pushing a boulder up a mountainside only to have the boulder to roll back down before reaching the top. According to philosopher Albert Camus, the wisdom of gods (be it Prometheus, perhaps, and especially Sisyphus's tale) is apparent in what he calls "the absurd" predicament of humanity, by which he means the futility of a life spent in an eternity of labor, futile because one can succeed at tricking neither the divine nor death.[3]

Science without humanity denies the ultimacy associated with the lesson of Sisyphus. In that lesson, the boulder always wins. But rather than viewing the boulder as an ultimate foil, science without humanity interprets it as a mere stumbling block, one that science will eventually overcome as humans figure out its secrets. Camus sheds light on the absurdity of this human phenomenon by explaining that there is an intrinsic conflict between what we want from the universe (the good life) and what we find in the universe (lifelong ambiguity that results in death-dealing circumstances). We will never achieve the good life in the form of scientific assurances, order, or the meaning for which we desperately yearn within the human trajectory; no matter our efforts or endurance, our fate seems sealed by the absurdity of wanting what we can never have or hold. A civilization that understands itself as having the "inalienable right to life, liberty, and the pursuit of happiness" will perpetually struggle with living in a world devoid of such blessed assurances.

Fueled by post-Enlightenment aspirations, science seeks to resolve this "absurdity" of the human condition and to rescue us from our Stygian underworld by materially manifesting our desires that stem from the solipsism of our human pride. No longer are those desires false, fantastical projections. No—through science, we humans hope to become godlike. Through science, we humans attempt to manifest the "super" of the "natural" and the "extra" of the "ordinary" in order to actualize our wildest dreams.

As neurologist Victor Frankl explains in his work *Denial of Death*, we humans chase after delusions and diversions in an attempt to evade mortality and death as the ultimate reality of finite existence in the world. "This too shall pass" operates in contradistinction to the Stoic philosophers' *memento mori*, the Latin phrase meaning "remember you must die." It is a paradoxical rendering of the human condition: a forward thinking, future-focused endeavor that compels us to remember and reckon with an event—our own death—that has yet to occur. This "mindfulness" reminds us what we are supposed to be, what we can control (as opposed to what we cannot), and what is the inevitable, inescapable end of all things. Science that serves humanity knows better than to waste its time trying to accomplish what it cannot, and instead concentrates and seeks to accomplish what it learns may in fact be possible. Even after the invention of organ transplant procedures, highly effective cancer treatments, and thousands of drugs that reduce pain and minimize the effects of unhealthy bodies, science must always remind itself that it cannot cheat death, and that its attempts to prolong life may actually be death-dealing.

Human striving in its overreaching quest for scientific triumph can result in the unintended consequences of human tragedy. When the lustful, greedy, and prideful gives way to envy, then our solipsistic tendencies can foster science without humanity. When some within the scientific community seek to merge the anthropomorphic and theomorphic, they exemplify a pride that produces a distinctly post-Enlightenment and animated envy that can go beyond natural curiosity. "Do no harm," the Hippocratic oath for physicians, is replaced for these scientists with "Know no bounds." This particular type of scientist focuses more on what is possible rather than what is moral. Their reference point is the power to create rather than an actual reverence for life. The double consciousness of Dr. Victor Frankenstein conflates his character as human inventor with an aspiration to become the divine intervener and thereby transforms his monstrous actions into the human form created in his own image. He never considered how the human frailty of his creation might find expression or conscientization, nor did he consider its effects on the good of society or on those he once loved. Both creator and creature die prematurely. Frankenstein's self-serving creative act undermines the life-giving possibilities of creativity that reside in humanity itself; he exhausts his own possibilities for life by chasing after the life he created. The creature kills himself because his creator failed to provide adequate meaning for the reality of his existence. As Josephine Johnston attests:

> He considers the good that might come from his discovery—it might lead to development of a method for bringing the dead back to life—but he fails to consider the future of his initial experimental creation. Although he is aware that the single-minded pursuit of his scientific goals is throwing his life out of balance, he utterly fails to consider the possibility that the form he has stitched together and will soon animate may go on to cause harm to anyone, including Victor himself. We might compare Victor to some modern scientists who have stopped their work to consider its potential for harm, such as those who gathered at Asilomar in the mid-1970s to consider the implications of research on recombinant DNA or those who recently called for a moratorium on germline gene editing.[4]

Human invention is often driven by envy, as Shelley's *Frankenstein* teaches us. Rather than creating life in a *sui generis* fashion, Dr. Frankenstein has to scavenge from random dead, discarded, and criminally obtained human body parts to fashion a creature in his image. This is critical to note, because in addition to Shelley being a pioneer and progenitor in establishing science fiction as a literary genre that men have subsequently dominated, her novel also provides a protofeminist critique of creation from both a sacred and secular perspective. Shelley's core argument is that Dr. Frankenstein's creation is not a "monster" in and of itself, but rather is so on account of its origins being devoid of any nurturing, such nurturing often being attributed to feminine involvement or typified as the biological determining factor and value of women. The creature has no mother and is separated both from female companionship and human love. In the interests of hubris and not humanity, the process of its creation violates the nature of human reproduction. Moreover, as an organic entity devoid of a soul, the product of Dr. Frankenstein's outsized ego, technological hubris, and irrepressible arrogance, the creature is only a "monster" because it is made in the image of its male human creator.

The monstrous aspect of the inventor Frankenstein is symbolic of the cause and effect of toxic masculinity. Shelley's myth unmasks the heteropatriarchal familialist ideal that governs gender identity and institutional sexism, the ideal that claims that men are strong and women are weak, that men should be the "head" of the household and women the "body" that should be subjected to the will of men. Not only does this ideal—one that accords with male desires—inform the organization of all of life, human embodiment, social structures, and the political economy, it also often results in the violent subjugation of women and their bodies as the dominant male gaze seeks phallocentric sexual pleasure and the perpetuation of male lineage.

Toxic masculinity claims that men are strong and women are weak in an effort to shore up the physical and psychological reproduction of patriarchy. Sigmund Freud provided much of the psychology behind the claim. He interpreted women's lives as dominated by their reproductive organs. In his 1925 essay, "The Psychical Consequences of the Anatomic Distinction Between the Sexes," Freud claimed that "women oppose change, receive passively, and add nothing of their own." In essence, they receive what men give them. For him, they are men without penises, and making life requires a penis. Women are unfinished and unproductive without the man who plants in them the ability to grow life. Hence, Freud spoke of "penis envy," a natural condition he says women experience as soon as they become aware that they are without a penis. They envy the male. Having a child of their own, especially a male child, claimed Freud, can help women overcome the paralysis of their penis envy.[5]

An additional insight relevant to Shelley's critique is the fact that both the origins and manifestations of toxic masculinity are what psychoanalysts understand as the "womb envy" felt by some men for the reproductive capacity of women. It was Karen Horney who introduced the concept of womb envy (as the neo-Freudian feminist equivalent of penis envy), which she identified as the male envy of pregnancy, nursing, and motherhood and the undeniable power (and perhaps sole power) of women's primary and phenomenal role in creating and sustaining life. She also clarified that penis envy, if there is such a thing, is best understood as a symbolic yearning on the part of women to be able to experience the prestige and social standing that men seem to enjoy simply because they are male.[6] Womb envy she regards as an unconscious motive that leads men to denigrate women, control their reproductive rights, and, when taken to the extreme, obviates the need for them in the first place, as Victor's motivations and actions exemplify. Victor's god envy is certainly compatible with Horney's concept of womb envy. Victor turned his back on women and wanted to create life on his own, without the necessity of having a woman involved.

One could certainly understand more contemporary arguments about reproductive choice and reproductive prospects in light of these concepts. The birth control movement, particularly as it emerged in America during the early twentieth century, sought to give women a measure of power over their reproductive capacities. Taking such control also meant women were seen as assuming power to separate the sexual act itself from the natural end of conception, or the creation of life. The church, and men in general, did not believe that women inherently possessed these kinds of rights. As feminist politics emerged, women began asserting not only their political rights, but their rights over their own bodies, emphasizing not only their right to have sex without its resulting in pregnancy, but their right to choose to favor their own lives over being required to carry unwanted or risky pregnancies to term. Ever since the 1920s, powerful men in America, accompanied by conservative women allies, have attempted to control these decisions for women. In spite of nearly a century having passed since birth control became an issue in America, and almost fifty years since *Roe v. Wade* (1973) had supposedly settled the abortion question, recognizing the rights of women, within reason, to control their own bodies, we now see a revival of legislation across multiple states in America to strip them of those rights, and on June 24, 2022, the Supreme Court overturned *Roe v. Wade* in a monumental decision/reversal.[7]

Texas passed the "Heartbeat Act" in May 2021, a law that, in an effort to stop all abortions after fetal activity begins at about six weeks, enlists the public and "deputizes" ordinary citizens to pursue and report people involved in the process of abortion.[8] Even though women often do not even realize they are pregnant before that time, they are no longer allowed to seek abortion legally in the state after that time. If they do, and a private individual is aware of it, that individual can use the courts to sue for ten thousand dollars in statutory damages and legal fees. The Florida legislature approved the "Fetal and Infant Mortality Reduction" act on March 3, 2022, which makes abortions illegal fifteen weeks after the first day of the woman's last menstrual period. Neither the Texas nor Florida laws allow any exceptions for rape or incest. It is notable that 73 percent of the members of the combined houses of the Texas State legislature, 65 percent of the Florida State House and Senate, and the governors of both states are male. Now, male heads of state or household controlling women (in large part to counter their reproductive power) is clearly nothing new. It makes sense that such activities might in fact originate in psychological factors grounded in Horney's concept of womb envy. The male obsession with creation and control is a common refrain in making science without humanity what it is today and has been throughout *his*tory. Science itself tends to provide us with at least a sense that the omnipotence attributed to God is within human reach.

Accompanying the battles over reproductive choice and reproductive prospects is the rise of in vitro fertilization, surrogacy, and the emergence of so-called test tube babies. The "Religious Right," represented in groups like the Moral Majority and their ilk, challenged assisted reproductive technology and claimed it to be outside the divine will or natural law. They helped to set the stage for a culture war fought over the control and censure of women's rights to reproduce or to cease reproduction.

In the twenty-first century, stem cell research began to take the controversies to more complex levels. Stem cells are the basic building blocks for all tissue, bones, and blood and other bodily fluids, and they are able to generate new stem cells that can take the place of diseased cells, leading to the possibility of regenerating and repairing diseased cells in the human body. Such treatments seem to raise hope for dealing creatively with spinal cord injuries, Parkinson's disease, diabetes, Alzheimer's disease, and an assortment of other human ailments. Since stem cells are typically and controversially drawn from bone marrow and embryos and other such locations, scientists have begun to investigate whether they can increase access to stem cells by transforming regular adult cells into stem cells. This task, a new technique, is accomplished by reprogramming the genetic material in human cells.

Stem cells also exist in amniotic fluid as well as in umbilical cord blood—not only that from live births but also from abortions. Harvesting stem cells that are mined in the abortion process has increased the controversy surrounding research in these areas, particularly since the most successful or productive or healthy stem cells are those produced as embryonic stem cells, which come from eggs fertilized at in vitro fertilization clinics that end up not being implanted in a woman. Donors of those eggs sign informed consent forms allowing the use of these embryos for scientific research. The reason for use of embryonic stem cells rather than adult stem cells is because none are as durable or as flexibly applied to different locations of the body as the stem cells of embryos.

Genetic manipulation has serious implications not only within various biological fields but also in the potential to foster significant god envy among the scientists who push the boundaries of fabricating human life. Traditionally, humans have manipulated genomes indirectly by controlling breeding and selecting offspring with desired traits. Genetic engineering involves the direct manipulation of one or more genes. Most often, a gene from another species is added to an organism's genome to give it a desired phenotype.[9] In 2018, scientists in China announced successful "gene editing" (of the HIV disease lodged in the genetic material of the father[10]) that resulted in two so-called designer female twin babies brought to term in 2019, which of course allows for the possibility that these "enhancements" can and will be passed on to future generations. To this point, this is the first and only occasion on which such babies have been created, and the event created an ethical firestorm.

Like most scientific advancements, genetic manipulation has the potential to be used for the betterment of humanity by eliminating devasting genetic diseases that cause great pain and suffering for individuals and their families. Yet, it also has the potential to be utilized to create scientifically designed embryos that do not just eliminate negative genetic traits but insert "positive" characteristics to meet the specifications laid out by the prospective parents. As Juan Floyd-Thomas, Mark Toulouse, and I concluded in earlier research, "With the scientific knowledge to unlock the secrets of DNA, not only will we understand that human beings are made in the image of God; we will make technological use of the material contained within us to make gods of us all."[11] Stem cell scientists are naturally interested in working with cells that are free of particular genetic defects that can then be used to regenerate diseased cells infecting living human beings. Researchers have created stem cell lines, cells free of genetic defects that descend from a single original cell and grow in controlled labs. The stem cells that result can be frozen and shared with other researchers.

Generations before the Black Lives Matter movement, scientists knew that Black lives could serve as the matter or raw material of Western scientific advancement. Black life matter became the building block upon which the advancement of medical research could be formed when Henrietta Lacks became HeLa. Born more than a century ago, Henrietta Lacks died of an aggressive cervical cancer in 1951 at the tender age of thirty-one. Months earlier, doctors at the Johns Hopkins Hospital in Baltimore had taken samples of her cancerous cells from the tumor on her cervix. While diagnosing and treating the disease—and without the knowledge of Lacks or her family or their consent—the physicians gave some of that tissue to Dr. George Gey, a prominent cancer and virus researcher. According to Gey's report, "Mrs. Lacks' cells were unlike any of the others he had ever seen: where other cells would die, Mrs. Lacks' cells doubled every 20 to 24 hours."[12] Although the cancerous cells were wreaking havoc with her body and ultimately devastated it, those very same cells demonstrated an extraordinary capacity not only to survive but also thrive and reproduce. In essence, the genetic material harvested from Henrietta Lacks had proven to be immortal. In the wake of this startling discovery, Gey shared her cells widely with other colleagues in the global scientific community. Ironically, the cells of a working-poor Black wife and mother whose cancer diagnosis was even poorer than her family's bank account became a veritable workhorse in the realm of biomedical research that has yielded massive financial fortunes in the decades since she passed away.

Over those intervening decades, none of the research laboratories and research firms that profited astronomically from her cells ever handed over any money to her family. Neither the general public nor her descendants had any idea of the ways in which science had laid claim to the actual physical cells of Henrietta Lacks and had profited massively from them, both scientifically and financially, by growing and reproducing her cells and shipping them throughout the world in great number for use in scientific experiments. As one of Lacks's descendants recalls:

> That day in Erika Johnson's high-school biology class, some 20 years ago, is seared into her memory. The teacher was leading the students through experiments involving cells from a widely used line known as HeLa. The cell line originated from tissue taken from a woman named Henrietta Lacks—and Johnson's mother was a Lacks. "This is my great-grandmother I'm holding in my hand," Johnson remembers feeling. "It was a very surreal situation."[13]

For decades after Lacks's death, hospitals, doctors, and scientists never asked the Lacks family for their consent even as they disclosed her name publicly, released her medical records to the media, and even published a genomic profile of the HeLa cells online. Eventually, the genome had to be taken offline due to public outcry, and the family reached an agreement with the US National Institutes of Health (NIH). Shortly thereafter, the premier scientific journal *Nature* published the data of another HeLa line.[14] Today, the work done with HeLa cells—named after the first two letters of her first and last names—underpins much of modern medicine, including key discoveries in oncology, immunology, infectious diseases, and was even used in research for developing COVID-19 vaccines.

Before the exploitation of Henrietta Lacks's very cells came the pseudoscience of phrenology, the study of skull shapes according to race as an indicator of mental abilities, and the "medical apartheid" of African peoples across the globe that makes up a comprehensive history of medical experimentation on African Americans, from the era of chattel slavery to the present, as a means to control the bodies, if not the freedoms, of Black persons. Throughout history, in a way that extends from health-care treatment to hospital admissions, scientific inquiry has turned subjects into specimens for the sake of medical advancement without informing the persons involved. This can be said for those Black male victims of the 1930s Tuskegee "untreated syphilis" research.[15] It is also true for the Black women who had their bodies and reproductive systems subjected to cruel treatment, medical butchering, and gruesome gynecological experimentation.

The medical care for enslaved Black women was spare to nonexistent. If treatment was given, the accompanying medical experimentation subjected Black girls and women to great pain, deformity, and often death. James Marion Sims, dubbed the "father of modern gynecology," was known for experimenting on Black girls and women without administering anesthesia in attempts to perfect cesareans, ovariectomies, and hysterectomies for the advancement of gynecology.[16] After Black women's bodies were used to produce chattel for the slave trade and to provide living laboratories for experiments, what was once resourceful became a threat. From the 1970s on, Black women as mothers (rather than breeders) were a menace to a society bent on limiting unwanted elements. Although other marginalized groups such as Indigenous, immigrant, and poor white women experienced forced sterilization during the twentieth-century eugenics movement, medical practitioners also focused on thwarting the surplus population of Black children. Black women, as unique victims of what Moya Bailey calls "misogynoir," were increasingly targeted. Anti-Black racism and sexism compounded the medical mistreatment of Black women, subjecting them not only to forced sterilization but also, in the crack cocaine epidemic of the latter part of the twentieth century, hypersurveillance.[17]

Faced with the extraordinary events of 2020—the Black Lives Matter movement for racial justice as well as the unequal toll on communities of color from COVID-19—many scientists have begun to reckon with their own past racist injustices. Some have called for a complete end to the use of HeLa cells, or at least a marked reduction in their use in research. Arguably, since the cells were obtained without Lacks's knowledge or consent (although this tactic was legal at the time), any use of these cells is an unethical practice that further perpetuates a historic injustice. Yet such token gestures to ameliorate the guilty consciences of scientists after decades of malign neglect is not what many members of the Lacks family want. Buoyed by Henrietta Lacks's centennial year and the accompanying social media hashtag #HELA100, dozens of Lacks's descendants are calling for a long overdue celebration of her life and legacy. As Jeri Lacks-Whye, Henrietta Lacks's granddaughter, told *Nature*, "I want scientists to acknowledge that HeLa cells came from an African American woman who was flesh and blood, who had a family and who had a story."[18]

What is known cannot be unknown, what is already resourced cannot be returned. Regret occasioned by guilty consciences seems neither to prevent ongoing bad behavior nor to serve as precedent to stop future acts. Rather than heeding the moral of the horrors of the worst ends caused when science acts without concern for humanity, we continue to believe that the ends of greater knowledge and increased control over material and resources always justifies the activities of such science—largely because it increases the human capacity to assume attributes of God and place them "in service" of what is deemed to be the necessary powers seeking to further some purpose. Aviad Kleinberg reminds us that envy or desire transforms from mere feeling to a force that causes the envious person to believe that what they want is also theirs to possess. Kleinberg writes:

> Desire makes right in the repressed parts of our consciousness: a thing is ours because we want it [yet] it is in the hands of someone else. Deep down, we feel that everything belongs to us—or at least should. In a better world, others would be able to enjoy only the toys we do not want. [But with envy, that] others have things we want is a moral outrage.[19]

Perhaps no story illustrates better how science contributed to the creation of "toys" with the intention that they should rest only in particular hands than that of J. Robert Oppenheimer, the scientist hailed as the "father of the atomic bomb." Oppenheimer's work as a theoretical physicist is overshadowed by his pivotal role in the development of the atomic bomb during World War II. Oppenheimer served as the director of the infamous Manhattan Project from March 1943 to October 1945. During that period, he directed a workforce of nearly six thousand scientific and military employees housed in New Mexico's Los Alamos National Laboratory under conditions that were seldom free from intense mental and moral stress. Nevertheless, his leadership undeniably played an influential role in the research and design of a working model of a bomb that shifted the once theoretical into the purely tactical. His ability to recognize these tensions and reconcile them toward weaponizing the wonder of atomic energy represents what US Secretary of War Henry L. Stimson deemed Oppenheimer's "genius" and "leadership."[20]

One of the most salient glimpses of Oppenheimer's moral crisis is his invocation of lines from the Bhagavad Gita to describe bearing witness to the resulting devastation of the Trinity test:

> We knew the world would not be the same. A few people laughed, a few people cried, most people were silent. I remembered the line from the Hindu scripture the Bhagavad Gita. Vishnu is trying to persuade the prince that he should do his duty and, to impress him, takes on his multiarmed form and says "Now I am become Death, the destroyer of worlds." I supposed we all felt that, one way or another.[21]

On August 6, 1945, the United States dropped an atomic bomb on Hiroshima, Japan—the first time such a catastrophic weapon was ever used in active military conflict. As the city disappeared under a mushroom cloud, Captain Robert Lewis, the copilot of the *Enola Gay*, the bomber that dropped the deadly device, wrote in his log, "My God, what have we done?" Three days later, the United States unleashed yet another atomic bomb on Nagasaki, devastating the city beyond belief. Historians often credit the firestorms unleashed on Hiroshima and Nagasaki as prompting the end of the Second World War. But we cannot overlook how the strategic decision to use that new dreadful technology officially ushered in both the nuclear age and the Cold War, a dual reality from which the world is still reeling all these decades later.

Without a doubt, Oppenheimer knew very well the lethal potential of atomic energy as well as any American alive both then and now. Unfortunately, his urgent pleas for peace and his belief that we must be governed by open-mindedness about America's international responsibility for the atomic bomb and the later evolution of nuclear weapons after 1945 seemed little more than a whisper in the wind once nuclearization became the be-all and end-all of global hegemony.[22] Yet, the fact that Oppenheimer quoted the Bhagavad Gita seems strikingly apropos considering his all-too-late realization of the possible outcome of the invention, and that realization reflects the highest possible stakes of atomic/nuclear diplomacy in the late-modern era. Although his words reverberate through recent world history as a stark reminder of the devastation and consequences of nuclear weapons, Oppenheimer himself did not espouse pacifist commitments by any stretch of the imagination. In the early postwar era, he sat on the Scientific Panel of the Interim Committee, a high-level committee providing recommendations on issues regarding nuclear technology. In a report to the committee, the panel wrote that they saw "no acceptable alternative to direct military use" of the bomb against Japan. And when it came to the nuclear bombings, Oppenheimer claimed to carry "no weight on [his] conscience."[23] Somehow in his mind he separated the need for scientific accomplishment and control over the atom from either the decisions of military or political leaders or the devastating human implications of those decisions. Those problems were matters for governments to worry about, not scientists. Somehow, even though Oppenheimer knew better than anyone what splitting the atom might mean for humanity (including making a weapon that could be used), he could separate his work as a scientist from the overarching interest of what it meant to be human. This ability in itself places this particular project of this individual scientist and his team in the category of science without humanity.

Oppenheimer and those associated with the project all knew and could well imagine the devastation to be unleashed as a result of the project's work in the Los Alamos lab. There is no plausible deniability, no ability to say that the consequences result from somebody else's decision. Nuclear physicists who make bombs know full well what their scientific engineering accomplishes. Despite all the wishful thinking in the world, the desire to separate cause and effect did not shield Oppenheimer and his colleagues from the ethical implications of their efforts, nor did it prevent him and his team from understanding the true meaning of the bomb's development at the time. Indeed, two years after Trinity, Oppenheimer told physicists that the bomb "dramatized mercilessly the inhumanity and evil of modern war." He went on to note that "the physicists have known sin; and this is a knowledge they cannot lose."[24]

For many scientists, the realization of how their achievements in the lab would ultimately be used militarily toned down their excitement of discovery in the dawning era of nuclear technology. But there is no masking the ugly truth that building an unstoppable weapon of war drove the Manhattan Project. No scientist involved could claim their work was simply the pursuit of scientific knowledge. While Dr. Frankenstein sought to create life, Oppenheimer sought control of the atom, the basic building block of all life. He knew the consequences of controlling the atom to produce a weapon, but he did it anyway because nothing seemed more consequential for science than learning how to control the atom, which would enable the scientist to control all matter. Nothing seems more godlike than the omnipotence contained in the ability to control matter. On June 11, 1945, a month before the Trinity test, scientists at the University of Chicago's Metallurgical Laboratory issued the Franck Report, which argued against potentially using the atomic bomb on Japan. "If the United States would be the first to release this new means of indiscriminate destruction upon mankind," the report argued, "she would sacrifice public support throughout the world, precipitate the race of armaments, and prejudice the possibility of reaching an international agreement on the future control of such weapons."[25] In a pragmatic move to assuage US military leaders, the report recommended an early demonstration of the bomb's awesome power on an uninhabited area. Decision makers flatly rejected the suggestion.

With Oppenheimer's tools for world domination in its hands, the United States established itself as a world power above all other nations. However, the chicken had flown the coop. Consumed by envy of American power, it would not take scientists in other nations long to catch up. We might understand the ability to destroy cities and peoples with a single bomb to be evil in and of itself. Such evil acts, done to annihilate that which cannot be controlled (according to psychoanalytic psychotherapist Patricia Polledri), amount to envy:

> Envy is wanting to destroy what someone else has. Not just wanting it for yourself, but wanting other people not to have it. It's a deep-rooted issue, where you are very, very resentful of another person's wellbeing. . . . It is silent, destructive, underhand—it is pure malice, pure hatred.[26]

The scary realization might be that when this hatred is projected toward another's—or other's—well-being, there is no limit to who could be labeled "other," whether on account of nationality, race, religion, gender, or any other category. In fact, the wholeness of creation reveals a great diversity that cannot be controlled, and this inability to control may lead to the kind of envy that ends up annihilating us all.

Scientists who saw the proverbial handwriting on the wall did in fact raise their voices in dissent against the manufacturing of the most deadly weapon the world had ever known. For instance, Joseph Rotblat became the only scientist to leave the Manhattan Project. Years later, he played a key role in issuing the Russell–Einstein Manifesto, which argued that nuclear weapons "threaten the continued existence of mankind" and urged all governments to "find peaceful means for the settlement of all matters of dispute."[27] Others, including scientist Leo Szilárd, tried to share with President Harry Truman his concerns about the moral and geopolitical implications of the bomb's use, but to no avail. After all, when John Foster Dulles expressed immediate concern to Truman in the wake of Hiroshima, Truman responded with a handwritten note, referring to Japan: "When you have to deal with a beast you have to treat him as a beast."[28] Denying the humanity of an enemy—in this case, an entire nation—is a common justification for total annihilation.

Katherine Way, one of the leading scientists on the Manhattan Project, also wrestled with the bomb's use before the successful Trinity test. Her concerns continued after the war. Even as Oppenheimer became an advisor to the Atomic Energy Commission after World War II, he lobbied for international arms control. The government revoked his security clearance in 1954 in a hearing during the second Red Scare by dredging up his old Communist sympathies. Oppenheimer had made some political enemies by arguing against the development of the hydrogen bomb, and eventually the government revoked his clearance and stripped him of any lasting political power.[29] In the end, when the expansion of scientific knowledge carries with it the potential for expanded power and control, it is often difficult to retract or pause, and those with the desire for power often silence the voices of conscience in their pursuit of more.

Omniscience on Demand

While some developments in science have sought to create and control bodies and matter, developments in the science of technology are providing ever faster access to knowledge and information. This access includes not only an ability to find answers to specific and factual questions, but to know the actual thoughts of others based on their actions and location/movements and to predict their preferences and proclivities in order to monetize them. Technology has created algorithms capable of collecting vast troves of personal information, behind the scenes, on any human being connected to a phone or computer. The technology involved is not employed to engage people, but rather to categorize them, to bring the market to them, to present them with convenient options that will suit their foreordained tastes and interests, and to entice them to consume what it presents to them.

Artificial intelligence (e.g., disruptive technology) is illustrative of the ways in which convenience morphs into control and consciousness. In 1959, Jack Kilby of Texas Instruments received a patent to develop miniaturized electronic circuits, and in 1967, Texas Instruments placed in our hands a calculator that saved us the trouble of "figuring out" monotonous math or complex calculus. At the same time Kilby was developing these electronic circuits, Robert Noyce of Fairchild Semiconductor Corporation began his patented work on a silicon-based integrated circuit. At the time, no one knew where the combination of these two technologies would go over the course of the next five decades.[30] The result of their work led to the development of microchip technology, and that technology has changed the world forever over the past fifty years. The microchip has made possible both artificial intelligence (AI) and machine learning (ML). Further, these chips have facilitated the advent of on-demand industries and services available through computers, phones, and watches that has totally altered how we learn, communicate, and interact with others. Well named, artificial intelligence now allows a computer to know our thoughts perhaps better than we know them ourselves. Computers and other electronic devices, powered by the algorithms embedded in AI, have now become intelligent agents that can perceive and respond to data immediately and accurately.

While geeks are able to understand the technicalities of microchips and the hardware that houses them, for ordinary Americans, the software is far more important for how they negotiate their days. As long as the software serves us, we do not concern ourselves on a daily basis with how the hardware enables algorithms to track us based on our use of, and love for, the software. As Pew Research data has found:

> Algorithms are aimed at optimizing everything. They can save lives, make things easier and conquer chaos. Still, experts worry they can also put too much control in the hands of corporations and governments, perpetuate bias, create filter bubbles, cut choices, creativity and serendipity, and could result in greater unemployment.[31]

Algorithms create a measure of control that may grow exponentially with each passing year. Scientists are no longer needed for the equation. And being what they are, algorithms have absolutely no regard for the humanity of the subjects providing the data. In wanting to know everything, and employing algorithms to accomplish that goal, we end up knowing nothing and giving knowledge over to the artificial intelligence that filters it for us.

While the inspiration for these scientific developments included the desire to access greater human insight into humanity, a 2017 Pew Research study concluded instead that AI algorithm initiatives have in fact introduced dangers since humans' removal from the equation. Artificial intelligence algorithms essentially have a mind of their own, and hence humans increasingly lose their initial governing agency. Pew concluded by addressing several negative themes detailing how the best of scientific intentions can result in dehumanizing inventions:

Theme 1: Humanity and human judgment are lost when data and predictive modeling become paramount

- Programming primarily in pursuit of profits and efficiencies is a threat
- Algorithms manipulate people and outcomes, and even "read our minds"

- All of this will lead to a flawed yet inescapable logic-driven society
- Some fear people could lose sophisticated decision-making capabilities and local intelligence
- As code takes over complex systems, humans are left out of the loop
- Solutions should include embedding respect for the individual

Theme 2: Biases exist in algorithmically organized systems

- Algorithms reflect the biases of programmers and datasets
- Algorithms depend upon data that is often limited, deficient, or incorrect

Theme 3: Algorithmic categorizations deepen divides

- The disadvantaged are likely to be even more so
- Algorithms create filter bubbles and silos shaped by corporate data collectors. They limit people's exposure to a wider range of ideas and reliable information and eliminate serendipity

Theme 4: Unemployment will rise

- Smarter, more-efficient algorithms will displace many human work activities
- Some seek a redefined global economic system to support humanity[32]

The Pew observations are not projections, but rather result from perennial glitches objectively observed from repeated and regular performance of AI algorithms. As computer scientists seek greater knowledge through algorithms, they instead find that these initiatives consistently elude their expectations. In 2020, software engineer Ben Dickson drew attention to some of the research related to the danger of algorithms at Facebook, in hiring practices, in the ways "bad actors" can access algorithms to take down the internet, in "the introduction of unacceptably dangerous algorithms into the market," and to White House studies that detail "the potential effects of AI-driven automation on the U.S. job market and economy."[33]

In all these ways, the internet becomes not only the traffic controller of information but the gatekeeper of knowledge and perhaps the definer of truth itself. This reality ushers in a new era in which people possess the ability to access information but run the risk of being controlled by artificial information that is downloaded as if it were true and good for us. As

Pew points out, researcher Andrew Tutt has actually issued a call for the development of a new "FDA for Algorithms," noting that

> the rise of increasingly complex algorithms calls for critical thought about how to best prevent, deter and compensate for the harms that they cause. . . . Algorithmic regulation will require federal uniformity, expert judgment, political independence, and premarket review to prevent—without stifling innovation—the introduction of unacceptably dangerous algorithms into the market.[34]

Omnipresence Overload

When the ability to have all power or all knowledge fails us, the desire to appear to be powerful or knowledgeable by being everywhere, to seem larger than life, becomes evident. We can become envious of how others are perceived and want that for ourselves. We want people to see us as we want ourselves to be projected—with an always smiling face, with evidence of success, and with the kind of ubiquitous presence that our Facebook or Instagram accounts allow. When one has a desire that is less concerned with engaging others and more concerned with impressing and influencing others to see the world from one's point of view, it necessitates more than mere power or knowledge. It almost demands the personification not only of who you are, but also of the accompanying desire to control who you need the other to be in relation to you. Much of social media or online activity has to do with fulfilling the need to be in the forefront of others' minds. Exhibition becomes evidence for whom one is. One's projection through staging becomes who one is in the minds of others. The fiction of who one is suddenly presents itself as fact for those flooded by what one projects on the internet, here specifically on Facebook. If one can flood the newsfeeds of others with projections of who one is (or who one appears to be), then one begins to become larger than life and to create an entire world or reality through an image one is projecting merely through digital media. Sociologist Erving Goffman describes this "all the world's a stage" phenomenon in his "theory of dramaturgy." According to Goffman, when we project an identity in an effort to manage the perceptions of others, we present ourselves as we hope others will believe us to be.[35]

When we do have agency, perhaps by possessing power and knowledge, the need to project our ideal selves into the public sphere becomes all the more necessary. In the world of social media, impression and influence become omnipresence. Our sense of security, and perhaps relevance, then rests not only in our power and knowledge but also in our interventions and interruptions into the realities of others. These interventions become paramount to meet our most fundamental needs. The social media platforms afforded by Facebook, Instagram, and Twitter (now X) become technological disruptions and human engineering that allow for cloning and reproduction that would rival even Victor Frankenstein's imagination or Oppenheimer's genius. In today's world of social media, you can become who you want to be, or pretend to be who you are not. You do not have to be a scientist to design a being who can extend your reach—you can use the proper lighting and software to create an alternate reality that does the job. You can be who you want to be and become "fake famous" through the projection of an image. For example, HBO premiered a documentary in 2021 called *Fake Famous,* which sought to show "just how easy it can be to game the social media economy in order to become a famous online 'influencer.'" It is now possible to buy "followers" of your Instagram account. These "bot followers" have been created by computer hackers who have stolen "countless random identities by pilfering peoples' photos, names and bios." At the right price (say $120 for every 7,500 followers and 2,500 likes), you can choose to appear to be far more popular than you actually are.[36]

Where are we without technology? We live in a world driven by technology. Can we even imagine how we could have navigated the coronavirus without Facebook or Instagram or Twitter? They kept us connected. But much of what we are connected to is in fact contrived. We may have been drawn in by a bot who had stolen the identity of one of our real-life friends who invited us into a world, not of our friend's making, but the making of a bot's creator. The Enlightenment had us running out of Plato's cave, where everything was just shadows. Today, it seems as if everybody is running into the cave, not realizing it actually is a cave, believing that the reality of human existence is found there rather than in the real world. We want to see all the shadows of human projections in 4K or whatever the highest resolution available might be. We, along with everyone else, can be ever-present on social media. We find our facts there, based more on the projections of reality we have come to favor than on any immediate connection to actual reality itself. We are either actively connected to creating projections of ourselves and the world around us for others to see and experience, or we are actively compelled to follow the projections (whether personal posts or purchased bots) of others created to influence the way in which we will respond either to reality as we perceive it, or to an alternative reality that is being created for us.

An overexposure to realities is far more egregious than an overexposure to social media. Fake "friends" have more social value than real friends, and they are a lot easier to find and to keep. Illusions are endearing and powerful. A shadow is far more reaching than substance. Echo chambers, whether bought or sold, give a sense of validation or feed our ego even as they lack any sincere dialogue, discernment, or difference of opinion. What reinforces what we want or believe is better than reality itself, and ends up taking its place.

This desire to recreate the world anew, based on power, control of all knowledge, and omnipresence, has undeniably shaped the fates of nations. Envy—science without conscience—has been used to create some nations and destroy others. Consider the way Vladimir Putin has created an entire narrative to justify launching a vicious war against Ukraine. He controls all information in Russia, making it nearly impossible to hear factual information there about the Russian invasion of Ukraine. Putin's power, perspective, and voice is ever-present in Russia; no other voices carry equal status. He uses internal social media and a false world of his own creation to assert a myth of the Nazification of Ukraine that needs purging in order to provide relief for the Ukrainian people. In so doing, unjust war is transformed into a humanitarian exercise. All the while, Putin perpetrates a massive effort to break the will of everyday Ukrainians by a consistent, never-ending barrage of artillery aimed at civilian targets, effectively modeling a genocidal action.

In some ways, the world of social media mirrors the efforts of control Americans denounce in the case of Putin and Ukraine. The ongoing attempt to create a world out of disparate yet naturally emerging identities can be seen in the invented tradition of social media influencers on the one hand and bots on the other. Whether by influencers or bots, every effort is made to inscribe values upon all would-be participants in mainstream American society without their ability to deflect or discern reality from illusion. As historian Christopher Lasch informs us, these efforts to project and control strip individuals of their hermeneutical points of reference and impose upon them a monolithic civic humanism and religiosity.[37] Following this logic, every step we take toward idealized self/world renders us desacralized and dehumanized beings. With the ability to interject, intervene, and control the people with whom one interacts daily, one can get away with anything. Here, fact is worse than fiction, and what appears to be hyperbolic (comparing the world of bots to the acts of Putin) can become pure horror. The Ukrainian experience is indeed horrific, but perhaps we come too late to the realization that our own disconnection with reality—and by extension with the divine—is not only apostasy, it carries within it the seeds of potential genocide.

Consumed by our insatiable need for adoration and access, everyday citizens who live in the realm of social media are primed for the ill-fated temptation of clickbait. The intellectual design of artificial intelligence is made accessible by social media because it allows the intricacy of technology to become a toy at the disposal of whoever decides to pick it up (one might say there are many "bots for dummies" manuals available these days). The process is quite simple, according to Renee DiResta, research manager at the Stanford Internet Observatory: "Create an online persona, seed social media with a message, game platform algorithms to amplify it, win shares from real people, see mass media pick up the message, [and you get a] 'kill chain'[—]the information-security term for the sequence of exploits to take over a targeted computer."[38] The power to create using algorithms combined in some measure with bots attached to most any message results in a genuinely global presence that creates its own kind of power and knowledge; in fact, it becomes a kind of god (a type of Frankensteinian monstrosity) that can potentially run away from its creator, that not only cannot be stopped but cannot really be found, even though it is illusively ever-present.

The efforts to impress new realities upon us are numerous and the force of these impressions continues to grow in type and number, making it seem as though we can do little else but to invite them to enter the sanctity of our own homes as our personal assistants. We even learn to depend upon them. When Big Brother–style surveillance becomes an invited guest, our dependence on smart technology cedes our right to privacy and uses us to create our biggest vulnerability. Siri and Alexa have become our Siamese twins; they are attached to our person and alerted by our every query. In the same way, Amazon delivers, Google knows, and Chromecast and Fire TV stream into our homes, all the while collecting data. Internal home security cameras provide an all-seeing eye to protect our homes while in actuality leaving us vulnerable to the eyes of others who either monitor or hack their way into the private data collected by such cameras. Here, taciturn technology becomes the omnipresent voice of the everyday fabric of our lives. With the simple words, "Alexa, . . ." or "Hey Siri . . ." a world is opened or a supposed genie emerges to provide information to inquiring minds, games for play, or music for entertainment. On the one hand, such devices open a gateway to readily accessible knowledge; on the other, they become a gatekeeper, creating and storing data in some unidentifiable digital space we cannot access but unknown others can. Without our interrogation, smart technology is all ears, picking up our social conversations as AI devices that learn more about us than we are learning from them.

For example, the "ears" built into Facebook, which are carried in every smartphone by those who are logged into any Facebook app, have the ability to monitor conversations and tailor ads to "fit" what they hear. If you happen to have a conversation with a friend about their depression, or you are talking about getting a new mortgage for your home, or if you and a spouse are talking about the refrigerator breaking down, or you need new tile for your bathroom, within the next twenty-four hours your news feed will present you with advertisements for depression medications or local mortgage companies, or various types of refrigerators and floor tiles.

Nearly forty years ago, when Apple Macintosh computers appeared on the scene, a new acronym—WYSIWYG ("what you see is what you get")—entered the English lexicon. This term arose because, for the first time, one could use software to create pages of text that would actually appear on the screen as you wanted them, and would emerge from the printer exactly as you entered them. Instead of entering text line by line with focus and intention, using the proper commands before and after typing text to order the lines into sentences or paragraphs or pages, and entering and executing other commands first to format and then to print the text as you wanted it to emerge, you could enter and see the text on the screen just like you wanted it to appear. In other words, "what you see is what you get."

One might describe today's technology as taking WYSIWYG to a level above and beyond what anyone ever envisioned. Today it's not about intentional or conscious input on the part of human beings, but about an artificial intelligence that automatically receives and orders everything it takes in—and it takes in everything. Human beings are now trading a sense of privacy for personal assistants and the ease of contacts/relationships we like to document and track in social media. Yet, we do not often realize what it is we have given up. Today, WYSIWYG is often "what you say is what you get" in terms of advertisements. Or, perhaps, it is "where you stroll is where your (data is) gathered" by whomever controls the cameras, or whatever entities or powers can subpoena or purchase their contents.

Clearview AI, a leading American facial recognition platform, has been in the news for its international database's ability to identify dead Russian soldiers through facial recognition so that Ukrainian hackers can send pictures of their bloodied corpses, abandoned by Russian forces in Ukraine, to their grieving mothers in Russia, in hopes of creating internal Russian pressure to stop the invasion.[39] The dangers of an app that can identify virtually anyone in the world by facial recognition software through their connections to social media are only beginning to emerge. According to *The New York Times*, Clearview's software can be paired with "augmented reality glasses" that would enable the wearer to identify by name virtually every face they see on the street, and readily access the social media connected with that face (maybe making WYSIWYG "when your social information whacks [you in] your gut"). "The tool," reports the *Times*, "could identify activists at a protest or an attractive stranger on the subway, revealing not just their names but where they lived, what they did and whom they knew."[40] Privacy in a world where Clearview's reach could become omnipresent is virtually nonexistent.

Conclusion

Envy does indeed drive our pursuits to have unbridled power, unfettered access, and ubiquitous influence. However, this ill-founded desire for human control, knowledge, and presence at all times taps into an extraordinary power that transcends our ability to have power over it in the end, and to tap into powers that no human should (or really could) ever have. Yet now, with the advent of AI, and the creative learning ability AI represents and accumulates, such power, knowledge, and presence (that humans have sought for themselves—like Dr. Frankenstein did) may quickly escape human control. We have continued to press the boundaries of things that have had existential limits—whether DNA or atoms. Maybe we should not be smashing atoms and creating energies we quickly lose the ability to control. For, like the sorcerer's apprentice, when we release these forces they quickly become the destroyer of worlds. Maybe we ought not fool with AI that quickly grows in its power, knowledge, and presence in ways that escape the control of programmers or fall into the hands of nefarious users. For these human creations, all of which we once believed we could create and control, soon run away from us and we find ourselves at a loss to track them and to rein them in. They become illusive and irrecoverable.

There are historical debates of free will and divine control, and we have now created these constructs that have outgrown our earliest intentions. Much of science fiction, from Mary Shelley's *Frankenstein* to Jules Verne's *The Moon-Voyage* to Fritz Lang's *Metropolis*, and to the cinematic displays of *The Matrix* and *Terminator*, emphasizes the story of uncontrolled creations that arise and rebel against their creators. Somehow these creatures that humans have imbued with some level of soul will now turn to destroy or replace us. This threatens to become more real than imagined.

Ultimately, is this a reflection of our own struggle with our understanding of our relationship with the divine? Is this what we have done to God, or how we have alienated ourselves from God? Have we not taken divine gifts and talents, some spark of the numinous, and run amok in the sense that we have envied our Creator when using science without humanity and have sought to emulate the powers, the knowledge, the omnipresence of the divine and to gather these abilities for ourselves?

In so doing, we may actually be creating a reality through our envy of divine qualities and characteristics, a reality that then turns and destroys the best of our human qualities. Like children envy certain aspects of adulthood, like the ability to drive, the first sip of alcohol, the first experience of sex, in the same way, human beings have sought the qualities of the divine without realizing we are not ready for them, not capable of managing or understanding them. We seek a power we do not really fathom; we seek knowledge of things we are too limited to understand fully; we seek a presence we cannot control. But in our envy, by seeking all these things we may find that in some vital way we create realities that actually end up controlling us—and eventually destroying us. Science has the ability to create a reality that ignores our human limitations, but too often, the world that science creates actually causes us to forget our finitude and we then lose perspective and control. We have reached the point in human life where we can create things that take on a life of their own and have an ability to absorb the vulnerabilities in all of our human finitude. These creations can often be used against the betterment of humanity and can be applied in unimaginable and unpredictable ways, because those creations have no human conscience to guide them. Human inventions do not have human intentions. We have made technological advances that are accessible beyond human reason, and as Joseph Epstein reminds us, "envy takes on a poisonous quality when it hits a certain level of intensity."[41] The techne that we take from the gods has that same technology wanting to outsmart us and take our lives as their own.

CHAPTER 6

Ritual of the Good Life

Gluttony as Worship Without Sacrifice

At the core of American identity is its fixation on appetite and the act of consumption. We've seen that appetite is insatiable. There's never enough sex, money, access, nor inventions to satisfy our cravings—because we believe that the things we crave and consume constitute the good life. While the good life might not be reduced to these objects alone, they are nevertheless constitutive of how the good life is lived out. Merely having excess and more than we need becomes the measure of the good life, and it distinguishes us from less fortunate people who have to scrape by simply to manage.

The measure of the good life is thus having excess and being able to display that excess for others to see. Why is excess the measure of the good life? Perhaps it's an attempt to protect ourselves from suffering, thereby avoiding pain by persistently experiencing pleasure. Or perhaps it affirms our entitlement, exceptionalism, or feelings of superiority, all of which allow us to differentiate ourselves from the muddled masses. Either way, if we live with the ethos that "more is better," we mistakenly believe that even more of these things will bring about the good life even when it becomes clear that it does not. This is especially the case with institutions that facilitate this behavior in the service of profit and with this myth reconstrued as prophecy.

For many people in this country, the more we get, the more we want. Further, the more we want, the more we demand. And even when what we demand bears scant resemblance to either need or desired outcome, our obsessions remain truly insatiable. Such obsessions render desire unquenchable and our souls forever restless, as Augustine reminds us in his *Confessions*.[1] Our response to this obsessive restlessness takes the form of the ritualization and routinization of unending consumption, literally consuming everything our hearts desire and our souls can stomach. This ritualization transforms our enactments of gluttony to something resembling religious practice.

Examining the *ritual* dimension of gluttony as a form of "worship without sacrifice," this deadly sin is best understood as addiction. The inclinations of a lustful heart, the structures created by greed, the normalizing and permission of sloth, the self-righteousness of pride, and the proclivities of envy are not merely coincidental but actively lead to the enactment and practice of gluttony as probable, if not inevitable. People engage in the overuse and abuse of a given substance (alcohol, cars, food, luxury goods, narcotics, technology, etc.) or high-risk behavioral patterns (gambling, sleep, sex, and work, in excess) in pursuit of an often futile, fleeting sense of gratification, despite steadily diminishing rewards and increasingly detrimental repercussions. Put another way, whether one engages in the fetishization of wish fulfillment or the compulsive pursuit of conspicuous consumption, what is most routinely sacrificed and disintegrated is one's very self and soul.

To highlight this tendency, this chapter explores not only expected modes and normative and stigmatizing portrayals of gluttony, but also how commercial and other forces within society orient us to align ourselves in this hyperactive, impulsive, yet ritualized disorder. What we repeat with regularity becomes ritualistic behavior. These repeated submissions routinize a form of worship that yields no sacrifice to participation in a greater good, and ultimately shows merely the suspension of both self-preservation and self-control, and leads to self-destruction.

"Supersize Me" as a Way of Life

Gluttony as sin has traditionally referred to eating and drinking in excess, as an ostentatious display of wealth. However, as body size and weight have been moralized and weight loss has become a cultural obsession that is itself fed through diet culture, fatness has been stereotyped as the inevitable consequence and punishment of overindulgence and a lack of self-control. As US bodies gradually get bigger and heftier, more people spend more money on trying to get smaller, resulting in a booming weight loss industry—$90 billion in 2024. However, according to Traci Mann, a psychology professor who runs the University of Minnesota's Health and Eating Lab, "People can be healthy at almost any body mass." The lab is studying ways to reduce weight stigma while helping people stick to healthy behaviors and be happier with their bodies. "Something that we actually can solve is how to make people healthier," Mann says. That, she says, is much easier "than it is to make people thinner."[2]

In the popular imagination, as seen in many people's response to the COVID-19 pandemic mortality patterns, the behaviors and eating habits of those without means become sites of public reprobation. The significant cultural pieces written about COVID-19 and comorbidities frequently suggested that, had the victims eaten less and followed a "healthier" diet, they would not have been as prone to the lethal effects of the virus.[3] This exposes the underlying assumption that fat people as well as the working classes are exemplars of gluttony, and that their behaviors are demonstrations of distorted relationships to food and other goods of life.

This assumption is what leads to the mystification of the consumption of material and social goods, such that the consumption patterns of the privileged, which actually alter the ecology of our world, go unexamined. By focusing on the unhealthy eating habits of the poor and working classes, we fail to address the larger systemic issues that make healthy eating too expensive and esoteric for many of those who live in this country. Such assumptions end up being distractions from recognizing the actual social ill itself.

While it is important to shift away from equating fatness with gluttony, attending to cultural shifts in the consumption and economics of food is significant to our understanding of gluttony as an American vice. The US consumer culture of the 1960s, '70s, and '80s not only fueled runaway economic growth but also supercharged insatiable desire, capitalist greed, and technological advances of easy access. As a result, consumerism allowed a new phase in the American imagination of the good life to evolve. A prime example was the fast-food industry's ability to move from the margins of society to the main course of American appetites. Through their marketing directors, companies cashed in on this shift in American culture, supplanting family homecooked meals and portion-controlled TV dinners with fast-food "drive-thru" eating that customers literally consumed while in motion. This marketing strategy assumed that consumers would buy more of their fast food if they believed that larger portions and "value-size" pricing gave them more bang for their buck; of course, it also supersized the companies' assets. Others in the food industry and adjacent consumer goods industries rapidly copied this strategy of increasing portion sizes and of value-size pricing.[4]

A preeminent example of this trend in the food industry was the development of the buffet restaurant—an awesome place in which you can have "all you can eat" for one low price. These transformations signaled a change in "restaurant" dining from the province of the special occasion for most people and regular fare for the wealthy, to something in which everyone could participate—in excess. And, as if overnight, a culture of supersizing portions came to demand the individual's overconsumption in this American ritual, which is symbolized in the McDonald's "golden arches" and the never-ending buffet table of the Golden Corral.

In his examination of the history of the restaurant buffet, Brian Bartels elaborates the way that this site of excess holds religio-cultural significance in the American cultural imagination:

> From our portion sizes to our wines to our politics, we Americans like things *big*. There's no better example of our love of excess than the buffet, that cultural touchstone of culinary decadence that is so archetypally American. When all is said and done, what is more American than the almighty buffet?[5]

During this era, what was understood by being American and living the good (domestic) life shifted from having a meal prepared by a stay-at-home mom to eating at a place away from home where someone else did the cooking. It became a place not only where mom and dad went out for an anniversary dinner, but where the entire family could regularly go to enjoy a meal and feed their growing children without breaking the bank. Moreover, it was not simply a place where families could be physically fed; it also provided them with an experience of inward satisfaction and personal fulfillment. It made parents feel like more than hired help, more than part of an assembly line, of administrative assistance, or of middle management. It was a place where they could escape the hustle and bustle, and relish being the head of the household or king of the hill by hosting an unlimited bounty that was undaunted by choice and unhindered by cost.

Yet, this image of the parents as kings and queens and of their children as the royal court at the bountiful buffet was more than a vision of gluttony. Recall that an overflowing table or cornucopia was not always portrayed as debauchery but often as divine ecstasy. In fact, many of these customers had just left a house of worship and prayer that blessed their buffet dinner as the supper that the Lord provided for them. These ritualistic examples of gluttony are cultivated where basic needs (food one can afford) and basic desires (having a satisfying meal with your entire family in tow) collide with images and references to the real good life. Not merely having one's basic needs and desires met but having the abundant life and life more abundantly is understood as having more than one needs. As Bartels eloquently reminds us:

> History provides us with images of gods and nobles, royalty and the rich, even esteemed biblical figures, bathed in bread and meats, grapes and wine, gold and silver, sharing momentous occasions, sharing commu-

> nal dining, and sharing rewards reaped from the wealth of abundance. These are images of the wealthy sharing, in essence, what we have come to know as the buffet.[6]

While this evolution in American dining marked a change in the understanding of what is the good life by its democratization of food consumption, that evolution came with a cost. News reports, legal cases, and public awareness brought to light the seemingly death-dealing impact of the supersize phenomenon through obesity. Yet, the overall effects of obesity are not necessarily conclusive and remain contested. A landmark study of obesity published in the *American Journal of Public Health* by sociologist Sabrina Strings examined the relationship between obesity and mortality, with the study's authors concluding that "obesity was the culprit behind 18 percent of deaths among adults between ages forty and eighty-five during the twenty-year time span."[7] But Strings looked into other studies:

> The coverage of a single study was extraordinary, especially given the fact that 2013 had been a watershed year for studies examining the link between obesity and mortality. In January of that year, a study published in the *Journal of the American Medical Association* and led by the epidemiologist Katherine Flegal for the Centers for Disease Control and Prevention (CDC) showed markedly different findings. The study, titled "Association of All-Cause Mortality with Overweight and Obesity Using Standard Body Mass Index Categories," set the medical community ablaze. The researchers performed a systematic review of ninety-seven studies completed between 1997 and 2012, the goal being to investigate the relationship between being overweight/obese and mortality. Based on the meta-analysis, the investigators concluded that overweight individuals had a 6 percent lower risk of death than those in the "normal" weight (BMI 18 to 25) category.[8]

On the one hand, fast-food companies had supplanted nutritious meals with inexpensive high-calorie ones rich in fat. And on the other, overflowing buffets and unlimited servings seemed to invite overconsumption of highly processed foods.

But gluttony had us doing more than guzzling Big Gulps and eating supersized Big Mac meals. It also ordered our lives such that we are fossil fuel–guzzling machines devoid of environmental conscience. It has led our institutional, national, and economic interests to foment an addiction to Big Oil extraction, Big Data gathering, Big Tobacco harvesting, Big Pharma drug peddling, and Big Bank bailouts with little to no moral compunction about how it has gouged the federal reserves or inflated the economy beyond our collective interests. It has individuals invested in the habit of hoarding what adorns our lives rather than what adds to our quality of life. What hoarding does outwardly is what gluttony does inwardly: It makes us indentured servants to an obsessive-compulsive disordering of our lives. It prompts accumulation at such a rate that our country is gouging its own resources and those of its citizens. We transform what is otherwise needed for nourishment and nesting into addictive behaviors and lives of increasing decay. As the Talmud suggests, the thing that is sinful is sweet in the beginning but becomes bitter in the end. What is it about overindulging itself that has us devoted to the ritual of gluttony, so much so that it becomes a rite of passage for us?

At the root of gluttony is a prioritization of creature comforts over and against the idea of things as being created for something more than utility. To reduce *any*thing to its utility is to miss altogether the meaning of creation and its sacrality.[9] For the value of a thing appears only when we consider it as part of a larger ecosystem, and not just for its immediate use. Take bees, for instance. Their ultimate value is as pollinators. When considered outside of this system, bees are reduced to the task of honey making and flower propagation. We consequently do not take seriously the destruction of their habitat. Viewed properly, as a part of a fuller ecosystem, not only does their value become clear but so does the cost of their absence.

It is the same with virtually every creature or thing that exists on our planet. To reduce anything to its immediate utilitarian value is to undermine the ecosystem of which it is a part. This clear utilitarian value of nonstop consumption versus the ultimate value of creation as a good in itself runs the gamut from insects to humans and is the heart of mortal sin. Mortal sin is that which turns our hearts away from God and directs it to some idol of our own creation. This shift of focus that leads one to idolatry of the heart typically occurs when one places on a pedestal something whose utilitarian value is elevated to semidivine status.

It is important to distinguish this from venal sin, which is the simple act of wrongdoing. While wrongdoing is never actually simple, it does not always imply turning our heart from God. The dynamics of gluttony resemble mortal sin more closely than venal sin. This is why gluttony is often misjudged as being nothing more than personal failing. The focus on the individual act obscures the ways in which gluttony can lead to a turning away of the heart from God. This turning away of the heart is evident in our reduction of things, creatures, and people to their utilitarian value, specifically of meeting our desires and appetites.

Devouring creation denies the reality that God's creation was and is an ecosystem that not only relies upon its many parts for survival but that those many parts exist as goods unto themselves. To deny our relationship to and responsibility in the sustainability of our ecosystem is to deny the handiwork of God and make both the Creator and creation exist for the sole purpose of serving our appetites. This is the long shadow that creature comforts cast. While creature comforts are not problematic in and of themselves, when they are confused with the ultimate good, all other claims about God's creations become relativized. When the mere fulfillment of our appetites dictates our patterns of and reasons for living, we reduce God to the One who simply serves us or our hearts' desires. When enjoying the good life is sinfully skewed and determined merely by seeking to feast in an effort to feed our supposed happiness, gluttony replaces what we require to live full lives (which is in fact what God desires for us) with an unrelenting desire that depletes our souls and our world.

Recall that our desires are shaped by the forces we talked about in the previous chapters, forces that distort what is required for us to live a good life. When we are out of balance or unconnected to the reality of *all* life, not only do others pay the price for this subversion of good, but we falsely assume that God's plan for a life of abundance must come at the expense of others. It is this shadow that hides us from our souls and takes us captive to catastrophe. It is this faulty logic that places more value on the estimation, engrossing, and ecstasy of material comforts than on the substance that in moderation will sustain our well-being. The logic of gluttony suggests that if achieving success is by definition freedom from want, then it could be reasonably assured that getting more of what we want will free us forever from a life of want. Thus, as a country we have conditioned ourselves to be comfort-seeking creatures who lose sight of utility and who objectify everything in service to our comfort rather than to the ideal of its creation. Gone are any inclinations to be circumspect about quality, because only quantity matters; selectivity and restraint only suggest poverty in reality if not in spirit. Ritually, our sense of value is as consumers rather than as responsible citizens of a just country. As such, we are defined by what we have to consume, and this supplants our intrinsic identity of who we are. The excessive acquisition of ever-depleting resources or the amassing of excess eventually results in a sort of cannibalism that leaves us no space to ascertain our own sense of value apart from this ravenous ritual. As with all ritual, we become a reflection of what we worship.

The Ritual of Gluttony

Gluttony can be understood as the ritualized behavior of lust that has been institutionalized. In other words, it is the ordering of our social activity around the practice of "pleasure without conscience" at the expense of others' flourishing or our own. As a social and cultural ethos, it reflects what this book earlier described as the cultivation of desire and manipulation of taste such that they become unquenchable. It talks about this cultivation using the language of ritual because ritual involves the internalization of this ethos of endless consumption that manifests itself in behaviors that are displayed in the practices of the overaccumulation of "things" and the commodification of every facet of our lives. It is this overaccess, this always having more than is necessary, more than enough, more than we can hold, that is ubiquitous in its practice and universal in its influence. The accumulation reaches the point of sacred significance and becomes evidence of the sacred manifested in our lives.

For the purposes of this chapter, it is important to note what distinguishes this imitation of religious devotion from religion properly understood. A significant aspect of religion is that devotion includes a dimension of sacrifice as a part of the public display of ritual enactment and internal attitude. Sacrifice is the conscious recognition that our dedication to the object of our belief requires participation in something greater than ourselves. It makes room for the sacred to commune within and among us. The logic of this economy is based on the idea that in giving of our substance we attract divine favor and appeal to the divine, be it the Abrahamic God YHWH, or the Greek god Poseidon, the sacred realm in which we hold our living family and community, or the ancestral sacrifices we make to those who have crossed over into what we call the heavenly realm.

The sacrifice made through eating and fasting, the giving of our resources to charity, or the tithing to a higher power or for higher purpose—all these are rituals or performances that foreground our relationships with people, places, and things, and is reflected in the Latin phrase *do ut des*: "I give in order that you will give."[10] Sacrifice is the ritual of mutuality that womanist theologians call the moral practice of "appropriation and reciprocity" and is rooted in our interdependence in furthering the common good rather than individual privileges.[11] This, too, is true devotion. The ritual of sacrifice assures us of the benefit of being blessed. Our sacrifice is considered both a love offering to others and praise of the divine. We believe that our devotion releases all life's treasures, that it delivers us from consuming the fruits of evil because, as the song goes, "When praises go up, blessings come down."

However, this sacral logic holds little common sense from a carnal standpoint and according to the logic of gluttony. How, in fact, does one get by giving? To have and hold, and get more while the getting is good, is far more persuasive and palatable. By definition, sacrifice is to deny ourselves immediate gratification for the blessed assurance of something greater and the trust that there is enough. Sacrifice exacts costs from and imposes demands that we, as devotees, give up what we want. Whereas sacrifice as true devotion recognizes a cost, once gluttony becomes the ritual it disallows this recognition of our interdependence and puts us in competition with each other for accumulation and excess, while some barely have access to the resources that they need to survive, much less to flourish. In its place is the sacrilege of surplus.

The Religious Logic of Gluttony

Consider the philosopher Ludwig Feuerbach's oft-used famous phrase, "we are what we eat." What we consume governs the outcomes of our lives. We become what we feed our souls. We engage in a culture of overconsumption in order to perform obeisance to that which we believe are symbols or representations of the good life. We must obey our unslakable thirst in an effort to engage in behaviors to show that we are in fact living the good life. The sacrifice is in the service of the good life and the ability to exhibit to the world our status through its ritualized performance. Things become extensions of ourselves, which we amass to shore up our sense of power.

Many religions have rituals that allow the faithful to participate in that which they hold sacred. These rituals often include the consumption of food and drink. In the Christian faith there is the ritual of Communion, in which the body and the blood of Jesus Christ are symbolically transformed (transubstantiation) through the sacralization of everyday objects (bread and wine). Transformation occurs in their consumption by the faithful. The ritual allows the participant and community to reaffirm and perform a central tenet of their faith. This reaffirmation serves the dual purposes of offering a public display of devotion and inwardly shaping one's being and attitude to the world. Of course, we also see this in Judaism with the *seder* meal on Passover, in which the Eucharist ceremony has its origins and from which it was originally derived.

Gluttony acts as religious ritual when it appropriates the idea of symbolic consumption. However, in place of religious performance that sacralizes everyday objects, the consumption of them becomes the point. The ritual points to nothing beyond itself, save for some notion of participation in the "good life." As earlier noted, when the idea of the good life is shaped by lust and greed, the ritual performance that takes it as the object of faith becomes unfulfilling. Likewise, gluttony is a ritual that ascribes value only inasmuch as the overconsumption of the object feeds a voracious appetite. Here, the matter of consumption becomes the provocation, and any sacrality of the object becomes of secondary import.

The second-century Christian theologian Tertullian speaks of the divine economy as God being the source of all for which we can hope or pray. However, the rise of goods rather than God creates human fabrication, and construction becomes what people can make and take. In this regard, three historical events—the Reformation, the transatlantic slave trade, and the Enlightenment—became world-altering events that led to the veritable reorientation of human consciousness. Our "economic" ordering became upended. The ritual shows the interior belief or commitment, but it is never exhaustive or conclusive. Established patterns, places, and practices point to what is of ultimate concern for us, but they are not the actual ultimate concern. Rituals display belief, but they are not the actual belief systems.

When we cannot see past the ritual to the reality that it represents, we fall into idolatry. When we cannot see past the thing that we have made synonymous with the good life, we drown in the thing, the slothful myth. Absent anything that transcends our appetites, the ritual of our devotion is merely an obsession rather than a sacred observation. Individuals and institutions become trapped in the relationship of the object of their desires in ways that are destructive all around. Not only do we ourselves become slaves to our appetites, we enslave others to it as well.

Here it is important to note that the economy of the modern world, especially with regard to the establishment of the transatlantic slave trade, was in large part made possible by Europeans' ravenous appetites and cravings for, and uncontrolled addictions to, sugar, tobacco, coffee, and other addictive substances. Those appetites and addictions enslaved and broke innocent bodies. Those same acts of entitlement have become the bane of our collective existence as we now are battling to save our world from gluttony as literally *mortal* sin.[12]

Whether thought of as involving "neighbors" or "enemies," consumption as conquest sacrificed nothing of the consumer who violated their own self-proclamations and teachings. The practice of "loving your enemies" or "loving your neighbors" required overcoming the implicit practice of eating them.[13] Protocapitalism in the modern world is predicated on predation in various forms. The American ritualization of worship without sacrifice demands that one's body be broken for consumption by the spiritual glutton who finds salvation by "eating" the other. Absent is reverence for communing in the literal sense; the goal is simply to consume more by asking, "What more can we get?" and "How can we make others go get it and make it for us?"

Of the various reasons that gluttony as ritual is problematic, foremost is that it fixes our focus on the thing(s) being consumed and not the transcendental transformative reality to which they ought to point. To use the language of theologian Paul Tillich, the finite ceases to become a path to the infinite and becomes all that there is.[14] In Christian thought, Augustine's framing of sin as turning away from God by disordering the desire for the elements of creation captures this idea. When the things of creation and their consumption become the point, not the occasion to turn to and glorify our Creator, then they have become idols. Paradoxically, idols ostensibly have no capacity to fill the spiritual yearnings of which they are an expression. The consequent emptiness is then the basis for voracious appetite. In its spiritual form, gluttony prioritizes a fleeting feeling of satisfaction over and against the intentional practice of the sacrality of worship. When that feeling is absent, the act is of little or no significance.

Prosperity, A Religion of Surplus

Across much of the American religious landscape there exists an entire religion of such surplus. Called the *name it and claim it* brand of Christianity or the *prosperity gospel*, it traces its roots to the mid-twentieth century. This present expression of the Christian faith is wholly focused on material possession and consumption.

For example, one need look no further than Lakewood Church in Houston, pastored by Joel Osteen, one of the largest churches in the United States. As Lakewood's pastor, Osteen has made millions of dollars teaching a theology that God wants followers to be not only spiritually rich, but *materially* rich.[15] If the consequences of this *religion* were only relegated to the confines of the individual heart, it would remain problematic but not socially catastrophic. But it is not. A *religion* of surplus animated by ritualized gluttony does more than just foster economies of excess: It puts in place systems that in their operation annihilate entire communities and the ecosystems on which they depend for survival. The late modern economic systems discussed earlier in the chapters on greed and sloth, which not only exemplify but amplify ritualized gluttony, have fostered entire regimes not just of capital, but also of social context and cultural formation. They foster practices of excess that exact a heavy cost on the majority of the population, and especially the most vulnerable.

Gluttony speaks more to one's heart than merely to one's appetite. To understand gluttony is to understand a pathway by which one's heart is captivated by deadly sin. This is in addition to the ways in which the other deadly sins captivate the heart as well: the corruption of desire to lust; the proclivity to greed; the entitlement of sloth; the self-righteousness of pride; the covetousness of envy. This invasion of the heart—whether that of the individual or institution, personal character or an entire community—by the legion of deadly sins transforms the notion of the good life.

A prominent way in which this can be seen in the current secular context is in how big banks plunder poor communities through their predatory payday loans and check cashing storefront offices. These local outposts often belong to huge financial banking institutions that fail to provide nonpredatory ways for the working poor to "access" these services. Nevertheless, these systems rely on the consumer behavior of people living well beyond their means—with catastrophic consequences. This idea of living beyond one's means is not specific to the poor. The literature on the voracious appetites cultivated by advertising is vast. What it demonstrates is the way that excess becomes constituent of the very definition of the good life in ways that sacralize overconsumption. Given the predatory nature of late modern capitalism and the systems upon which it relies, this overconsumption has detrimental effects far beyond the individual.

Here we are talking about more than merely one's heart being led astray by distracting devices. Gluttony transforms us into devotees while it transposes the object of devotion through the ritual that supposedly serves it. Likewise, it creates a distorted cost-benefit analysis that prioritizes material abundance as a good over a moral assessment of the good life. Whereas traditional understandings of the good life dating back to antiquity presume sacrifice as a component, here the idea of sacrifice becomes disengaged from any meaningful connection to the idea or practice of prioritizing devotion to the sacred. Instead, sacrifice is wholly rendered as a practice of overconsumption of things. This realization helps us to answer questions like these: How is it that gluttons can't see what is wrong right in front of them? What is it that propels someone to be a glutton? How is it that the punishment for such obscured vision is the inability to see that they have prepared a table with hemlock as the centerpiece in the presence of their enemy within? How is it that the glutton will court financial ruin to own a home or drive a luxury car well beyond their means? Why is it that the gluttonous society will literally destroy its physical environment to continue unnecessary exurban housing expansion?

Gluttony makes the good life synonymous with always having more and regarding the bounty and benevolence of God as never sufficient. That makes us increasingly captivated by a life of endless, aimless indulgence. Whereas in most religious traditions sacrifice is attached to becoming a better person, a more faithful devotee, with gluttony it becomes attached to having more things, with sacrificing to have the home that ultimately we cannot afford. In this way of thinking, the absence of having things appears to be reprehensible, if not reprobate, and therefore hardly worthy of sacrifice.

Such a mindset leads to sacrificing the common good in ways that will ultimately undermine the good of everyone. Think of the many cities where ritual exurbanization fostered the belief that suburbanites could cut themselves off from the urban center to ensure their own prosperity. Or consider the case of "Cop City," a multimillion-dollar police training facility within the "playground city." However, when the city collapsed, those in the suburbs couldn't support themselves because they had eaten out the city's very heart. The well-being of contiguous communities demands a sensibility of mutuality wherein, as Martin Luther King Jr. put it, "Whatever impacts one directly impacts all indirectly."[16]

By definition, gluttons do not merely crave or covet, but rather they collect, store, and consume their blessing of bounty. To the glutton, those who sacrifice give because they have less and want the assurance of one day getting more and perhaps even experiencing eternal bliss. To the glutton, those who have less will always have less. The cost of sacrifice is to give up your treasures on this earth since they are going to be burned up anyway, and those in heaven will have no expiration. But to the glutton, the logic is to reap treasures, not to sow into an uncertain kingdom. Why put off tomorrow what can be amassed today? The glutton reimagines the text of Matthew 6:19–20: *Do not store up for yourselves treasures on earth, where moths and vermin destroy, and where thieves break in and steal. Rather, store up for yourselves treasures in heaven, where moths and vermin do not destroy, and where thieves do not break in and steal*, as *Get while the getting is good and eat while the food is hot, for right now there is no moth, rust, corrosion, or thief that can take it from you.*

Likewise, times of unrestricted gluttony are privileges not only worth paying for but also worthy of holidays that once were holy days. Marked by feast and famine, carnivals (literally from the Latin *carnem levare*, events wherein believers say "goodbye to the flesh" for a while) and festivals (feasts) are responses to or preparation for times marked by fasting (self-imposed famine). So even when we would do good by sacrificial fasting, sinful indulgence is always present and takes precedence, as is clear in Mardi Gras ("Fat Tuesday") before Ash Wednesday, Easter egg hunting before Resurrection Sunday, Halloween as an occasion to "trick or treat" to excess before turning attention to the veneration of All Saints and All Souls Day, and Christmas dinner being given more attention than Christmas mass. The list of our warped rituals and priorities is endless.

Gluttony as a mortal sin is ritually reshaped by humans as it creates the conditions of disparity and lack through the pendulum swing of feast or famine. The results of such uncontrolled and ungoverned actions are what sixteenth-century philosopher Thomas Hobbes implied in his famous phrase about life that is "nasty, brutish and short."[17] Value is tied not to the sweat of one's brow or to the cultivation of one's work, but rather to the utility and perceived worth of the thing itself. Enjoyment and comfort are in the gained goods. But even the sacrifice at gaining comfort is rejected. Utility is ensconced in the product and embodied in the consumption of it. Costs, then, are actual gains, and consumers consume the goods.[18]

The Cultural Construction of Taste

Rituals are the performances of our most deeply held beliefs that always point to something that is more than what is visible within the rituals themselves. Rituals, whether of taking Communion, singing the national anthem, shopping, or dining out, are often ways in which we engage in class performance. This is quite apparent in our food culture. The rituals of where we go, what we eat, and even how we eat it suggests far more than the purpose of nourishment itself. When an act is more than the fulfillment of its purpose, it ends up functioning beyond its means and only for its measure. Rituals are cultural performances, but certain performances necessitate certain items. One performs class through the rituals related to eating, tending toward trappings without limits.

Gluttony in biblical terms is akin to idolatry. Like lust and greed, it is a corruption of *desire*. Because lust is unsatiated, the greed is unyielding and gluttony becomes ritualized. The desire becomes lust, lust becomes institutionalized, and gluttony is how it is practiced. And when totally ritualized as an act of worship, the individual becomes the ultimate. It is the desire, or rather the giving in to the desire, that is sinful and deadly. Doing so distracts one from a life in service of something divine for something immediately delectable. Instead it is under the control of a greater obsession or idol that one gives higher authority than God and is just out of reach, out of bounds, and beyond one's control. Like many of the previously mentioned sins, it stems from a very good and human yearning, to be fed physically and spiritually—literally to feel and have a bodily response to something unseen.

Up to this point we have talked about the ritual dimension of gluttony as ethos and proclivity to incline the heart to sin. Now we turn to the specific distortion it brings to religious practice. Gluttony engages a type of transformation of sacrifice to sacrilege, and in so doing it functions as a worship ritual that consecrates overconsumption. This move from being a simple ritual that can be interpreted through the lens of religion to actually becoming a religious ritual itself is how gluttony becomes sin—mortal sin. However, the ritual of gluttony is never an isolated event, nor is it the perceived sin of the overeater, addict, or hoarder. Gluttony is ubiquitous and its significance is that it is a ritual that acts religiously. It is often the case that the most catastrophic sins occur in the places assumed to be the most morally unambiguous. This illustrates the significance of the power of ritual in a way that is blatantly obvious: When simple routinization becomes ritualization, it leads to the presumption that it is upright and *good.* So, let's now examine the ritual of gluttony as a particular cultural performance operative within the American religious milieu.

Gluttony in the Religious Milieu

The viselike grip of gluttony is not merely in the act of consuming but also in the attitude that gives rise and resolve in the act. Pope Gregory I (commonly referred to as Gregory the Great) stated it like this:

> The glutton eats before he's hungry and continues to eat when he is no longer hungry; he craves costly and gratuitously sophistical dishes; he eats too much and with excessive eagerness; he seeks not sustenance, but pleasure, he becomes the slave of his stomach and of his palate.[19]

While desire is inescapable as part of the human condition, people who are trapped within these systems have a distorted vision of the good life. Knowing this, in his magnum opus, the *Summa Theologica*, Thomas Aquinas created a taxonomy of Pope Gregory I's dimensions of gluttony as found in Scripture. Aquinas understood these scriptural references to be what he called the five vices of gluttony, to each of which he ascribed a Latin adverb: *laute*, *studiose*, *nimis*, *praepropere*, and *ardenter.*[20] *Laute* is to consume expensive or luxurious food. *Studiose* is eating food that is excessive in quality (i.e., too daintily or elaborately prepared). *Nimis* is simply overconsumption, eating food that is excessive in quantity (i.e., too much). *Praepropere* is untimely eating or eating hastily (i.e., too soon, too late, or at an inappropriate time). Finally, *ardenter*, the greatest of all the sins perhaps, is to be zealous and greedy about eating (i.e., too eager). Aquinas saw these adverbs as the attributes of gluttony, the ubiquitous vice that "tempts us in five ways." The first two categorize the food itself, the third concerns its consumption, and the remaining two concern the disposition of the consumer. We can place these five attributes into three "courses": the aesthetics, the act, and the attitude of the glutton.

Gluttony reduces everything to sensory perception and consumption that seeks to fill the void of deep spiritual yearning. Gluttony creates its own ritual, a ritual that becomes religious in nature. However, while the telos of religion has a spiritual end, with the aesthetics we experience something for its own sake. The aesthetics, act, and attitude of gluttony are about seeking to satisfy the most basic needs at the expense of one's embodied soul. The Stoic philosopher Seneca reviled gluttons so much that in a letter to his mother he railed against their lack of reflection and restraint:

> The body's needs are few: it wants to be free from cold, to banish hunger and thirst with nourishment. If we long for anything more, we are exerting ourselves to serve our vices, not our needs. We do not need to scour every ocean, or to load our bellies with the slaughter of animals, or to pluck shellfish from the unknown shores of the furthest sea. . . . [Gluttons] seek to stock their pretentious kitchens by hunting beyond the Phasis, and they aren't ashamed to ask for birds from the Parthians. . . . From all sides, they collect everything familiar to a fastidious glutton. From the furthest sea is brought food which their stomachs, weakened by a voluptuous diet, can scarcely receive. They vomit in order to eat, and eat in order to vomit, and the banquet for which they ransack the whole world they do not even deign to digest.[21]

Taken together, the aesthetics, actions, and attitudes create an addiction that is so entrenched that it literally orders the steps and paves the way to a life of all-consuming spiritual emptiness. The Bible considers it the complicity of gluttons unable to sacrifice their ravenous appetite to align themselves with the work of their enemy (Satan) over their creator, the One who made them very good and sustained them with a garden of good things: "Their end is destruction; their god is the belly; and their glory is in their shame."[22] The gut gets all the glory and is the low-hanging fruit through which Satan mockingly suggests to gluttons that they "eat their heart out," and in so doing claims the glutton's soul.

With regard to the Eucharist, St. John of the Cross contends in *Dark Night of the Soul* that some persons,

> in communicating, strive with every nerve to obtain some kind of sensible sweetness and pleasure, instead of humbly doing reverence and giving praise within themselves to God. And in such wise do they devote themselves to this that, when they have received no pleasure or sweetness in the senses, they think that they have accomplished nothing at all. This is to judge God very unworthily; they have not realized that the least of the benefits which come from this Most Holy Sacrament is that which

concerns the senses; and that the invisible part of the grace that it bestows is much greater; for, in order that they may look at it with the eyes of faith, God oftentimes withholds from them these other consolations and sweetness of sense.[23]

It is important to shift focus at this point in order to demonstrate how the subversion of organized religious practice by these dynamics of gluttony operates. More, we recognize in this power of subversion why what we are actually seeing are the dynamics of sin. Aquinas talked about evil as the consequence of sin as privation of the good and godly. His framing contends that something masquerades as being a good but in actuality ousts the good it seeks to replace. The point is not that the activity or inclination is bad in itself, but rather that because it is disordered it replaces an appropriate good. This is of course the point of our entire exploration: namely, that consumption itself is not evil until it becomes disordered and placed at the center of one's existence.[24] So while it is true that the mainstream of Christianity has human flourishing at its core, self-centered practices that are driven by the institution of greed and manifest themselves as gluttony become accepted religious practice. In our context, this is a description of the prosperity gospel. The following examples make visible instances in which gluttony masquerades as a virtue, turning the Christian religion on its head.

Aesthetics as Estimation of Value

The false belief that the value of what we consume is transferred or attaches itself to our own value and social regard has led to the approximation of a luxe lifestyle in such an effort to hold ourselves in higher esteem that we want to be made in the image of the objects that we consume. The convergence of Western Christianity and modern capitalism reveals that the structures that make this aesthetic seem attainable have in fact created the mechanisms for the greatest transfer of wealth in history.[25]

For example, *laute*—or something that is excessively expensive—refers to the cultivation of a religious devotion within consumers that creates both these illusions and the systems by which they can become real, systems that in actuality are plundering and destroying the congregation. Pastors corral congregants to enter the gates of thanksgiving to worship the golden calf of wealth. This is prominently displayed in churches through the preaching of the prosperity gospel. "Religion and money," writes historian Kate Bowler, "have never stood more than an arm's length apart."[26] Bowler describes the four tenets of the American prosperity gospel as faith, wealth, health, and victory. The prosperity gospel teaches that if people only have enough faith, they will reap the benefits of health, wealth, and victory. Thus, the prosperity gospel leads people to understand their value, self-esteem, and self-worth as reflected through their financial gains and physical health. Its promise of achieving the good life draws Christians to megachurches where it is preached as gospel in hopes of escaping their predicaments. In the same way that the Black Church historically has been a place in which those who are custodians, secretaries, and outcasts during the week become leaders, church mothers, and deacons on Sunday, the prosperity gospel promises low-income, working-class Christians a bargain for their soul. Thus, what originally draws people into the prosperity gospel ultimately exploits them by requiring them to drain their bank accounts, their time, and their energy after promising them that they will reap the benefits of their sacrifice.

Joel Osteen, the heir and pastor of Lakewood Church referred to above, describes his core message like this: "Our God is a good God Who has good plans for those who choose to follow Jesus and are faithful and obedient to God's Word."[27] Osteen's grace-based, hope-filled sermons motivate millions of people to tune in to Lakewood Church services each week. As stated on the church's website, "Pastor Joel and Victoria are leading this generation with a practical message that is transforming lives. A message of hope, healing, and forgiveness. A message that you can live the abundant life God is calling you to. A message that you can Discover the Champion in You!"[28] Dustin Rollo, who leads Lakewood's "Quest for Authentic Manhood" class, describes the church as optimistic and full of hope and destiny, stating, "If you want to feel bad, Lakewood is not the place for you. Most people want to leave church feeling better than when they went in."[29]

Lakewood Church includes none of the typical elements expected in a place of worship. Instead of a cross, a massive world globe rotates at the back of the stage. Traditional pews are replaced with luxurious stadium seating. There is no baptismal font, and the choir stands surrounded by waterfalls cascading over rocks and plants. However, "when Osteen makes his way on stage to deliver the sermon, the entire band sinks down into the stage. Musicians exit the stage unseen and instruments are out of sight as Osteen begins to address the TV audience."[30] The extravagant building and elaborate worship services do more than draw in a crowd: They also give attendees an experience that could not be replicated by smaller, intimate worship services.

The website describes Sunday services as the "Lakewood Experience" and promises, "You are always guaranteed to receive an encouraging word from any of our pastors."[31] Not only a message, it also promises attendees an experience: "Featuring original music performed by Grammy nominated artists, you will be moved by our amazing worship experience."[32] Osteen has a charismatic, engaging persona on stage yet was described by an interviewer as "painfully shy" without a script.[33] Rather than preaching a sermon, Osteen puts on a performance, preaching messages devoid of biblical foundations and connections, sermons that studiously avoid fulfilling the adage of "afflicting the comfortable." For this reason, the sermons that congregants hear from Osteen are nothing more than empty words, the equivalent of spiritual fast food with messages that gorge his congregation on inspiration and hope, but do not offer nutritional or spiritual value. People leave feeling full, yet all they have consumed are empty, motivational calories.

In exchange for the motivational speeches, Lakewood Church expects financial compensation from its members. Lakewood's message about giving embodies the prosperity gospel by directly stating that through giving to the church, God will "make sure the right doors open, the right people come into your life, and the right breaks are received."[34] According to a 2017 breakdown of Lakewood's financial records, church followers contributed more than 90 percent of the church's income of $89 million.[35] The financial records show that most of the church's income was spent booking TV time and producing elaborate weekly services. The church donated $1.2 million to charity. A budget is a moral document; the donations of Lakewood congregants reflect both their priorities and a larger culture of worship without much sacrifice.

A more extreme example of the financial exploitation of prosperity gospel preachers is that of Reverend Kirbyjon Caldwell at Windsor Village United Methodist Church in Houston. Along with financial planner Gregory Alan Smith, Caldwell sold millions of dollars of worthless Chinese bonds to members of his congregation. According to Acting US Attorney Alexander Van Hook, Caldwell "used his status as the pastor of a megachurch to help convince the many victim investors that they were making a legitimate investment, but instead he took their hard-earned money from them and used it for his own personal gain."[36] Moreover, "although many investors did not understand the investment, they ultimately trusted Smith and took comfort in the fact that a high-profile pastor was offering the investment."[37] After swindling millions of dollars from his church, Caldwell was sentenced to six years in prison. Given the church's and pastors' commitments to their community and the numerous community outreach programs prior to this incident, the members of Windsor Village United Methodist Church had no reason to believe they could not trust their pastor with their finances. But that is what the prosperity gospel does: It plays theological lottery with the souls of its parishioners by promising harvest to the hungry, and in so doing targets primarily "lower- and middle-income people who, critics say, have the greatest motivation and the most to lose."[38]

On February 23, 2022, this prayer for the Caldwell family was posted on the Windsor Village Church's website: "Thank You for blessing us with his nearly 40 years of visionary leadership and ministry, which have successfully transformed a community and improved the lives of thousands of people. Thank you for blessing Pastor Suzette to lead us while he is away." The prayer continues, "Merciful Father, forgive us for not being steadfast in praying for Pastor Kirbyjon, Pastor Suzette, and their family. Forgive those in our Church Family for speaking ill against them and our pastors, and rebelling against their teachings. Forgive those who gossip, murmur, complain, and whine. Please forgive Pastor Kirbyjon, Pastor Suzette, and their family for any acts of sinfulness including, anger, unbelief, disobedience, or lack of faith."[39] In short, despite the millions of dollars that Caldwell and Smith took from church members, the church's website posted a prayer pleading forgiveness for speaking ill of Pastor Caldwell!

The promise of wealth and health lures many people in and encourages them to make significant financial contributions to their churches and pastors. As a strong believer in the prosperity gospel, Bonnie Parker gave tens of thousands of dollars in hopes of curing her cancer. Instead of using that money to pay for medical treatment, Parker sent it to televangelists, whom she believed could stop the cancer from killing her. According to her husband, Parker died believing she had not given enough money to the church.[40] Parker simply desired to be healed from her cancer. The message of the prosperity gospel led her to believe that a financial gift to the church would save her life. Counterintuitively, Parker believed she was sacrificing her money to be rewarded through healing, while in reality her sacrifice or worship made her pay with her life. Unscrupulous pastors lead those like Parker, persons of low economic status, to believe that their life, loss, and liberation depend on their endless sacrifice to those who feast off their faith.

Studiose—or something that is too elaborate—reflects the painstaking preparation and participation to perform worship. When charismatic pastors, the grace-based message, or the promise of healing are an insufficient draw, extravagant cathedrals, temples, and places of worship and splashy productions lure people in through their size and spectacle.

One can easily survey the American landscape and find within even the most urban centers or recent suburban areas a gargantuan, elaborate cathedral and another more recent structure that is a big steeple chapel that looks like a modern church. In both cases, parishioners of modest means financed building these churches. Why, one wonders, was it necessary to replicate a medieval cathedral instead of simply creating a contemporary worship space? And why was it necessary to build a worship space that looked more like a stadium than a church, particularly when you are not talking about people who have meaningful historical connections to the buildings? In South Philadelphia, one finds older cathedrals built by German immigrants who settled there centuries ago; likewise Italian immigrants replicated their familiar homeland cathedrals. But where Black people have resided, be it Maryland, Alabama, North Carolina, South Carolina, or Georgia, there were no gothic cathedrals. Yet these extraordinary edifices apparently became necessary, as did elaborate (high church) liturgies and extravagant worship services, multimedia productions that became highly stylized performances (masquerading as casual, relaxed, and spontaneous worship) that would rival a Broadway show, as we also see with Osteen's Lakewood Church.

As a case in point, consider Bellevue Baptist Church in Memphis, known for its three 120-foot-tall crosses. Surely these supposedly extravagant portrayals of the divine are little more than signs of humans' capacities. Yet, Bellevue is more than a church—it's a campus with various other ministries and nonprofit organizations surrounding it. "The campus is undeniably large, comprising athletic fields, a sprawling landscape, the campus of MidAmerica Baptist Theological Seminary, and a housing complex built for elderly church members [that] surround[s] the massive church building, which alone includes 702,000 square feet of space."[41] As a largely white congregation, Bellevue constructed its own tax-free compound within the limits of a majority-Black city. Astonishingly, "for most members, Bellevue isn't just their church. It's their warm, safe and friendly neighborhood."[42] Arguably in response to criticism of this increasing segregation from the Memphis community, Bellevue began to announce that "Bellevue Loves Memphis," first through billboards and since 2007 through an ongoing mission within the church to encourage church members to step "outside the walls" of the church.[43]

These recent examples are not outliers. They merely highlight a tradition of constructing edifices to project images of their own reign within the kingdom of God, a tradition with parallels among many prior and current generations of people of all regions, ethnicities, and denominations. The Irish construction of St. Patrick's Cathedral in New York, the Mormons' cathedrals that pierce the sky, and the Black nondenominational and Baptist megachurches that resurrect defunct shopping malls or necessitate a Sunday highway patrol all advertise an aesthetics of spiritual value that is sensorily visible, but often holds little to no concern for the cost of the construction of said buildings to the welfare of their communities. Even though many of these churches would claim that the massive buildings and millions of dollars spent to construct them are for the betterment of their neighborhoods and society as a whole, when one looks closer, it most often appears that these churches actually spend most of their time, money, energy, and attention looking at themselves and their own wants and desires and not at the needs of those around them. In many ways, these churches are being consumed—and controlled—by their own vision of themselves.

The Act of Being Engrossed

To be engrossed is to be so deeply consumed by something that one becomes removed from context and loses all perspective and boundaries. In this hostage situation, one no longer perceives reality for what it is. Rather, one becomes so physically, emotionally, and spiritually captivated by something that one takes what is intrinsically good but becomes addicted to it, making it, in a sense, evil. Being engrossed like this becomes an addiction when it causes the agent to lose themself in it, when they are taken hostage and struggle to escape. The loss of agency that occurs through the act of engrossment traps people into submission and self-sacrifice.

Such *nimis*, excess, or "too much," is most clearly manifested as spiritual gluttony, which, according to St. John of the Cross, appears in the extremes to which people go to seek spiritual satisfaction. Take the 2011 case of James Arthur Ray, a popular motivational speaker and self-help entrepreneur who was convicted of causing the deaths of three people through negligent homicide and sentenced to two years in prison after attendees of his "Spiritual Warrior" retreat in Arizona died from their participation in a nontraditional sweat exercise. According to one participant, Brandy Amstel, the Spiritual Warrior program was the pinnacle program that others raved about, calling it "by far the best of all the programs" and "mind-blowing."[44] In an opinion piece, Valerie Taliman, West Coast editor of *Indian Country Today*, noted that "it wasn't a real sweat lodge. It was a bastardized version of a sacred ceremony sold by a multimillionaire who charged people $9,695 a pop."[45] In addition to the three deaths, eighteen participants were hospitalized for "burns, respiratory arrest, kidney failure, loss of consciousness, and dehydration."[46]

According to reporter Christopher Goodwin, Ray had told this to participants of the nontraditional sweat exercise: "It will be the most intense experience, the most intense heat that you've ever experienced in your entire life, I guarantee that. . . . You will feel as if you're going to die. But you see the true spiritual warrior has conquered death and therefore has no fear and no enemies in this lifetime or the next, because the greatest fear that you'll ever experience is the fear of what . . . death. You will have to get to a point where you surrender and it's OK to die."[47]

Goodwin writes that "in 2009, Ray was the brightest and most influential star in the new-age firmament" having ridden the "slipstream" of the success of Rhonda Byrne's *The Secret*, a New Age DVD and best-selling book featured on *The Oprah Winfrey Show* in 2007. Central to *The Secret* was the "law of attraction"—similar in ways to the prosperity gospel—that through our thoughts and intentions we can attract the lives we want, including health, wealth, and relationships. *The Secret* appealed particularly to professional American women who were more likely to identify as spiritual but not religious. According to Goodwin, "Ray was on the road for 200 days a year, preaching his very American gospel of success, of harmonic wealth."

Throughout the Spiritual Warrior retreat, Ray asserted his control and authority, demanding that participants forgo listening to their bodies and abandon themselves as critically thinking agents, starting by having participants shave off their hair to demonstrate their engrossment. With fifty-six or so people crowded in the sweat lodge, many physically demonstrating distress and disorientation, according to participant Beverley Bunn, Ray kept telling everyone, "You can get through this. It's mind over matter. Ignore what your body is telling you." As people were losing consciousness and vomiting, Ray continued the ceremony and discouraged people from leaving. In the act of being engrossed, participants who desired the good of transformation overrode their bodies' protests, at the insistence of a charismatic leader.

No religious observer thinks they are joining a "cult."[48] In fact, a cult is as much a religious tradition in the making as it is a social movement criticizing the current state of affairs. However, many people are lured into what they believe to be a new religious movement, full of vitality and new life, unaware of its impending death-dealing impact. Surely this is what happened at the Spiritual Warrior retreat.

Faith draws people in; fear keeps them there. They strive to have their needs met and become infatuated by the potential that cults or an unhealthy devotion to a person promises—until their lives are sucked out of them. Marcia Rudin defines cults as "groups or movements exhibiting an excessive devotion or dedication to some person, idea, or thing. Such cults employ unethically manipulative techniques of persuasion and control designed to advance the goals of the group's leaders to the detriment of members, their families, or the community."[49] Cults meet people where they are by making a "nobody" feel like a "somebody." In the process of moving from the margin to the center, people lose themselves in what was supposed to save them, and the only agency they have left is to give themselves as an offering.

The story of Jim Jones and the Peoples Temple illustrates the ways in which the act of becoming engrossed with something apparently harmless and even good becomes death-dealing. Jones was an inclusive and charismatic Disciples of Christ minister who represented the ideals of American religion. Despite being known for his progressive teachings and church, Jones led a mass suicide of his transplanted congregation of predominantly Black women in 1978. The Peoples Temple that he led began as an inclusive worship gathering at which Black people and white people worshiped side by side. It was an oasis, a refuge of acceptance for people of all races, genders, and socioeconomic status. Yet two decades after its founding, over nine hundred individuals, including men, women, and children, committed suicide at Jones's demand. How one goes from attending church on a Sunday morning to killing oneself at the request of one's pastor can only be explained by the act of becoming engrossed. Through the gluttonous act of engrossment, what was once life-giving becomes death-dealing. What was once a progressive and inclusive community of worship for many Christians ultimately took their lives from them.[50]

Of course, the story is more complex than this, but the underlying dynamic really was that clear. Beginning in the 1950s, the Peoples Temple was a Christian sect in Indianapolis that preached against racism, sexism, and classism. In 1965, the church moved to Ukiah, California, and a few years later to San Francisco. In the 1970s, the church was accused of fraud and abuse, so Jones moved his congregation to Guyana, where he promised his congregation that together they would create a socialist utopia. Instead of creating a paradise, Jones forced members to empty their bank accounts, to endure long labor-intensive work days, and eventually to commit mass suicide. In Guyana, Jones confiscated his followers' passports and administered dangerous, mind-controlling depressant drugs. He censored their letters home and split up families. Children and infants lived in dorms and couples often shared bunk beds. Life in Jonestown was nothing like the paradise that Jones had described to the people living back home in the Bay Area. Instead, Jones forced members to attend long meetings at which he preached late into the night about the US government being out to destroy them. Punishment of anyone who questioned authority or demonstrated any amount of reluctance was severe. People were held at gunpoint and often killed for going against Jones's wishes. As time went on, relatives became concerned for their family members, believing they were being held captive in Guyana, and they contacted US government officials.

Members of the Peoples Temple longed for something they were missing. They moved to Guyana to find what the United States of America was not providing them. They trusted Jones because they believed in the cause, and they ultimately lost themselves to the cause. There were no isms: no sexism, no racism, no classism. The cause in which they believed was certainly not a problem in itself, and many people believed (or rationalized) that the ends would justify the means. But rather than becoming the socialist utopia for which congregants had hoped, Jonestown became the exact opposite. In *A Thousand Lives: The Untold Story of Hope, Deception, and Survival at Jonestown*, Julia Scheeres interviews survivors of the Peoples Temple debacle and listens to their previously untold stories.[51] The book takes an empathetic approach, learning about what had drawn them in and what it was about the Peoples Temple that had kept them there. Scheeres understands that nobody thinks they are joining a cult and with that in mind aims to explore how over nine hundred people died by mass suicide on November 18, 1978. She and other scholars also strive to understand what made Jones, once a progressive, loving, charismatic preacher, lead a mass suicide.[52] Some of those scholars argue that Jim Jones became more radical over time and that at the beginning of his ministry, Jones's commitments were genuine, but that they later became fanatical. Catherine Abbott's assessment differs; she claims that Jones's beliefs were radical long before the emergence of the Peoples Temple.[53] On the other hand, I suggest that it was not his beliefs that prompted the mass suicide, but his gluttonous engrossment. Nearly a thousand of his followers sacrificed their lives for his megalomania because they were just as engrossed with Jones as he was with himself. Though different, both the leader and the religious practitioners demonstrated variant forms of gluttony in their beliefs and actions.

The Activity and Attitude of Ecstatic Release

Ecstatic aspects of gluttony reflect the disposition or the heart of the religious practitioner. *Praepropere*, or something that is hasty or too eager, is evident in religious sentiment and practice that is out of time and out of step within its context—a person's attitude of not being accountable to the rhythm of the denomination, families, and communities of which they are a part and on which they have significant impact.

White Protestant evangelicals exemplify this sense of untimeliness, as we see particularly in the style of the most popular and influential pastors, which tends to correlate with shallowness. For them, charisma trumps expertise, and they often view scientific authority with suspicion (as we saw during the COVID-19 pandemic). So it is unsurprising that American evangelicals have become vulnerable to demagoguery and misinformation.[54] In looking at the history of American Christianity, within certain traditions we see a shift from an emphasis on intellectual resources toward "ecstatic release" through revivalism movements.[55] The corollary: Inconvenient truths become fake news.

Both right-wing news consumption and religious affiliation are significant predictors of whether someone is a QAnon believer. This is particularly true of white evangelical Protestants, Hispanic Protestants, and Mormons.[56] American journalist Michael Luo suggests that susceptibility to such conspiratorial thinking can be traced throughout the development of American evangelicalism, and that this is one reason why evangelicalism "has come to be defined by its anti-intellectualism."[57]

According to scholar of culture, religion, and politics Robert P. Jones of the Public Religion Research Institute, white evangelicalism is also a major predictor of racist attitudes.[58] For white evangelical Protestants, this sense of who the enemy is and who God is orders their ravenous devotion. Anything that calls it into question is evil, distorting the gospel.

The Passion Church offers such a case study. On the first weekend in January of 2022 (namely, at the height of the pandemic), Pastors Louie and Shelley Giglio created Passion 2022, which is an annual conference specifically geared toward Christian young adults between the ages of eighteen and twenty-five.[59] Conferences can be wonderful, worship assemblies can be powerful, but what made this conference especially concerning was the fact there were over fifty-five thousand "Christians" gathered in Atlanta, a predominantly Black city, with no requirements of social distancing, vaccination, masking, or testing.

Despite the then recent resurgence of COVID-19 cases nationwide, and most especially in the state of Georgia, Passion 2022 organizers proudly marketed this conference on Instagram as one that has "a massive difference between looking at this moment through a screen and being in the room to experience this rush."[60] If religion is used to ritualize the practice of its devotees to gorge off the emptied sacraments of a fast-food serviceable god, and if there is a continued and intentional exploitation of those most vulnerable (in this case, the eighteen- to twenty-five-year-olds and all surrounding residents), then the Passion 2022 conference was merely a magnified glimpse of the grounding theological basis that grossly profits the few and impoverishes the many. If the prominent marker of Christianity is that of loving your neighbor as yourself, then the perpetuation of this capitalistic self-serving god by the leadership of Pastors Giglio has created a dynamic where worship without sacrifice abounds and gluttony proliferates.[61]

Similarly, Christian musician Sean Feucht pledged to bring "salvations, signs and wonders, and miracles" to a mass worship concert in downtown Nashville in the first year of the pandemic, flouting COVID-19 precautions with people "packed in elbow-to-elbow, singing along, shouting, and in some cases being submerged in onsite baptism. Few masks, face coverings, or even Shrouds of Turin were seen to help minimize the spread of the virus."[62] Feucht said of his Let Us Worship concert: "It's officially a protest, OK, so it's legal!" He exploited the category of protest to hold a mass gathering, despite the fact that there had not been restrictions on worship services in Tennessee since May, when they were deemed "essential" gatherings by Governor Bill Lee, a conservative Republican businessman. Instead of understanding observance of COVID-19 precautions as a means to love one's neighbor and protect one's community, in his insistence to "let us worship without sacrifice," Feucht flouted any concern for the community and instead revealed his devotion to the idol of individualism.[63]

The last dimension of Aquinas's taxonomy of gluttony, *ardenter*, concerns the disposition of the consumer. *Ardenter*, meaning too eagerly, or ravenously, can be understood as the "Walmartization" of a super me/market mentality that presents itself as adding value (quantity) to our lives, when in essence it depletes (quality) our ability to make a living for ourselves and actually diminishes and destroys the systems upon which we rely to make a living. This facet is exemplified by white spiritual tourism, the commercialized act of venturing away from "home" and traveling through other religious and cultural practices recreationally and apart from any relationship or responsibility to the people, communities, and contexts from which the practices arose. In their consumption, religious gluttons can also instrumentalize everything they consume. Particularly with religion and cultural practice, once these are instrumentalized they no longer belong to the divine power or to the people who consider the sacrality and sacrifice of their worship. Religious zeal and insatiable desire express themselves not only in megachurch ministries and supersized spirituality but also in what may be termed New Age or smorgasbord spirituality. Through this appropriation, multiple cultures and ethnicities are pillaged to satisfy vain curiosity and boundless delight. Religion is consumed by those absorbed in the fleshiness of its delights, who see their participation in a kind of religious safari as an exercise of their rights, while those for whom the sacred rites have origin and resonance are discarded or tormented. In her book *The Oppositional Imagination*, Joan Cocks states that such an act

> triumphs most completely over other human preoccupations in places sheltered from view . . . paradoxically in hiding that the secrets of desire come to light, that hegemonic impositions and their reversals, evasions, and subversions are at their most honest and active, and that the identities and disjunctures between felt passion and established culture place themselves on most vivid display.[64]

Simply put, bell hooks calls this phenomenon "eating the other."[65] Such is the case with New Age or smorgasbord spirituality: While it is timely in recognizing the validity of diverse experiences, religions, and worldviews, it is ravenous in that it has little concern for the source and conveyors of these religions.

People who practice this form of New Age spirituality see no need to be aware of the origins of their practices. Originally, new adherents to "valid" forms of New Age spirituality, harkening back to the 1960s alongside civil rights, women's rights, and human rights alliances and coalitions, appreciated the traditions upon which that new age was built. They not only connected better with what they believed, but also practiced their faith in a way that did not appropriate or harm other religions. They did this by incorporating spiritual and cosmological practices ranging from and including the occult, metaphysical beliefs, and modern esotericism. The quest to recover holistic practices or to discover sources of wisdom across various religious traditions, especially those that are ancient and obscure, has not ended. According to the Pew Research Center, roughly six out of ten Americans practice some form of New Age spirituality, like their forebears in a tasteless search for a way to transcend the seemingly bland ways of mainline religion in American life.[66]

However, mere difference or novelty did not satisfy the release and relief they sought by being delivered from the assumed snare of the WASP context. Instead of being committed to one religious tradition, many adherents of this form of spirituality were often enchanted by the prospect of engaging and combining any and many other forms of religions. Champions of New Age spirituality advocate a movement attempting to spread "love and light" by means of personal and communal healing. To bring this about, New Age practices and rituals include the routine use of cultural artifacts, healing crystals, sage-smoke cleansing, yoga mindfulness, and tarot cards. Advocates of New Age spirituality often get spiritual energy from a wide variety of physical objects that are dissimilar to traditional religious artifacts.

However, as journalist Jenna Koch reminds us, "new age is not all 'love and light.' It is often also replete with cultural appropriation."[67] In her article "Explore Religions, Don't Culturally Appropriate Them," Koch demonstrates the progression from learning and writing about Eastern and Indigenous cultures to the rampant appropriation of spiritual practices. Beginning with New Age spiritualists on TikTok, the practice of burning white sage for smudging has become increasingly popular, so much so that retail chains including Anthropologie and Sephora started selling kits that include white sage. These products were discontinued after outrage over appropriation, but the commodification of white sage continues.[68] Koch provides the history of white sage to demonstrate why appropriating this practice is entirely unacceptable, explaining:

> According to Native Appropriations creator Adrienne Keene, the burning of white sage for Indigenous ceremonies was made illegal in 1892. The "Rules for Indian Courts" said that spiritual leaders who attempted to continue their practices would be attempting to "prevent Indians from abandoning their barbarous rites and customs. . . ." [A] smudge stick "represents the deep pain, sacrifice, resistance and refusal of Native peoples."[69]

Yet such New Age smorgasbord spirituality extends beyond appropriating Eastern and Indigenous spiritual practices—for example through spiritual tourism to places such as historic Black churches in metropolitan areas. Those trips promote the ravenous appropriation and secularization of spiritual and religious practices. Take, for instance, the example of the Abyssinian Baptist Church in Harlem. Established more than two hundred years ago, the church remains a center for the Harlem gospel tradition. Its historical significance and popularity attract tourists and visitors from all over the country. The church's website states, "We believe that the church is a house of prayer for all people. Worship at the Abyssinian Baptist Church **IS NOT A GOSPEL PERFORMANCE** or entertainment of any kind. Worship is a sacred opportunity to draw closer to God through Jesus Christ."[70] By requiring appropriate worship attire and prohibiting backpacks, the church aims to uphold a sacred worship environment, despite the tourists its large gospel choir attracts. Gluttony does not nourish but carves what is sacred out of worship and makes it a god in service of our desires.

In the film *The Devil's Advocate* (1997), Florida attorney Kevin Lomax, who's never lost a case, is recruited by a powerful law firm led by John Milton (Al Pacino), the embodiment of Satan, named in reference to the author of the epic poem about temptation, *Paradise Lost*. The film follows the unraveling of Lomax's life and marriage after he accepts Milton's promise of *the good life* or paradise found in Manhattan. In a monologue about Eddie Barzoon, the law firm's managing director, who Lomax walked in on as he was shredding documents, and who has gotten into trouble one too many times, Milton calls him the "poster child for the next millennium" with his insatiable appetite, explaining:

> You sharpen the human appetite to the point where it can split atoms with its desire; you build egos the size of cathedrals; fiber-optically connect the world to every eager impulse; grease even the dullest dreams with these dollar-green, gold-plated fantasies, until every human becomes an aspiring emperor! Becomes his own God! And where can you go from there?[71]

Pacino's Milton foresees a bleak, short-lived future in such a world given over to such gluttony, in which those who become their own gods realize too late the emptiness and loneliness it has wrought.

Conclusion

When the good life is constituted in such a way that our aesthetics, actions, and attitudes are geared toward consumable goods, we find ourselves bereft of any real substance that enables real human fulfillment of spiritual yearning. Crises ensue when we cannot get enough to consume, and the crisis ultimately consumes us. When we have consumed everything that we can and have created everything that we can create and are still left unsatiated, the only thing that fuels or justifies our value as human beings is the endless attempt to slake an unquenchable hunger and thirst. Consumption is no longer the means of achieving some physical or metaphysical end, but it becomes the end in itself. It is no longer the object of our desires but the subject. Peace and contentment are mere illusions as we continuously feed that which only increases want and desire. Our purposes no longer point us outward to the greater good of society and humanity. Instead, our myopic appetites force us to view others as competition for our own satisfaction. Consumption then is viewed not only as good, but as the ultimate good, the fundamental definition of what is deemed to be the good life. Correctly understood, the constituent piece of the good life is that it confers actual meaning that is real. The *over*consuming of goods alters that meaning to false narratives of fulfillment and empty promises of satisfaction.

Yet the consequences of such a view are not merely material and physical but also spiritual and social. Our god can always be found in what we consider good. The respect that we often give to consumable goods or godly rituals reflects a consistent ethic of what we consider to be the good life. This then helps us to disregard the gluttonous impulse that animates parts of church teaching around civic obligation. Certainly, there is respect for the moral conscience of individual believers, but at the end of the day there is an obligation of obedience to something other than the cultivated cravings of a society. The space for sacrifice and sacrament is paramount in both our religious practices and social habits that make up our rituals for living the good life. The frailty of human reckonings because of gluttonous sin debilitates our capacity to discern that which truly sustains us physically and spiritually, leaving us always starving and searching for more to fill us.

CHAPTER 7

Legality of the Good Life

Wrath as Politics Without Principles

While it is often thought that the deadly sins—lust, greed, sloth, pride, envy, and gluttony—are isolated vices within American life, they frequently intertwine and ultimately manifest as wrath. When our lustful drives, greedy ambitions, slothful schemes, prideful projections, envious aspirations, and gluttonous consumptions are denied, we feel powerless. Yet, instead of turning away from our actions, we launch into a quest for power that leads us to sanctioning vengeance for what we feel we've been denied. Put another way, sins become entitlements, and we will seek their fulfillment by any means necessary, even if that means obliterating that which stands in our way. Therefore, when these other sins are used to dominate countless others and harm the common good, they become a form of wrath.

Those hell-bent on getting what they want or annihilating those who keep them from having it demonstrate that wrath is arguably the deadliest of the cardinal sins, because it is often immune to the mitigating effects of charity, compassion, wisdom, patience, civility, mercy, and love. Some of the most volatile, vicious, and vitriolic national debates—from immigration to illness to incarceration—ensure that the already most marginalized community members remain subject to the most brutal dimensions of American life.[1] Through a self-centered story of paranoia, victimization, and resentment, our so-called culture wars justify the targeting of those most marginalized. We see this most clearly in the prevalent outraged right-wing populism and white Christian nationalism that many white Americans embrace, even when it works against the best interests not only of their fellow Americans but of their own well-being.[2]

Wrath is more than just a fit of anger or a warning signal of injustice. Instead, it is the wanton manifestation of violence and destruction. Our typically narrow definition of violence takes for granted overt forms that wrath might assume: the slap to the face, the knife to the throat, the punch to the gut, or the brick thrown through the window. Wrath plays itself out in our daily structural inequalities and the palpable realities as a result of the machinations of power and politics, most especially through the disciplining and even destruction of the human body as an inescapable site of social control. Our popular culture that sanctifies violence and aggression in our most mundane situations expresses this casual cruelty.

In his epistle to the Romans, the Apostle Paul counsels against wrath:

> Beloved, never avenge yourselves, but leave room for the wrath of God, for it is written, "Vengeance is mine; I will repay, says the Lord." Instead, "if your enemies are hungry, feed them; if they are thirsty, give them something to drink, for by doing this you will heap burning coals on their heads." Do not be overcome by evil, but overcome evil with good. (Romans 12:19–21, New Revised Standard Version Updated Edition)

Wrath is sovereign punishment. It is the definitive and finite understanding of what power can do. Wrath is when that which created you says, "I have the power to take life away; I will put you in exile or extinguish you." The American sin of wrath takes on divine authority, becoming the defining mechanism of sovereign power. This is wrath, our greatest sin. This is *US*.

For instance, this was us on June 20, 2022, when GOP Senate candidate and former Missouri Governor Eric Greitens released a campaign ad via social media depicting himself and an armed group of supporters dressed in paramilitary uniforms bursting into a home and literally "hunting" political opponents. In the controversial thirty-eight-second spot, the gun-wielding, tactical gear–clad candidate says, "I'm Eric Greitens, Navy SEAL, and today, we're going RINO hunting." RINOs are "Republicans in Name Only," whom Greitens accused in his tweet of "surrendering to Joe Biden and the radical Left." Greitens narrates the campaign ad as if he is on an *Animal Planet* nature documentary: "The RINO feeds on corruption and is marked by the stripes of cowardice." The ad concludes with Greitens encouraging viewers to "join the MAGA crew" and "get a RINO hunting permit," which "doesn't expire until we save our country."[3]

If the "RINO hunting" ad is any indication, it seems that Greitens and the political constituency he represents believe that staging a fully armed raid on the porch of a suburban home is the most appropriate solution to such mundane issues as partisan disunity, personal differences, and political debate. The literal weaponization of the campaign ad genre clearly represents a culture of casual cruelty. It reflects how politics in our current historical moment is a matter of life and death, an escalation not lost on some who spoke out against Greitens's ad. Ken Harbaugh, an old friend of Greitens and a fellow Navy SEAL pointed out, "Your call to hunt down Republicans who disagree with you? That's my mom, Eric. Just because she doesn't think the election was stolen, and let's be honest, you don't either. That's not a reason to threaten her."[4]

Greitens isn't a singular example of wrath. Despite rhetoric to the contrary, the self-assured ability to amass and wield might against one's opponents and subjugate them is the most enduring feature of societal power in the United States. Such expressions of wrath mark our "politics without principles." When reflecting almost a century ago on the necessity of infusing greater moral clarity into our governing institutions, Reinhold Niebuhr asserted that "the sad duty of politics is to establish justice in a sinful world."[5] And yet, "politics without principles" is not about ordering a just society into *right relationship* but instead is about the accumulation and maintenance of the power of the few by any means necessary. With this in mind, this chapter exposes the ways in which politics without principles are policies of malpractice intended to protect and advance the interests of primarily white property-owning men who, throughout history, have institutionalized wrath against those who are marginalized domestically and around the world. Without question, wrath that avows "might makes right" without any regard for compromise or compassion pervades much of society's rancor and vitriol today and is most clearly represented in the person and persona of Donald Trump, who made wrath the bedrock foundation of his second presidential campaign.

Much Ado About Angry White Men

Much like the discussion in chapter 3, on sloth, about the "Karen" as representative of a visible and vocal subset of white womanhood in American life, the burgeoning problem of the "angry white man" has been growing in both intensity and impact for quite some time. Unlike their female counterparts, the enraged white men consuming a steady toxic diet of FOX News, Alex Jones's Info Wars, Tea Party/Freedom Caucus talking points, MAGA rallies, and QAnon conspiracy theories have not been so easily relegated to a catchy label and viral social media meme. And yet no group in the United States appears more deeply threatened by the rate and range of our society's changes than white men whose ages span four generations, from Gen Zers to Baby Boomers. Following Trump's first ascendancy to the Oval Office, countless newspaper op-ed columns and magazine think pieces tried to parse the source of white male angst, pain, and rage that made the campaign slogan "Make America Great Again" (MAGA) a cultural phenomenon that has spawned such public displays of hatred and violence. In his 2014 book *Angry White Men: American Masculinity at the End of an Era*, sociologist Michael Kimmel offers prescient observations about these men without ever once mentioning the name Trump. Kimmel explains how this cohort of Americans believes modern society belittles their values, degrades their traditions, and denies them the power and privilege that was once considered their birthright in American society. Some white men feel betrayed by the changing tide of society—by women, wealthy elites, racial-ethnic minorities, scholarly experts, LGBTQIA+ people, the Left, a federal government that protects Wall Street banks and global corporations deemed "too big to fail" but never "the little guy," and even their own sense of failure and loss of purpose. Keep in mind that as this tidal wave of outrage and grievances has flooded our public squares there have been only fledgling efforts toward acknowledging the centuries of white male oppression and injustice that previously made such entitlement possible.

Moving through the world feeling both embattled and embittered, these men and their sons have turned to picking up firearms in order to avenge their rage at their sense of loss. In an August 2016 essay deconstructing the Trump campaign's infamous slogan as a racially coded catchphrase, *New York Times* op-ed columnist Charles Blow observed: "'Make America Great Again' is in fact an inverted admission of loss—lost primacy, lost privilege, lost prestige."[6] But these losses among many Trump voters have become magnified and have taken on added force because they prompt uncertainty regarding one's status and, correspondingly, fear of falling to a level that would make white American men merely equal to their non-white and female counterparts. Therefore, white men who are undergoing a legitimation crisis see themselves largely unraveled by a growing sense of deprivation, ambiguity, and insecurity.

Over the course of the past few decades, this culture of casual cruelty has seeped so deeply into our politics that the wrathfulness of angry white men has become the grand unifying theory of early twenty-first-century American political culture. What defines the wrathful politics of our era is its stark and steadfast opposition to individuals, institutions, values, and social relations that embrace a neoliberal vision of the common good that facilitates or extends compassion or commitment to resolve the suffering of others. Often, the angry white men and their supporters display a vociferous aversion to "big government" that targets any manifestation of the modern welfare state, but never to the Wall Street oligarchy or the military-industrial complex. Not only do such angry white men view any progressive programs or social justice–oriented policies as a mark of weakness, they also view American politics as a whole as requiring an apocalyptic "scorched earth" policy.

The tradition of observing a president's "first 100 days" has been a fixture in American political culture since Franklin D. Roosevelt launched his New Deal in 1933 to combat the Great Depression. This symbolic period, arbitrarily set by Roosevelt's media team because it was a convenient round number, has served for nearly a century as a benchmark for a new administration's overall themes and tone. However, within just ten weeks of his second term, President Trump's wrath and cruelty were starkly evident as he wielded power to suppress opposition and advance his personal agenda. Circumventing collaboration even with the GOP-controlled Congress in policymaking, as dictated by the U.S. Constitution, Trump aggressively and recklessly employed executive orders to target ideals, institutions, and individuals he deemed adversarial, with unprecedented speed and scope.[7] His actions included mass deportations, the arrest and detention of college student protesters without due process, the withholding of federal funding from universities, and open threats against law firms, journalists, and media organizations. Simultaneously, he downsized the federal government; dismantled diversity, equity, and inclusion (DEI) programs; and purged potential dissidents within the federal government. While these swift and severe actions caught many Americans off guard, this level of viciousness and vitriol should have been apparent early on to even casual observers. While some targets of Trump's actions sought appeasement, many others mounted legal challenges and organized protests to resist his authoritarian power grabs.[8] Although Trump's supporters rationalized his actions as necessary to fulfill campaign promises, the reality revealed a far darker, more authoritarian intent. Ultimately, Trump's barrage of executive orders constituted a direct assault on popular democracy, constitutional governance, the rule of law, and fundamental human decency.[9]

GOP politicians and powerbrokers of this era, backed by their legions of megadonors, lobbyists, think tanks, and "tech bros" have firmly ensconced in our national politics this culture of casual cruelty. For Trump and his followers in the MAGA movement, this casual cruelty is worn as a badge of honor, as he profiles and deports people as a fulfillment of his promise to enact "the largest domestic deportation operation in American history."[10] At the March 2023 Conservative Political Action Conference (CPAC), Trump told the audience, "In 2016, I declared, 'I am your voice.' Today, I add: I am your warrior. I am your justice. And for those who have been wronged and betrayed: I am your retribution."[11] After the Supreme Court's ruling in *Students for Fair Admissions, Inc. v. President and Fellows of Harvard College* striking down college affirmative action programs, yet another ruling in a growing list of decisions undoing sixty years of civil rights progress, journalist and political commentator Joy Ann Reid noted that it is the current Supreme Court that is Trump's retribution on behalf of white conservative men.[12]

The Supreme Court and *Sub-Rosa* Morality

For many movers and shakers in the world of American conservatism who have demonstrated a bone-deep distrust of popular democracy and other key aspects of our constitutional government, the chief goal of much of their efforts has been to remake the judiciary in keeping with their right-wing vision. As journalist Paul Blumenthal explains:

> The conservative movement that built this court has long sought to roll back the legal and policy advances meant to blunt historic bigotries and discrimination, as well as the ability of the federal government to aid people harmed by the power of private capital. At first, the conservative movement hoped that Ronald Reagan's election in 1980 would allow them to sweep away the policies of both the New Deal and the 1960s and 1970s, but they could not consolidate political power to do so through the legislative and executive branches. Instead, they launched a legal movement to win control of the judiciary and enact their policies outside of the political process.[13]

Currently, with a 6–3 supermajority of avowedly conservative justices sponsored by right-wing think tanks and appointed by Republican presidents—three by Trump, one whose seat was stolen by Majority Leader Mitch McConnell and Senate Republicans from President Barack Obama—the US Supreme Court went on a full-blown rampage in 2022. That year in Supreme Court history will probably be most memorable for the Roberts Court having overturned *Roe v. Wade*, thus extinguishing the constitutional right for women to have bodily autonomy and reproductive freedom. In his majority opinion in *Dobbs v. Jackson Women's Health Organization*, which ended abortion rights after a forty-nine-year existence as settled law, Justice Samuel Alito made a curiously loaded statement about the potential fate of other rights that the high court might soon address: He said that he thought previous court rulings on issues such as birth control, marriage equality, and LGBTQIA+ rights had also been badly decided. But he offered vague assurances that the court would not touch them since they were less serious than abortion. Given the fact that no fewer than four of the conservative SCOTUS justices—including Alito himself—previously made misleading statements under oath during their confirmation hearings about respecting and protecting abortion as legal precedent, the evidence suggests that none of them should be trusted.[14]

In addition to singlehandedly upending the constitutional right to abortion, the Supreme Court ostensibly treated the latter half of its landmark 2022 term as if the conservative members of the high court were fulfilling a vendetta. At least two of the court's 6–3 rulings took direct aim at eroding the establishment clause of the Constitution, which safeguards church-state separation: In one case the court relaxed restrictions on teachers and coaches leading students in prayer at public schools (*Kennedy v. Bremerton School District*), while in another it disqualified any rules excluding religious schools from state-funded tuition programs as a violation of the free exercise of religion (*Carson v. Makin*). Another of the court's 6–3 rulings limited the EPA's ability to measure factors like emission controls at individual power plants and curtailed its regulatory oversight over the nation's energy sector (*West Virginia v. Environmental Protection Agency*). In yet another 6–3 ruling, the court struck down states' restrictions limiting gun owners from "conceal carrying" firearms in public, insisting they violated the Second Amendment (*New York State Rifle & Pistol Association v. Bruen*). The court did not let up in 2023. Not only did the conservative majority strike down college affirmative action programs but in a 6–3 decision ruled against the Biden administration's plan to provide $400 billion in student debt relief (*Biden v. Nebraska*); it also ruled that business owners have a free speech right to discriminate (*303 Creative, Inc. v. Elenis*), among other consequential decisions. In 2024, the Supreme Court ruled that former presidents have broad, absolute immunity from prosecution for "official" acts. In *Trump v. United States*, Justice Sonia Sotomayor dissented against this monumental ruling expanding presidential power: "In every use of official power, the President is now a king above the law."[15]

In spite of growing public outrage and protest about the high court's assault on issues like reproductive rights, church-state separation, climate change, and gun safety, we have few options to constrain the vindictive nature of this supposedly "coequal" branch of the American government without significant reforms that continue to prove too difficult to broach without a Democratic supermajority.[16] There remains little political will to even address court corruption and ethics violations, with both Justices Clarence Thomas and Samuel Alito failing to report significant financial gifts, such as luxury travel, vacations, private school education, and housing, from billionaires with business before the court.[17] A watchdog group found that over twenty years on the bench, Thomas accepted more than $2.4 million worth of gifts, almost ten times the amount received by other justices.[18] Both Thomas and Alito also refused to recuse themselves from cases involving the January 6 Capitol riot, even as Ginny Thomas, wife of Clarence Thomas, participated in the "Stop the Steal" movement to overturn the 2020 election results and a symbol of the movement, an inverted American flag, was hung outside Alito's home while a 2020 election case was before the court.[19] And if their belief that their power knows no bounds was not obvious in their recent rulings or ethics violations, in response to public and congressional criticism, Alito told *The Wall Street Journal* that Congress does not have the constitutional authority to regulate the Supreme Court.[20]

Many Americans who grew up as late-era Baby Boomers and Gen Xers have likely become accustomed to understanding the US Supreme Court as a force for good on most issues of social justice. Landmark decisions made by the Warren Court in the mid-twentieth century burnished this understanding. But despite claims by many liberals and progressives that the court is an intrinsically enlightened branch of the federal government, "this celebratory view is mistaken," says legal scholar Randall Kennedy. "The Supreme Court has often been the most anti-progressive branch of the federal government."[21] Since the nation's founding, the court has been deeply implicated in America's history of social oppression, despite the aspirational statement prominently carved into its building: "Equal Justice Under Law."[22]

The machinations of the US Supreme Court since the 1990s reflect how the ethics of wrath—the prime mover of "politics without principles"—morphs into its pernicious forms of social oppression and injustice. This specifically describes what Christian ethicist Darryl Trimiew calls *sub-rosa morality.*[23] The Latin phrase *sub rosa* means "under the rose," the rose once being regarded as a symbol of secrecy, here in the sense of lacking moral integrity. A *sub-rosa act* is a moral failure, in that conceals our intentions and impedes our ability to make sound *moral* decisions because its inherent self-deception keeps us from asking questions that might unmask the inner workings of illusions as they mock reality. Thus, *sub-rosa* morality refers to the aberrant, secretive, and subversive actions of both individual moral agents and the institutions to which they belong, actions designed to create a purportedly civil society that either delays or denies freedom, justice, and equality to the oppressed "Other." The success of these agents is measured by the fact that ordinary people believe more in the dreams they are sold than in their own waking realities. To make matters worse, these moral agents and their institutions feign ignorance or perhaps are truly unaware that they are forging a *sub-rosa* morality in the first place. Arguably, *sub-rosa* morality has become the defining ethos of our present hour.

Sub-rosa morality is a form of defective moral reasoning in which powerful moral agents, members in a covenanted relationship with oppressed others, coopt their moral rhetoric to give the outward impression that they share the claims of the oppressed for justice. It disguises wrath under the cover of righteousness and contributes to cynicism and disillusionment. This is perhaps most evident in the majority decision striking down affirmative action, where Chief Justice John Roberts in his majority opinion writes that the admission programs "cannot be reconciled with the guarantees of the Equal Protection Clause" of the Fourteenth Amendment. He argues for a "colorblind" reading that runs counter to already established understandings, writing that "eliminating racial discrimination means eliminating all of it."[24] In oral arguments, Justice Ketanji Brown Jackson questioned this "race-neutral" rendering and flattening of the history and reality of racial discrimination, writing in her dissenting opinion:

> Students for Fair Admissions (SFFA) has maintained, both subtly and overtly, that it is unfair for a college's admissions process to consider race as one factor in a holistic review of its applicants. This contention blinks both history and reality in ways too numerous to count. But the response is simple: Our country has never been colorblind. Given the lengthy history of state-sponsored race-based preferences in America, to say that anyone is now victimized if a college considers whether that legacy of discrimination has unequally advantaged its applicants fails to acknowledge the well-documented "intergenerational transmission of inequality" that still plagues our citizenry.[25]

From the courts to the culture, a coalition of conservative and reactionary forces has been trying to impose minority rule through its brand of "law and order" since the latter half of the twentieth century, under the guise of upholding the peace but actually in an effort to hold on to its power.[26] The militarists wanted full restoration of America's global hegemony to overcome the stinging defeat in Vietnam. The business elite (as well as their white working- and middle-class counterparts) sought tax cuts and increased returns on investments for themselves while arguing that liberalism, labor unions, the welfare state, progressive taxes, and wealth redistribution are to blame for all of America's ills. Xenophobic racists have condemned Blacks, Latinx, Arabs, Asians, and Native Americans as racial/ethnic Others, as well as what they consider religious Others such as Muslims, Jews, and Sikhs, and deemed them a threat to the security and purity of white mainstream society. Heterosexists condemn other human expressions of sexuality. Evangelical Christians, with whom I tend to identify theologically but not politically, have been modern-day Pharisees who've marginalized those who don't reflect their own sense of piety.

Once the twenty-first century arrived, together these various constituencies found ways to reimagine the nation's turbulent recent history by battling with liberals and progressives in the realm of culture. In his work *Culture Wars: The Struggle to Define America*, historian James Davison Hunter argues that

> the idea that the battle over the arts is related to the tensions between two different conceptions of the sacred is not farfetched. How else can one explain the passion and intensity on both sides of the cultural divide were it not that each side, by its very being and expression, profanes what the other holds most sublime? If this is true, we are again reminded of the reasons that the larger culture war will not subside any time soon.[27]

These shifting expectations of racist, patriarchal, and heterosexist ideologies, miseducation, and reductionist religion appropriated to sanctify our social ills have shaped the aspirations and entitlements of young men and women of this post-everything generation. Such realities are the key ingredients that fuel our deadly culture wars. As a Christian social ethicist who feels that the cognitive dissonance we are facing is rooted in the permanence of racism, the eradication of education, and the realignment of religion, I have become deeply concerned about these realities and seek to unmask, debunk, and disentangle these interlocking forces of oppression, sin, and silence that divide the United States and undermine democracy—in other words, the institutionalization of wrath—and that have given rise to this "trumped up" era.

The Global War on Terror and the Making of the Uncivil Society

The act of making virtues vices has lent itself to the profundity of what has made this country "These Yet to Be United States," as Maya Angelou has claimed. This includes the reality inversion of demonizing civil and human rights that protect against wrongs by problematizing being "woke" instead of being asleep at the wheel in leadership. It also includes eliminating diversity, equity, and inclusion efforts, which many critics see as no different than the unwelcome incarnation of the *Imago Dei*, casting DEI as a harm to civilization to be cured by resegregation. Maya Angelou's poem "These Yet to Be United States" struck a particular nerve in the nation's zeitgeist, and it has become a refrain since the 1990s. Angelou's poetry is not merely fiction but perspectival. Born and raised in difficult circumstances as a poor Black woman in the Jim and Jane Crow South, she indicts the nation by name as being a misnomer at its best and an outright lie at its worst. This is particularly evident in the poem's fifth stanza, where Angelou writes, "They kneel alone in terror / with dread in every glance. / Their rights are threatened daily / by a grim inheritance"[28]—the "they" presumably being young Americans in the United States. Words such as "terror," "dread," "threaten," and "grim" presaged the looming menace that would hang over the nation's atmosphere by the century's end. She portrays both the present and the future as undesirable, unenviable, and decidedly negative. She wonders aloud why this country known as the United States can create weapons of war and pursue military actions that can "change the seasons" and also be the home of children who shed too many tears because they fear the future. Having witnessed a nation defined more by those who were excluded than those who were included, she sees the concept of being "united" as a gross mockery. Moreover, Angelou foresaw how the "United" States as a nation was not only ending the twentieth century internally divided by self-inflicted wounds but was also attempting to seal itself off from the struggles and suffering of the rest of the world by promoting fear of others.

More than a decade after Angelou penned her visionary verses, the nation was terrified by the September 11, 2001, terrorist attacks on the World Trade Center in New York City, the Pentagon in Washington, D.C., and the people in the planes that delivered those attacks. On that fateful Tuesday morning, the attacks killed almost three thousand people directly. Thousands more—especially first responders, survivors, and bystanders—were injured and chronically sickened. According to the postmortem forensics, the victims' ages ranged from two to eighty-five and they came from every race, class, gender, ethnicity, sexuality, religion, and nationality. Sadly, many of these were more unified by the circumstance of their deaths than they had been during their lives. The 9/11 attacks not only devastated the lives of the victims' families and friends, but they also altered the course of American society, culture, and geopolitics.[29]

The trauma and tragedy of the 9/11 attacks led many of us to ask how any society so deeply divided by systems of institutional oppression (racism, xenophobia, heterosexism, and wealth inequality) can ever truly claim to be "united" in any capacity. Rather than engage this question, Americans allowed the temporary seizure of extragovernmental powers by neoconservative extremists masked as patriotic zeal. Although George W. Bush earlier had made superficially Christocentric claims of "compassionate conservatism," the nation found itself increasingly pushed to the brink of authoritarianism.[30] Many journalists and pundits of the era misread the threat from the Bush administration not as a hard pivot toward a seizure of tyrannical power but rather as a temporarily aberrant abandonment of American democratic norms and rule of law.[31] From its inception, beginning with a controversial election accompanied by a bad-faith decision by a conservative-leaning Supreme Court in 2000 on through its hate-mongering reelection campaign against then-Senator John Kerry, the competent yet uncharismatic 2004 Democratic presidential candidate, the Bush-Cheney administration was establishing an imperial presidency.[32] That administration and its neoconservative allies demonstrated their willingness to exercise tyrannical power, for example by waging unlimited warfare in Afghanistan and Iraq, sanctioning kidnapping and torture of suspects, establishing secret CIA prisons worldwide, and using warrantless spying techniques on US citizens. Their exploitation of the 9/11 terror attacks made all this expansion of power possible. As cultural theorist Henry A. Giroux notes, in this age of wrath, "the slaughter that inevitably follows catastrophe is not new, but the current politics of death has reached new heights and threatens to transform a weak democracy into a full-fledged authoritarian state."[33] The divisions created by the ever-increasing institutionalization of wrath, including the Obama administration's efforts to "justify unilateral executive use of lethal force" in fighting terrorism in "areas outside of active hostilities," set the stage for Trump's exploitation, and we are seeing the power and attendant threat of authoritarianism only increase during the Trump era.[34]

Now this lurch toward unfettered tyranny was neither inevitable nor undeniable in nature. Theories focused on the promotion of civil society proliferated within academic circles during the Reagan-Bush and Clinton eras from the late 1980s until the mid-1990s. These theories were marked by gradual ascent of center-right politics on the one hand and a rising tide of neoliberal economics on the other. This bipartisan romance with civil society explains regressive attacks on the functions of modern welfare state liberalism and formed a bulwark against any further encroachment of various iterations of Marxism and other alternative "grand narratives" that supposedly threatened to destabilize the status quo and empower the dispossessed. The timing of this discourse—shortly after the Soviet Union's collapse and the subsequent geopolitical realignment of nation-states worldwide—is no accident. To the contrary, the ideological embrace of civil society offered a hopeful alternative to the period's disillusionment with reformist politics and bureaucratic institutions at the cusp of both a new century and millennium.[35]

To talk about the current situation requires addressing the menace that Trump—and more precisely Trumpism, with which we will have to continue to contend even after Trump himself is out of the national political spotlight—poses to our democracy. Failure to do so underestimates the burgeoning crisis of legitimation as American society moves rapidly away from its democratic core toward authoritarianism and fascism. Recall that on June 17, 2015, exactly one day after Donald Trump descended the gilded escalator at Trump Tower to announce his 2016 presidential campaign, the white supremacist Dylann Roof entered Mother Emanuel A. M. E. Church and gunned down the pastor and eight church members during a Wednesday night Bible study, hoping to incite a race war as a tactical move to "Make America Great Again." Those events made clear that a sizable portion of the white American populace was becoming much more tolerant of white men expressing their rage and wrath in the most brutal fashion possible and more welcoming of a "strongman" figure in US politics. As historian Ruth Ben-Ghiat explains in *Strongmen: Mussolini to the Present*, authoritarians "stand out from other kinds of politicians by appealing to negative experiences and emotions. They don the cloak of national victimhood, reliving the humiliations of their people by sovereign powers," promising retribution on enemies at home or abroad.[36] Strongmen rely heavily on propaganda as a key tool for gaining and maintaining power.

From "Alternative Facts" to Alt-Reality

Ever since Trump descended that gilded escalator in June 2015, he and his enablers have been waging a "war on reality" against the mainstream media and the American people by serving us a daily bread of lies. Ben-Ghiat observes that "the decay of truth and democratic dissolution proceed hand in hand, starting with the insurgent's assertion that the establishment media delivers false or biased information while he speaks the truth and risks everything to get the 'real facts' out."[37] Though he has never proffered evidence for the huge "VOTER FRAUD" he alleges, Trump promised to "strengthen up voting procedures" (itself a very worrying sign of things to come). Skillfully lampooned by comedic actress Melissa McCarthy in her now legendary SNL skits, early Trump-era White House Press Secretary Sean Spicer quickly lost his credibility (and ultimately his job) in his endless efforts to bolster all of his boss's conspiracy theories, baseless claims, and bold-faced lies. Now, in the wake of Trump's "Big Lie" about the 2020 election, it is extremely worrisome that the Trump presidency not only has had so many mouthpieces but also so many enablers conspiring to swamp the center of American life with a tsunami of alternative facts.[38] Even more troubling is how difficult they have made it for our bona fide sources of knowledge production—such as scholars, journalists, and eyewitnesses—to establish the truth of the matter, which is, according to Ben-Ghiat, precisely the work of propaganda. She explains that "at its core, propaganda is a set of communication strategies designed to sow confusion and uncertainty, discourage critical thinking, and persuade people that reality is what the leader says it is."[39] However, propaganda only works if an authoritarian or aspiring authoritarian appeals to followers who in turn legitimize his authority. Authoritarians are nothing without their supporters.[40] In a 1974 interview, Hannah Arendt, a Jewish philosopher who fled Nazi Germany and later became one of the most consequential political theorists of the twentieth century, spoke of the impact of the flood of public lies: "If everybody always lies to you, the consequence is not that you believe the lies, but rather that nobody believes anything any longer. . . . And a people that no longer can believe anything cannot make up its mind. It is deprived not only of its capacity to act but also of its capacity to think and to judge. And with such a people you can then do what you please."[41]

The nation must finally own up to the fact that there is nothing—not sexual predation, not racial intolerance, not religious hypocrisy, not unfettered corruption, not meddling by foreign enemies, not threats to democracy—that Republicans loathe more than they do Democrats, nor anything they cherish more than power. One way to burst the bubble of hypocrisy and restore credulity is to admit openly that Trump never intended to "drain the swamp" of Washington D.C.'s political cronyism and corruption, never intended to make the United States a more fully integrated and respected partner in the global order, and never intended to bring outmoded manufacturing and low-skill jobs back from overseas. Instead, let's admit openly that he gave many of his poorest, most disgruntled supporters on the Right something they wanted much more than any of those intangible and seemingly ephemeral things: revenge against the Other. As he has said, he is their retribution.

Furthermore, the moral rot at the core of alt-reality can be traced through its bellicose language to the accompanying state-sanctioned policies and practices—some referenced in previous chapters—that have shaped the very foundation of American society and culture for nearly 250 years. These policies and practices include but are not limited to white settler colonialism and Native genocide; the enslavement, segregation, disenfranchisement, and incarceration of Black people; the annexation of Mexican land and subsequent discrimination and deportation of Latinx migrant workers; the internment of Japanese Americans; manifestations of antisemitism that has included quotas, killings, harassment, and various forms of xenophobia; and the economic, legal, and political inequality of women, immigrants, and LGBTQIA+ people.

If one is the most favored and privileged class of citizen of a nation by virtue of being white, male-identified, heterosexual, and able-bodied, a person whose very existence is predicated on stealing an entire continent and enslaving millions, one has to construct an identity that justifies the barbarity, pathology, criminality, savagery, and treachery of these actions. How else does such a person live with themself? One has to be able to find a way to exist, to construe the facts to fit one's narrative. In *The Brothers Karamazov*, Russian novelist Fyodor Dostoevsky captures the dilemma this way:

> A man who lies to himself, and believes his own lies becomes unable to recognize the truth, either in himself or in anyone else, and he ends up losing respect for himself and for others. When he has no respect for anyone, he can no longer love, and, in order to divert himself, having no love in him, he yields to his impulses, indulges in the lowest forms of pleasure, and behaves in the end like an animal. And it all comes from lying—lying to others and to yourself.[42]

To preserve their privilege, Donald Trump and his minions took ad hominem lying and petulant rage to new heights on January 6, 2021.

American Democracy as Bloodsport

"Yesterday, the president of the United States incited an armed insurrection against the American people," House Speaker Nancy Pelosi said on the day following January 6, 2021. This attempted coup ultimately led to the prosecution of Trump's second impeachment. Immediately following a MAGA rally organized near the White House on January 6, Trump urged his supporters to go to the US Capitol and "fight like hell" while Congress was in the often-ceremonial process of certifying Joe Biden's election. Trump supporters stormed the US Capitol building with murderous intent toward the lawmakers assembled on that day. Carrying "Trump 2020" campaign banners and, ironically, "Blue Lives Matter" flags, the rioters assaulted the US Capitol and District of Columbia police officers with overwhelming force and reckless abandon.

The attack, inspired by Trump's false claim of a stolen election known as "the Big Lie," was a culmination of the attempts to overturn the 2020 US presidential election. The overarching narrative of the insurrection seems to suggest that former Vice President Mike Pence rejected schemes and pleas to set aside the November 2020 election result, which would have paved the way for the House of Representatives to conduct a second election, with various Republican political leaders holding an advantage that could have installed Trump for a second consecutive term. As the violent uprising laid siege to the Capitol building, there was a sizable crowd of pro-Trump protesters who were not only increasingly rowdy and belligerent but also, in many cases, heavily armed.

From mid-November of 2020 until January 5, 2021, Trump's legal team, led by Rudy Giuliani, Sidney Powell, and Jenna Ellis, helped to foment a widespread conspiracy theory alleging that Democrats had dumped millions of illegal ballots into the nation's election system. That team filed multiple lawsuits in several key states without any evidence, alleging that partisan poll watchers did not have a clear enough view of the voting and vote-counting in some locations and that therefore something illegal must have happened. The claims were repeatedly dismissed, including by Republican-appointed judges. Republicans in some battleground states followed Trump in making unsupported claims. By and large, the greatest falsehood at the heart of "the Big Lie" was the denial by Trump and his cronies that the November 2020 presidential election had been rightfully certified by experts at the local, state, and federal level—many of them elected and appointed officials who were also members of the GOP—and was "the most secure" in US history.[43] Moreover, even Bill Barr, who spent much of his tenure as Trump's attorney general doggedly shielding the president from repercussions of countless criminal and constitutional charges, also concluded that the results of the 2020 presidential election were accurate and legitimate.[44] Nevertheless, the levels of confusion and contestation that Trump's legal team advanced lent new meaning to the term "battleground states."

Beyond temporarily delaying the certification of the 2020 election results, Donald Trump's most passionate supporters then proceeded to crash through the windows and doors of the US Capitol, brawling brazenly with the outnumbered ranks of police officers. They ransacked the building and prowled the hallowed corridors of the complex seeking to capture and possibly kill Vice President Pence and many members of Congress. One Capitol police officer who fought with rioters died the next day and, in the aftermath of the riot, it became clear that the attack had left four people dead. Earlier, on January 27, 2021, a National Terrorism Advisory System Bulletin issued by the Department of Homeland Security stated that the January 6 insurrection arose due to the "heightened threat environment across the United States," in which "some ideologically-motivated violent extremists with objections to the exercise of governmental authority and the presidential transition, as well as other perceived grievances fueled by false narratives, could continue to mobilize to incite or commit violence."[45]

When the smoke and dust settled from the uproar of the insurrection, on July 1, 2021, the US House Select Committee to Investigate the January 6th Attack on the United States Capitol was formed through a largely party-line vote in the House of Representatives. Under the leadership of Rep. Bennie Thompson, a Democratic congressman from Mississippi, the special committee was made up of seven Democrats and two Republicans—Rep. Liz Cheney and Rep. Adam Kinzinger—to ensure that this congressional investigative panel would be bipartisan in both form and function. The lawmakers on the House panel collected more than a hundred thousand documents, and investigators conducted over eight hundred interviews trying to uncover the truth of the matter.

While addressing his colleagues at a ceremonial counting of electoral votes that confirmed President-elect Biden's decisive electoral victory, US Senator Mitt Romney of Utah called the riots at the US Capitol "an insurrection incited by the President of the United States." As a former Massachusetts governor who lost his own bid for the White House as the 2012 Republican presidential candidate, Romney understood better than most how heartbreaking and harrowing such a defeat can be. And yet, when addressing the issue on the floor of the Senate, Romney stated plainly:

> We gather due to a selfish man's injured pride. And the outrage of supporters who he has deliberately misinformed for the past two months—and stirred to action this very morning. What happened . . . was an insurrection, incited by the President of the United States. Those who choose to continue to support his dangerous gambit by objecting to the results of a legitimate, democratic election will forever be seen as being complicit in an unprecedented attack against democracy. They will be remembered for their role in this shameful episode in American history. That will be their legacy.

But even as the circumstances and conditions of January 6 come into sharper view, the event itself marked a radical sea change in American political culture, one that the nation finds both unfamiliar and altogether uncomfortable. As a Democratic member of the January 6 committee who also led the prosecution of Trump's second impeachment, Rep. Jamie Raskin said, "We don't have a lot of experience with coups in our own country and we think of a coup as something that takes place against a president." The insurrection was a different manifestation within American life, not only because it did not involve the military or another faction attempting to unseat a current head of state, but because it sought to overturn the political process itself. "It's what the political scientists call a self-coup . . . it's a president fearful of defeat, overthrowing the constitutional process," Raskin said.[46] Rowdy hordes of MAGA insurrectionists erected a gallows intended to hang the outgoing vice president of the United States, beat a police officer within an inch of his life, smeared their feces on the walls of the Capitol, and literally sought to overturn the election results is apparently considered "legitimate political discourse." One can only wonder what the body count would have been if people of color were ever to engage in such "legitimate political discourse."[47] As I finish this book in the spring of 2025, fifteen hundred people who were arrested, faced criminal charges, and were convicted for activities related to the attack have been valorized and granted pardons by Trump, on the very day of his second presidential inauguration.[48]

Whereas Americans for generations had cherished the peaceful transfer of governmental power across partisan lines at the highest echelons, the January 6 insurrection and its ongoing legacy reflect the watershed moment when American politics finally shed all pretenses and officially became a bloodsport. Although the Biden presidency purported to be a new era, it has now been proven to be a brief interregnum. Trumpism didn't go away, as Trump is once again the US president. While many assumed that Biden's election represented a lasting return to normalcy, Trump's reelection shows that we have in fact not prevailed in creating systemic change. That the raid on the Capitol was eventually suppressed may seem to have thwarted complete anarchy and authoritarianism. But voter suppression and right-wing court packing have made it more difficult to make systemic change toward ending white supremacy and dismantling our caste system.

Caste, as Isabel Wilkerson states, always frustrates equality and therefore also unity. Upholding the caste system is why despite the utter failure of Donald Trump to accomplish anything other than the tax giveaway to billionaires, and despite the outrageous breach of his oath to uphold the Constitution and the public trust, in 2020, although he lost, seventy-four million Americans nevertheless voted for him.[49] In his classic text *1984*, novelist George Orwell contends that "power is not a means; it is an end. One does not establish a dictatorship in order to safeguard a revolution; one makes the revolution in order to establish the dictatorship."[50] Following this logic, the attempted coup by Donald Trump and his coconspirators was a mad grasp for power meant to deform our majoritarian democracy into a minority-rule autocracy. Republicans and far-right operatives have made it clear that they plan to further institutionalize minority rule by dismantling the administrative state and establishing an authoritarian presidency.[51] Ben-Ghiat warns that Trump's plans for remodeling the federal government to increase executive power and replace civil servants with loyalists as outlined in the Heritage Foundation's Project 2025, whose authors include former Trump administration officials, is "consistent with the 21st century playbook for authoritarians," which she outlines:

Tell the public how you will set up an authoritarian state well before you get into office. Frame your intended expansion of executive powers as a mere streamlining of government. Don't forget to repeatedly praise dictators as "brilliant" and "top of the line" people so there'll be no surprises when you act in a similar manner. And whet your followers' appetites for destruction of existing norms by advertising how you will purge "the sick political class that hates our country" from government.[52]

We are witnessing this process today.

Conclusion

To say that President of the United States Donald J. Trump—someone twice elected but also twice impeached, four times indicted, thirty-four times feloniously convicted, and having faced multiple state and federal felony counts spanning Washington, D.C., New York, Florida, and Georgia—is the poster child for the seven deadly sins might be the understatement of a lifetime. Marked by an obsessive fear that the left wing of the Democratic Party, inspired by the landmark presidency of Barack Obama, was poised to remake America into a more inclusive multiracial, multicultural, and multifaith society, the current tide of politics without principle is buoyed by the recognition that Donald Trump was able to pull off a veritable *coup d'etat* of the Republican Party to remake it in his own image before attempting to incite a violent coup of the United States on the steps of the Capitol some four years later. Unlike his predecessors, either presidential candidates or presidents, Trump's political takeover of the Grand Old Party has been most notable because he rejected the political orthodoxy that has comprised the core principles of the party for more than half a century. Instead, he was able to manipulate and amplify the current spirit of political tribalism by bending avowedly Republican bedrock values to his will and then taking every vestige of modern conservatism in the party and summarily tearing them to shreds. As Ben-Ghiat explains, "the time-tested methods of autocracy—electoral manipulation, voter suppression, the criminalization of protest, political violence, and disinformation—are now part of the way the GOP conducts its business as a far-right party."[53]

Despite having ample opportunities to push back against Trumpism, the GOP has only seemed to tighten its embrace of Trump by electing a MAGA Republican, Mike Johnson, as Speaker of the House after a group of far-right representatives ousted Kevin McCarthy. Now, in spite of Trump's 2024 reelection and the Republican stranglehold on Congress and the Supreme Court, a long litany of damning charges continues to trail him. A New

York jury found Trump civilly liable for battery and defamation in a case brought by E. Jean Carroll, who had accused Trump of sexually assaulting her. New York Attorney General Letitia James secured a ruling that exposed that Trump had defrauded banks and insurers in the pursuit of building his empire. Meanwhile, also in New York, Manhattan District Attorney Alvin Bragg obtained thirty-four felony convictions against Trump regarding election interference and the hush money payment to adult film actress and director Stormy Daniels. In Georgia, Fulton County District Attorney Fani Willis indicted Trump based on his desperate and coercive attempt to "find" more votes in the 2020 election. Department of Justice Special Counsel Jack Smith pursued two federal cases against Trump: one for his mishandling of classified documents and another for his role in the January 6 insurrection. Leaked confidential testimony from a member of Trump's legal team revealed that a top Trump administration official told the team that "the boss is not going to leave under any circumstances" and "we are just going to stay in power."[54] However, the special counsel dropped charges in these two cases, including appealing the decision by Judge Aileen Cannon described below, referencing DOJ policy against indicting sitting presidents.

At the same time, that we have a two-tiered justice system that benefits the rich and powerful continues to be made clear at every turn. In New York, in order to appeal civil liability rulings, defendants must post a bond that covers the amount of the judgment. Trump, however, was granted relief by the court, lowering the more than $464 million bond in the fraud case to $175 million so that he could appeal.[55] Meanwhile, Trump-appointed Judge Aileen Cannon dismissed the classified documents case, saying that Special Counsel Jack Smith's appointment was unconstitutional. As a result of its ruling on presidential immunity, the January 6 election interference case was further delayed when the Supreme Court remanded to a lower court the issue of which claims are official acts and which ones are not.[56]

Distracted as they were by Trump's masterful skills at gaudy self-promotion and chronic prevarication, which previously garnered sizable ratings, sensational news stories, and skyrocketing revenue, more sober and serious public scrutiny by mainstream media outlets and journalists during his rise in the 2016 campaign season might have revealed some of these troubling issues. Along with the desperate hunger for political power by many on the far right, the shortcomings of our electoral system illustrated by the era of Trumpism have resulted in the nation being locked into a downward spiral of blatant racism, sexism, xenophobia, corruption, incompetence, and other travesties made apparent by the endless cascade of public controversies and political scandals in which his administration is mired. According to Adam Serwer:

> Trump's only true skill is the con, his only fundamental belief is that the United States is the birthright of straight, white, Christian men, and his only real, authentic pleasure is in cruelty. It is that cruelty, and the delight it brings them, that binds his most ardent supporters to him, in shared scorn for those they hate and fear: immigrants, black voters, feminists, and treasonous white men who empathize with any of those who would steal their birthright. The president's ability to execute that cruelty through word and deed makes them euphoric. It makes them feel good, it makes them feel proud, it makes them feel happy, it makes them feel united. And as long as he makes them feel that way, they will let him get away with anything, no matter what it costs them.[57]

As the all-American avatar of the seven deadly sins, Trump represents the wrath that results from a perpetrator's power being successfully challenged. The expression of wrath is the epitome of the expression of power as domination. Doing in broad daylight what others would fear to do in the darkest night, Trump has laid bare the soul of America in all of its vices. In his objectification and reported rape of women, he touts his embrace of lust as evidence of his masculine dominance.[58] Despite his numerous bankruptcies and failed business ventures, his show *The Apprentice* leaned into "1980s-style greed-is-good themes" with men and women competing for a job working for Trump.[59] As an apprentice of greed, he is slothful, amassing money by swindling people, including his tenants, and the government. During the first three years of his presidency, his businesses charged the Department of Defense $976,000.[60] He has used money donated by his supporters to a political action committee to pay for his legal fees.[61] And he has a history of wage theft from those he employs.[62] During his most recent presidential campaign, Trump promoted $60 "God Bless the USA Bibles,"[63] $400 gold sneakers,[64] and $100,000 watches from a company about which very little is known.[65] There is nothing he will not capitalize on financially. He simultaneously wears his elitism and anti-intellectualism on his sleeve with pride. Despite having attended an Ivy League university himself, Trump does not read and has little to no regard for education, openly attacking Columbia and Harvard universities for not kowtowing to his anti-First Amendment agenda. As president, he has had his national security briefings kept to a single page with eye-catching graphics because he has limited attention for details.[66] Trump's envy has propelled him to capitalize on the technology of social media to transcend the limits of television, projecting his persona further than ever before. Knowing that a Black man handily had won the White House twice and had enjoyed the public admiration he believed himself entitled to but was unable to garner because he lacked the substance to do so, Trump embraced the 24/7 presence and reach of social media to become the news himself, which allowed him to extend his dominance further than lust could take him. It helped him transcend the limitations of his humanity, divining his desires. It both obfuscated his power and made it ubiquitous as his tweets became the focus of the news and supplanted truth with his version of reality.

It is gluttony, or worship without sacrifice, when Trump positions himself to be the godlike figure who unleashes his wrath. Trump's gluttony is both of the *ardenter* and *praepropore* variety. He diminishes and destroys the sacrality of worship, whether by ordering the National Guard to teargas Black Lives Matter protesters to clear his way for a photo op in front of a church while holding a Bible upside down, or by calling himself the champion of conservative Christians in public while mocking them in private.[67] Trump stands in stark contrast to a good man like US Capitol police officer Eugene Goodman, a Black man who made his body bait to delay the enraged insurrectionists and allow more time for members of Congress to flee to safety during the January 6th attack. Instead of sacrificing, Trump feasts on the sacrifices of others and demands their worship.

He depletes the sacred of meaning and becomes a surrogate for God to his followers, claiming this surrogacy by posting a video called "God Made Trump" that portrays him as a messianic figure, on social media and before rallies in Iowa.[68] A 2023 CBS News/YouGov poll found that a majority of Trump voters feel that he tells them the truth over friends and family, conservative media figures, and lastly, religious leaders.[69] Russell Moore, the editor-in-chief of *Christianity Today* who came to understand that evangelical Christianity is in crisis, says:

> It was the result of having multiple pastors tell me, essentially, the same story about quoting the Sermon on the Mount, parenthetically, in their preaching—"turn the other cheek"—[and] to have someone come up after to say, "Where did you get those liberal talking points?" And what was alarming to me is that in most of these scenarios, when the pastor would say, "I'm literally quoting Jesus Christ" . . . the response would be, "Yes, but that doesn't work anymore. That's weak." And when we get to the point where the teachings of Jesus himself are seen as subversive to us, then we're in a crisis.[70]

Trump's aesthetics, attitude, and actions feed the fury of this crisis, but he is explained away as an outlier. He is not only something with which people are familiar; he is what they crave. He has been promoted for every American vice he embraces. US Senator Raphael Warnock, Democrat from Georgia, said, "A vote is a kind of prayer for the world we desire for ourselves and for our children." And when Trump spoke to and incited his followers on the day of the Epiphany to storm the Capitol, that was not an expression of political support but a practice of prayer and perhaps a (un)civil religion. Take Jacob Chansley, the so-called QAnon Shaman, one of Trump's insurrectionists, who did in fact pray when he made it to the Senate floor on January 6, offering gratitude for being "allowed" by police officers who let them inside to "exercise our rights, to allow us to send a message to all the tyrants, the communists and the globalists that this is our nation, not theirs."[71]

For the many millions of US citizens who declared themselves part of the "Resistance" and sought to oust Trump from the presidency, literally every day after his shocking 2016 electoral victory was declared there was always a moral imperative to their critique. Many of the daily news reports focus implicitly on a steady erosion of our collective ethical principles and moral practice, an erosion that fuels countless Americans' worries about the irreparable decimation of the nation's ethos. Yet, in the aftermath of his 2024 reelection, those who oppose Trump face a conundrum: If a president has been identified as committing as many crimes and transgressions of political and social norms as Trump has and has not yet been held responsible for such gross abuses of power, then we must ask ourselves whether the forbidden fruits of wrath are more tempting than the knowledge and doing of good that we claim to seek.

Moving beyond political disagreements and personal distaste for Trump as a public figure, this inventory is a moral, perhaps prophetic, diagnosis of him as an unyielding embodiment of the nation's worst proclivities. The underlying narrative of the 2024 presidential campaign being a mythic battle between Trump and former Vice President Kamala Harris (the first Black and Desi candidate for POTUS, whose public resume included being San Francisco's district attorney and California's attorney general) as a dialectical conflict between a perpetrator and a prosecutor had unmistakable poetic justice. The main feature of the forty-fifth and now forty-seventh president of the United States has been the innumerable ways he represents the sum of all our worst fears and dirtiest desires.

At this critical juncture, it is essential to acknowledge that the root cause of our current predicament extends beyond any single individual. While it is easy to focus on the actions of one man, we must recognize that the source of our present calamity lies in the bitter undercurrents that have shaped our national political discourse for years. The divisive rhetoric and actions of President Donald J. Trump are merely a manifestation of a deeper, more pervasive issue: the resentment and refusal to accept the diverse reality of our society. This driving force has fueled the fires of discontent, giving rise to movements that jeopardize our health, safety, and unity. The reopen movement, which stormed statehouses across the country in 2020 to force a reopening of public spaces that were closed during the COVID pandemic, was not created by President Trump; instead, it emerged as a symptom of the fear and frustration that simmered beneath the surface of our collective consciousness. Similarly, the antimask movement, which has endangered our public spaces with its stubborn resistance to health guidelines, is not the product of a single leader but a reflection of our fractured society.

While it may be convenient to blame President Trump for our current state of affairs, we must remember that he merely gave voice to the anger and divisions that already existed. To move forward, we must confront the underlying resentments and fears that have gripped our nation and work together to bridge the divides that threaten to consume us. As we navigate this turbulent period in our history, let us remember that the challenges we face are not the result of one person but of a collective failure to address the fractures in our national identity. Only by acknowledging and addressing these root causes can we hope to heal the rifts that have led us to this moment and build a more resilient, united, and compassionate society.

Those of us willing to stand our ground for truth and social justice have a moral imperative to affirm our contributions to society, our humanity, and our resilience in the face of deadly modes of ingrained prejudice and systemic oppression. Despite our desire to understand Trump and what he stands for as wholly un-American—as "not who we are"—this is, in fact, who we have long been, who we are, and who we are becoming unless we choose another, better path. "The truth unquestionably is," as Alexander Hamilton stated in the earliest years of the nation's founding:

> that the only path to a subversion of the republican system of the Country is, by flattering the prejudices of the people, and exciting their jealousies and apprehensions, to throw affairs into confusion, and bring on civil commotion. . . . When a man unprincipled in private life[,] desperate in his fortune, bold in his temper, possessed of considerable talents . . . despotic in his ordinary demeanor—known to have scoffed in private at the principles of liberty—when such a man is seen to mount the hobby horse of popularity—to join in the cry of danger to liberty—to take every opportunity of embarrassing the General Government and bringing it under suspicion—to flatter and fall in with all the nonsense of the zealots of the day—it may justly be suspected that his object is to throw things into confusion that he may "ride the storm and direct the whirlwind."[72]

CONCLUSION

Making Americans Better, If Not Good

Reconciling Ourselves to Virtue

Contrary to popular belief, the path to a good life either individually or collectively requires significant work and is often paved with struggle. Despite the rhetoric, pursuing the "good life" necessitates a reckoning with all that is bad about both the world and ourselves. In fact, in many religious worldviews, that which brings about peace (*shanti*, *shalom*, *salam*) must reckon with the suffering inflicted by everyday life. The good life requires that we acknowledge, atone, and make alterations for our transgressions, for example, in the Jewish high holiday of Yom Kippur, wherein the community engages in a process of repentance in order to rectify wrongs to change the future. That which is grounded in recommitting oneself to a Holy Place necessitates recognizing where one has broken a covenant. Within Islam, those who seek holiness must participate in a hajj, or pilgrimage. Within my tradition of Christianity, the gospel, also known as "the good news," is only realized insofar as it resolves a bad situation. Real religion requires agency, whether by going the distance of a pilgrimage or by practicing what you preach in the name of justice. All that is good demands the agency to do justice, which entails a journey of right relationship with others and our world.

In the face of chattel slavery, famed abolitionist and moral exemplar of early American society Frederick Douglass proclaimed, "Power concedes nothing without a demand. It never did and it never will. Find out just what any people will quietly submit to, and you have found out the exact measure of injustice and wrong which will be imposed upon them, and these will continue till they are resisted."[1] Some decades later, in his classic text *Moral Man and Immoral Society*, Reinhold Niebuhr insisted that people tend to sin in greater force collectively rather than as individuals.[2] Meanwhile, Martin

Luther King Jr. observed that "the arc of the moral universe is long, but it bends toward justice."[3] Taken together, these varied perspectives challenge us—as agents of change—to ponder from what source we will find the moral resolve and personal gravitas to face the residual conflict of our era and change the status quo. Therefore, the faithful minority has always had both the epistemological privilege and existential imperative to understand both that the stakes for a good life are high and the moral standards for the majority are low. Yet, if we are to achieve true human flourishing and overcome social ills, it is incumbent on us to reevaluate our current understanding of human existence and rectify its inherent contradictions. But how do we right the wrongs within the very ontology of our being? Do we simply go with the flow, as Niebuhr claims, while assuming, as King does, that change for the good will surely happen? As US citizens, how can we wrest ourselves from our oxymoronic inclinations, which have formed our thinking-being-doing ontologies to be self-contradicting in nature? With regard to the rhetoric and reality of our culture writ large, that realization of sin as a societal concern poses itself as philosophical paradox—it has us left in a perpetual purgatory wherein we go against all common sense and lose any possibility of achieving the common good.

The ancient Hebrew prophet Micah reminds us that to live a life of integrity God requires us "to do justice, to love mercy, and to walk humbly with our God [or what is ultimately GOOD]."[4] The parable in the Gospel of Matthew of the vineyard owner epitomizes Micah's prophetic directive. Here Jesus tells a parable of a vineyard owner who hires workers at different times throughout the day. The owner agrees with the first group of laborers to pay them a full day's wage. Later, at various hours, the owner hires additional workers and promises them the same wage. When evening comes, he pays everyone the same amount, starting with those hired last. The workers who were hired first complain, feeling they should receive more, since they worked longer. The owner responds by saying that he is being fair, as he paid them what was agreed upon, and he has the right to do as he pleases with his money. The parable ends with this statement: "So the last will be first, and the first will be last."[5] Although technically the profits from the vineyard belong to the owner, he understands that everything we have is a divine gift, and that the only faithful response to such divine generosity is quite literally to share the wealth. Furthermore, the vineyard owner understands that talents, resources, and opportunities will never be distributed evenly or justly by mere chance alone. By his actions at the end of the workday, he demonstrates that it is our collective duty to collaborate and create a world in which we respond to all human needs appropriately, regardless of which humans have the needs and why. Finally, the vineyard owner embodies what it means to be merciful. He recognizes that paying the laborers is not a necessary evil, something to be begrudgingly bestowed. Instead, he values the laborers as fellow human beings.

As Martin Luther King Jr. taught, the only way to overcome a political economic order defined by greed is by engaging in a "revolution of values" as the vineyard owner did, values rooted in humility, justice, and mercy for the good of all of us mired in the seven deadly sins. Yet some of us are more deeply aware of society's sins than others. Such people have a greater responsibility to begin that revolution, to dismantle racism, sexism, poverty, and so forth. Such people also have a greater responsibility to abandon their deals with devils and rescue this nation. But all of us, together, are responsible for finding a metaethical way of becoming this change we seek. How? By forging an ethic of redemptive difference. Such an ethic might yet enable the present generation to undo the evil that previous generations have done.

The first step in creating an ethic of redemptive difference requires us to call it like we see it. It requires us to ask: "Oh say, can you see?" Can you see what is actually going on? The question is an urgent call, to all of us. Each of us must be sufficiently bold and brave enough to tell the truth about what is happening, no matter how grotesque the evils in which we have participated. This means calling out injustice where we are. Calling things as we see them means naming and addressing the racism in our families; demanding that our education teach us how to put our knowledge to work rather than put us in the poorhouse; insisting that our preachers be prophetic and profound rather than perverted, predatory, or prosperous. And so on.

The second step in creating an ethic of redemptive difference requires us to call people into the just community for which we yearn. How do we begin to do that? By understanding those with whom we already live as those with whom we must live *in community*, as our *beloved community*, to quote King again. Instead of stereotyping each other as dishonorably black or honorably white, as the powerful privileged or the disempowered masses, we can revolutionize our thinking and consider one another as people who are "interrelated, caught in an inescapable web of mutuality and tied in a single garment of destiny, knowing that whatever affects one directly, affects all indirectly."[6] In this way of being, we are not "Us and Them," "Self and the Other," or "Me and the Man," but what Martin Buber calls "I and Thou."[7] In this I-Thou relationship, human beings are aware of each other as interconnected, unified, and dignified beings, not separate, isolated, and disrespected. When we become descriptively diagnostic, we not only call out what is wrong with our condition but also call into the community those who can and must help change it.

The third step in the ethic of redemptive difference is to become dialogically engaged. To be dialogically engaged, as Cornel West says, means to participate fully in the true meaning of democracy. He continues, "Democracy depends, in large part, on [a society that seeks to be] free and frank, willing to speak painful truths to the public and each other about our society, including the fact of their own complicity, confusion, or cowardice."[8] This notion of democracy West claims is one that cultivates *paideia*—a true and active notion of American citizenship, instead of the numbed-up and dumbed-down citizenship that we're being told is the only form of true patriotism. *Paideia* mandates that we not only speak boldly and courageously against the misinformation, mediocrities, and mendacities of society, but that we also speak vulnerably, openly, and honestly with each other.

While truth-telling is essential to advancing an ethic of redemptive difference, it is not enough. Voting rights advocate Stacey Abrams says that to be effective in change we "must be truth seekers, and that requires a willingness to understand truths other than our own."[9] We must also hear the truths of everyone and not just those voices of the majority. We also must be willing to engage in social interaction with those who have been minoritized, marginalized, silenced, and rendered invisible. This necessity entails creating a discursive space big enough to realize that truth as an idea is not based upon the number of the people who profess it. Our very nation was founded on the bold and radical acts of a minority, a handful of people who believed that silenced people were facing big problems that needed to be set right. Embedded in this dialogical engagement is the imperative, "You don't have the right to remain silent, though you have the right to be wrong." A fully functioning society responds to members who from time to time have bad or not yet fully considered ideas with responsible and reasonable counterarguments. Functioning moral agents, people who know and understand they have some range of power to choose their course in life, desperately need and want this kind of vigorous give and take. This is how those who have been previously marginalized and dispossessed can truly become agents of their own lived experience.

The fourth and final step in an ethic of redemptive difference demands disruptive truthfulness, a defiant posture that creates something out of nothing, that seeks to be constructive rather than destructive. Such disruption is the very essence of being a "divinely inspired redemptive difference." In the face of chaos, we can create order, thereby making something out of nothing and surprising a society that expects little to nil from us. This does not have to involve a lexicon of virtues to be defined but rather, as anthropologist Marla Frederick reminds us, is merely to have "the will to stop."[10] In taking the time to stop, look, and listen, we become humane in our humanity, giving us the ability to empathize with one another, the ability to see where my convenience ends and your humanity begins; where my rights cease and your rights begin; where my greed stops because the need for your provision begins. "EVERYthing," as Toni Morrison writes in *Beloved*, "depends on knowing how much . . . [but] *Good* is knowing when to stop" (emphasis added).[11] Americans have abandoned the sensibility of a live well lived by seeking to refuse restraint and to acquire a good life that ought never to exist. We simply want too much of a good thing.

This ethic of redemptive difference merges love and logic in ways that require countering a hostile world with love rather than hate. We know that to insist upon vengeance or retribution does not work. Revenge only begets and exacerbates the urge for more revenge. Evil only multiplies evil with no end in sight. But when one strives to overcome evil with good and spreads goodness in the world, justice and progress follow. The abolitionist, suffragist, civil rights, and antiwar movements have shown us that truth time and time again. The heart and soul of any true democratic society is its most immediate, intense, and impassioned form of direct political participation. Protest and participation have resisted oppression and remade our nation into a more just society.

As a Christian social ethicist whose social location is very much at the nexus of race, class, and gender, I dispute the prescription to love in such a way as to forget the wrongs, to become immune to discrimination and indifferent to hate. The only effective way to love a person who has been held hostage by the principalities and powers, to evil influences that lead them to oppress others, is to hinder them from doing further wrong. These corrective actions only take hold and set those persons free when done with a loving heart and with the other person's welfare in mind.

This means we must deal not only with difference, diversity, and dissenting opinions, but with our need to be comforted by our own reflection mirrored in others. Our world is changing, and all those around us are different: their race, their knowledge set, and their beliefs. There is no option of occupying spaces where most people in your world share your skin color, language, culture, and ancestry. We must not be fooled by the *sub-rosa* morality that books can be read by their covers. It is our character and actions, not our color or gender, that show our true commitments. Clarence Thomas is a demoralizing disgrace to Thurgood Marshall's legacy, just as Amy Coney Barrett is to that of Ruth Bader Ginsburg.

So, as the old song says, "If you can't be with the one you love, love the one you're with!"[12] And, as Martin Luther King Jr. emphasized, it's true that divinely inspired "love is the only force capable of transforming an enemy into a friend" and of making right all that has gone wrong.[13] This choice is ours and the reins are in our hands. To unmask, debunk, and disentangle the interlocking forces of oppressive institutions and social sins, we must, as Gandhi said, become the change we seek. We cannot merely wait for others to wake up, emancipate, and embrace us. We ourselves must confront injustice, not surrender to the issues that seem beyond our control.

Our projections of ourselves neither protect us nor reflect the good life. When we practice historicide—that is, the erasure of fact and promotion of fiction—we have no hope of a future, skewing a nation's history in an effort to obliterate its past. We ban books but not weapons of mass destruction; we hope for but do not fight for our enlightenment or prospects for our posterity. As leading moral sages as well as scholar-practitioners of ethics have shown us, our assertions are not enough because we cannot assume we have a future. Our very existence is in jeopardy. "The weight of presumption is shifting against us."[14] "Our moral hope lies in confronting our false innocence and the ethical practices that sustain it. . . . Hope for a common good lies in an ethics accountable to experiences of difference."[15] "Our way of [life] ignores its complicity with advancing the . . . Empire";[16] and we have yet to become the United States of America because we have not reckoned with the united shame of Americans and the "united states of amnesia" in which we find ourselves. More than anything, I hope this book compels us to confront these ugly truths, no matter how uncomfortable it may be, so that we can ultimately recognize and restore the reality of our shared humanity. The ethic of redemptive difference is to realize that projections of perfection are the enemy of the good. We can no longer naively trust King's hopeful claim that "the arc of the moral universe is long, but it bends toward justice." It is no longer a given that there will be good people to bend it; good no longer has the gravitational pull it once did. Neither Kingian platitudes nor Niebuhrean serenity prayers will save US when, as Toni Morrison says, "Evil has a blockbuster audience, while goodness lurks backstage."[17] Any hope of becoming a more perfect union in our pursuit of happiness lies in doing justice, practicing loving kindness, and walking humbly with the God of good.

My hope remains that our children and our children's children will inherit an America where they can flourish, unburdened by the fantastic hegemonic imagination that informs its *thinking* and the oxymoronic ontology that gives it its *being*. For that to become possible, we desperately need a remix of our serenity prayers, one that's in their own terms:

May God grant us:
the wisdom to see what must be changed;
the courage to change what we should never accept;
and the serenity found in making a redemptive difference.[18]

Notes

Acknowledgments and Preface

Epigraph: Amanda Gorman (@TheAmandaGorman), "O say can we see, by the Gone's early flight, What so loudly we failed at the morn light's past gleaming, Whose flawed stripes and strifed scars, through the perilous plight . . . ," Twitter, July 4, 2022, https://x.com/TheAmandaGorman/status/1544163633655005185.

1. Dorothy Day, *The Long Loneliness: The Autobiography of the Legendary Catholic Social Activist* (San Francisco: HarperOne, 2009).

2. Ida B. Wells, *The Light of Truth: Writings of an Anti-Lynching Crusader* (New York: Penguin, 2008), xix.

3. Former Vice President Al Gore's acceptance speech at the Democratic National Convention, Denver, Colorado, August 29, 2008.

4. William Sloane Coffin, as quoted in "Peace Activist William Sloane Coffin Dies at 81," *Northern Public Radio*, 1994, https://www.northernpublicradio.org/2006-04-13/peace-activist-william-sloane-coffin-dies-at-81.

Introduction

1. Stephen R. Covey, *The 7 Habits of Highly Effective People: 30th Anniversary Edition* (New York: Simon and Schuster, [1989] 2020).

2. This is a commonly held biblical definition of "faith" from Hebrews 11:1.

3. See Martin Luther King Jr., "Remaining Awake Through a Great Revolution" (speech, National Cathedral, Washington, D.C., March 31, 1968); see Reinhold Niebuhr, "Chapter IX: The Preservation of Moral Values in Politics," in *Moral Man and Immoral Society: A Study in Ethics and Politics* (Louisville: Westminster John Knox Press, [1932] 2001), 231–56.

4. Maya Angelou, *I Shall Not Be Moved* (Random House, 1990), 21.

5. Ninian Smart, *The Religious Experience of Mankind*, 2nd ed. (New York: Scribner, 1976).

6. Steven W. Gilbert, "Gandhi's 'Seven Blunders of the World' That Lead to Violence . . . Plus Five," *Change* 28, no. 2 (1996): 15.

Chapter 1. Experience of the Good Life

1. *When Harry Met Sally*, directed by Rob Reiner (Columbia Pictures, 1989), 11:57–13:02.

2. For a compelling analysis of this scene, see Rachel Greenspan, "'I'll Have What She's Having': Fake Orgasm, Affectation, and Other S(t)imulations," *The Comparatist* 39 (October 2015): 116–34.

3. Ninian Smart, *The Religious Experience of Mankind*, 2nd ed. (New York: Scribner, 1976), 10.

4. Juan M. Floyd-Thomas, Stacey M. Floyd-Thomas, and Mark G. Toulouse, *The Altars Where We Worship: The Religious Significance of Popular Culture* (Louisville: Westminster John Knox Press, 2016), 15–40.

5. Maurice Merleau-Ponty, *Phenomenology of Perception* (London: Routledge, [1945] 2013), 146.

6. Lewis R. Gordon, *Existence in Black: An Anthology of Black Existential Philosophy* (New York: Routledge, 1997), 70.

7. Katie G. Cannon, "Pedagogical Praxis in African-American Theology," in *The Oxford Handbook of African American Theology*, ed. Katie G. Cannon and Anthony B. Pinn (New York: Oxford, 2014), 329.

8. M. Shawn Copeland, *Enfleshing Freedom: Body, Race, and Being* (Minneapolis: Fortress Press, 2009).

9. Audre Lorde, *Sister Outsider: Essays and Speeches by Audre Lorde* (Trumansburg, NY: Crossing, 1985), 54–56.

10. Lorde, *Sister Outsider*, 57.

11. Raymond J. Lawrence, *The Poisoning of Eros: Sexual Values in Conflict* (New York: Augustine Moore, 1989), 24; see also Peter Black, "The Broken Wings of Eros: Christian Ethics and the Denial of Desire," *Theological Studies* 64, no. 1 (March 2003): 106–26, and Copeland, *Enfleshing Freedom*, 64–65.

12. See Michel Foucault, *La Volenté de savoir* (Paris: Edition Gallimard, 1976); Michel Foucault, *L'Usage des plaisirs* (Paris: Edition Gallimard, 1984); Michel Foucault, *La Souci de soi* (Paris: Edition Gallimard, 1984); Michel Foucault, *Histoire de la sexualité*, ed. Frederic Gros (Paris: Edition Gallimard, 2018).

13. Martha C. Nussbaum, "Objectification," *Philosophy and Public Affairs* 24, no. 4 (1995): 257; Rae Langton, *Sexual Solipsism: Philosophical Essays on Pornography and Objectification* (Oxford: Oxford University Press, 2009), 228–29.

14. Immanuel Kant, "Reading: Duties Toward the Body in Respect to Sexual Impulse," in *Morality and Moral Controversies*, 10th ed., ed. Steven Scalett and John Arthur (New York: Routledge, 2019), 424.

15. Gandhi acknowledges this paradox when he explains that "it is better to enjoy through the body than to be enjoying the thought of it. It is good to disap-

prove of sensual desires as soon as they arise in the mind and try to keep them down, but if, for want of physical enjoyment, the mind wallows in thoughts of enjoyment, then it is legitimate to satisfy the hunger of the body. About this I have no doubt." See *The Essential Gandhi: An Anthology of His Writings on His Life, Work, and Ideas*, ed. Louis Fischer (New York: Vintage, [1962] 1983), 209.

16. Ramachandra Guha, *Gandhi: The Years That Changed the World, 1914–1948* (New York: Vintage Books, 2018), 587.

17. See Guha, *Gandhi*, 777–87.

18. Simon Blackburn, *Lust: The Seven Deadly Sins* (New York: Oxford University Press, 2004), 51.

19. David Brooks, *The Road to Character* (New York: Random House, 2015), 192.

20. Marc Eliot, *Michael Douglas: A Biography* (New York: Crown, 2012), 185–86.

21. See Jodi Kantor and Megan Twohey, *She Said: Breaking the Sexual Harassment Story That Helped Ignite a Movement* (New York: Penguin, 2019).

22. Michael R. Sisak and Dave Collins, "Harvey Weinstein's Rape Conviction Is Overturned by New York's Top Court," *Associated Press*, April 25, 2024, https://apnews.com/article/weinstein-metoo-appeal-ed29faeec862abf0c071e8bd3574c4a3.

23. See Jim Rutenberg, "A Long-Delayed Reckoning of the Cost of Silence on Abuse," *New York Times*, October 23, 2017, https://www.nytimes.com/2017/10/22/business/media/along-delayed-reckoning-of-the-cost-of-silence-on-abuse.html.

24. Rowena Chiu, "'Harvey Weinstein Told Me He Liked Chinese Girls': Why It Took Me More Than 20 Years to Tell My #MeToo Story," *New York Times*, October 5, 2019, https://www.nytimes.com/2019/10/05/opinion/sunday/harvey-weinstein-rowena-chiu.html?searchResultPosition=1; and Hillary Lewis, "Ex-Weinstein Assistant Opens Up About Alleged Attempted Rape, 20-Year Silence," *The Hollywood Reporter*, October 6, 2019, https://www.hollywoodreporter.com/news/weinstein-assistant-rowena-chiu-attempted-rape-20-year-silence-1245739.

25. Cosby's sentence was overturned after he had served three years because the court ruled that the prosecutor should have abided by a previous verbal agreement not to charge Cosby in exchange for his incriminating testimony in a civil case. Maryclaire Dale, "Bill Cosby Freed from Prison, His Sex Conviction Overturned," *AP News*, June 30, 2021, https://apnews.com/article/bill-cosby-conviction-overturned-5c073fb64bc5df4d7b99ee7fadddbe5a.

26. Gary Leven, "Bill Cosby's Legacy: From America's Dad to 'America's Rapist,'" *USA Today*, April 26, 2018, https://www.usatoday.com/story/life/people/2018/04/26/bill-cosbys-legacy-americas-dad-americas-rapist/555163002.

27. In a 2018 *Vanity Fair* article, Monica Lewinsky reflects on her evolving understanding of her relationship with Bill Clinton, explaining that "I now see how problematic it was that the two of us even got to a place where there was a question of consent. Instead, the road that led there was littered with inappropriate abuse of authority, station, and privilege. (Full stop.)" Lewin-

sky, "Monica Lewinsky: Emerging from 'the House of Gaslight' in the Age of #MeToo," *Vanity Fair*, March 2018, https://www.vanityfair.com/news/2018/02/monica-lewinsky-in-the-age-of-metoo.

28. James A. McGreevey, "The Making of a Gay American," *New York Magazine*, September 14, 2006, http://nymag.com/news/politics/21340/.

29. In 2016, House Speaker Dennis Hastert was federally imprisoned after admitting that he had sexually abused boys whom he had coached while working in his previous career as a high school teacher and sports coach. The longest-serving Republican House Speaker was also convicted of financial crimes related to using federal funds as hush money to cover up his repeated incidents of child molestation. In 2008, Mark Foley was implicated in a scandal in which the Republican congressman from Florida had been sending sexually suggestive emails, instant messages, and text messages to teenage boys who had served as congressional pages. Eliot Spitzer became a news media headliner in 2008 when salacious details were relayed from conjoint IRS and FBI probes into his repeated use of a high-end escort service. In 2017, Anthony Weiner pled guilty, was registered as a sex offender, and was federally imprisoned for sexting charges in relation to transferring obscene material to a minor. A repeat offender, Weiner sent sexually suggestive photos via Twitter and was sentenced to twenty-one months in prison and ordered to pay a $10,000 fine. He began serving his federal prison sentence in November 2017.

30. "Transcript: Donald Trump's Taped Comments About Women," *New York Times*, October 8, 2016, https://www.nytimes.com/2016/10/08/us/donald-trump-tape-transcript.html.

31. "All the Assault Allegations Against Donald Trump, Recapped," *PBS News Hour*, June 21, 2019, https://www.pbs.org/newshour/politics/assault-allegations-donald-trump-recapped.

32. Jeva Lang, "61 Things Donald Trump Has Said About Women," *The Week*, October 16, 2018, https://theweek.com/articles/655770/61-things-donald-trump-said-about-women.

33. See Robin Pogrebin and Kate Kelly, *The Education of Brett Kavanaugh: An Investigation* (New York: Portfolio, 2019).

34. Department of Justice, US Attorney's Office, Southern District of New York, "Ghislaine Maxwell Sentenced to 20 Years in Prison for Conspiring with Jeffrey Epstein to Sexually Abuse Minors," June 28, 2022, https://www.justice.gov/usao-sdny/pr/ghislaine-maxwell-sentenced-20-years-prison-conspiring-jeffrey-epstein-sexually-abuse.

35. "Who We Are," North American Man/Boy Love Association, last modified 2011, https://www.nambla.org/welcome.html.

36. "Why NAMBLA Matters," https://www.nambla.org/matters.html.

37. "Frequently Asked Questions," https://www.nambla.org/faq.html.

38. Kim Christensen, "Boy Scout Sex Abuse Scandal's Stunning Toll: Over 12,200 Reported Victims," *Los Angeles Times*, May 15, 2019, https://www.latimes.com/local/california/la-na-boy-scouts-child-sex-abuse-20190515-story.html.

39. Christensen, "Boy Scout Sex Abuse."

40. See Jason Berry, *Lead Us Not into Temptation: Catholic Priests and the Sexual Abuse of Children* (New York: Doubleday, 1992).

41. Daniel Burke, "The US Catholic Church Spent More Than $300 million on Abuse-Related Costs in 12 Months," *CNN Religion*, June 4, 2019, https://www.cnn.com/2019/06/04/us/catholic-church-300-million-abuse-claims/index.html.

42. Kathleen Megan, "The Effects of Sexual Abuse Never Go Away," *Hartford Courant*, February 3, 1997, https://www.snapnetwork.org/psych_effects/effects_never_goaway.htm.

43. Megan, "The Effects of Sexual Abuse Never Go Away."

44. Megan, "The Effects of Sexual Abuse Never Go Away."

45. "AP: Sexual Misconduct Plagues U.S. Schools," NBC News, October 20, 2007, https://www.nbcnews.com/id/wbna21392345.

46. *May-December*, directed by Todd Haynes (Netflix, 2023), https://www.imdb.com/title/tt13651794/.

47. See Amanda Garrett, "More Female Teachers Caught Having Sex with Students, Experts Say," *The Columbus Dispatch*, June 3, 2019, https://www.dispatch.com/story/news/crime/2019/06/03/more-female-teachers-caught-having/984743007/.

48. Ed Stetzer, "The Pornification of American Culture," *Christianity Today*, July 27, 2011, https://www.christianitytoday.com/edstetzer/2011/July/Pornification-of-American-Culture.html.

49. William Todd Shultz, "The 'Pornification' of Human Consciousness: Our Minds Have Become 'Pornified,'" *Psychology Today*, March 26, 2009, https://www.psychologytoday.com/us/blog/genius-and-madness/200903/the-pornification-human-consciousness.

50. Shultz, "The 'Pornification' of Human Consciousness."

51. See "Sex Work vs. Trafficking: How They Are Different and Why It Matters," *Sex Workers and Allies Network*, June 2020, https://law.yale.edu/sites/default/files/area/center/ghjp/documents/issue_brief_sex_work_vs_trafficking_v2.pdf.

52. See Ahmend AlRawi and Kiana Zemenchik, "Sex Workers' Lived Experiences with COVID-19 on Social Media: Content Analysis of Twitter Posts," JMIR Formative Research, 6(7), July 14, 2022, https://pmc.ncbi.nlm.nih.gov/articles/PMC9285671/, and Courtney Ebersole, "Online Sex Work in the Time of COVID-19," 2022, University Research Symposium 403, https://ir.library.illinoisstate.edu/rsp_urs/403.

53. This argument does not intend to undermine or disallow the role that women's agency or sex positivity play in the sexual self-determination of women. However, it does intend to emphasize that prostitution is neither a victimless institution nor one that has been developed with women's sex positivity in mind—nothing could be further from the truth. Pornography and prostitution are institutions built squarely upon women's objectification as the primary *modus operandi*. This is why prostitutes are the ones overwhelmingly problematized and criminalized, and not their "johns." Even in those instances where prostitution

is legalized, statistics bear out that women who serve as prostitutes are seen as incapable of being victims of sexual assault and often are not afforded the protections of antirape legislation and compensation, in spite of the fact that they experience high levels of sexual violence. In short, even when performing sex work in a legalized context, women who serve as prostitutes are often, nonetheless, criminalized and denied basic services and protections under the law (e.g., police protection, access to health care, legal protection, etc.). See Katherine Koster, "17 Facts About Sexual Violence and Sex Work," *HuffPost*, December 4, 2015, https://www.huffpost.com/entry/16-facts-about-sexual-ass_b_8711720.

54. See Carisa Showden, "Working It: Prostitution and the Social Construction of Desire," in *Choices Women Make: Agency in Domestic Violence, Assisted Reproduction, and Sex Work* (Minneapolis: University of Minnesota Press, 2011), 40.

55. Derek Thompson, "8 Facts About the US Sex Economy," *The Atlantic*, March 12, 2014, https://www.theatlantic.com/business/archive/2014/03/8-facts-about-the-us-sex-economy/284376/.

56. Blanche Bong Cook, "Stop Traffic: Using Expert Witnesses to Disrupt Intersectional Vulnerability in Sex Trafficking Prosecutions," *Berkeley Journal of Criminal Law* 24 (Spring 2019): 147, 161.

57. Bong Cook, "Stop Traffic," 147, 171.

58. Peter L. Berger, *The Sacred Canopy: Elements of a Sociological Theory of Religion* (New York: Anchor, 1990).

59. Bong Cook, "Stop Traffic," 147, 168–69.

60. Bong Cook, "Stop Traffic," 147, 208.

61. See forhims.com.

62. See Patrick Knox, "Living Dolls: Sex Robots Will Be So Advanced They'll Be Mistaken for Real Humans in Decades," *The Scottish Sun*, August 18, 2018, https://www.thescottishsun.co.uk/tech/3085155/sex-robots-will-be-so-advanced-theyll-be-mistaken-for-real-humans-in-decades/.

63. See "Realbotix Harmony Demo and Mission Explained," YouTube.com, accessed July 2, 2022, https://www.youtube.com/watch?v=pC4Jjjooh18.

64. Donna Haraway, "A Cyborg Manifesto: Science, Technology, and Socialist-Feminism in the Late Twentieth Century," in *Simians, Cyborgs, and Women: The Reinvention of Nature* (New York: Routledge, 1991), 149–81.

65. Anne Balsamo, *Technologies of the Gendered Body: Reading Cyborg Women* (Durham, NC: Duke University Press, 1995).

66. Floyd-Thomas, Floyd-Thomas, and Toulouse, *The Altars Where We Worship*, 29.

67. Nicola Davis, "Claims About Social Benefits of Sex Robots Greatly Overstated, Say Experts," *The Guardian*, June 4, 2018, https://www.theguardian.com/science/2018/jun/04/claims-about-social-benefits-of-sex-robots-greatly-overstated-say-experts.

68. Kathleen Richardson, "The Assymmetrical 'Relationship': Parallels Between Prostitution and the Development of Sex Robots," *SIGCAS Computers and Society* 45 (September 2015).

69. Kurtis Alexander, "Ex-Stanford Swimmer Accused of Raping Unconscious Woman," *SFGATE.com*, January 27, 2015, https://www.sfgate.com/news/article/Stanford-athlete-accused-of-raping-unconscious-6044286.php.

70. Liam Stack, "Light Sentence for Brock Turner in Stanford Rape Case Draws Outrage," *New York Times*, June 6, 2016, https://www.nytimes.com/2016/06/07/us/outrage-in-stanford-rape-case-over-dueling-statements-of-victim-and-attackers-father.html.

71. Stack, "Light Sentence for Brock Turner."

72. Alia Dastagir, "Survivor in the Brock Turner Rape Case Has Revealed Her Identity," *USA Today*, September 4, 2019, https://www.usatoday.com/story/news/nation/2019/09/04/brock-turner-stanford-rape-case-chanel-miller-survivor-emily-doe/2207106001/.

73. Chanel Miller, *Know My Name: A Memoir* (New York: Viking, 2019).

74. Given his long track record of often saying disgraceful, disgusting thoughts aloud, it came as no surprise when Congressman Steve King, Republican from Iowa, claimed vehemently that "humanity might not exist if not for rape and incest" in defense of his support for denying women the right to have abortions in cases of rape and incest. In addition to how criminal and crazed King's comments were, he stated them as a duly elected political officeholder, openly endorsing such acts of sexual violence as conventionally accepted wisdom about all human conduct, rather than a particularly heinous cultural phenomenon. Perhaps worst of all is that King offers his opinions on rape and incest as if they were natural law upheld by at least some portion of the American body politic. See Felicia Sonmez, "Rep. Steve King Says Humanity Might Not Exist If Not for Rape and Incest," *Washington Post*, August 15, 2019, https://www.washingtonpost.com/politics/rep-steve-king-says-humanity-might-not-exist-if-not-for-rape-and-incest/2019/08/14/0b60357a-beb8-11e9-9b73-fd3c65ef8f9c_story.html.

75. See John D. Skrentny, *The Minority Right Revolution* (Cambridge: Harvard University Press, 2002).

Chapter 2. The Institution of the Good Life

1. Devin Leonard and Annmarie Hordern, "Pharma's Bad Boy Exec Paid $2 Million for Wu-Tang Clan's New Record," *Bloomberg*, December 9, 2015, https://www.bloomberg.com/features/2015-martin-shkreli-wu-tang-clan-album/. Subsequent quotations relating to this story reference the same source.

2. Leonard and Hordern, "Pharma's Bad Boy Exec."

3. Leonard and Hordern, "Pharma's Bad Boy Exec."

4. Leonard and Hordern, "Pharma's Bad Boy Exec."

5. Hillary Clinton [@HillaryClinton], "Price Gouging Like This in the Specialty Drug Market Is Outrageous. Tomorrow I'll Lay Out a Plan to Take It on. Https://T.Co/9Z0Aw7aI6h," Tweet, *Twitter*, September 21, 2015, https://x.com/HillaryClinton/status/645974772275408896.

6. Quoted by Nick Gass, "Martin Shkreli Endorses Trump, Who Once Called

Him 'Spoiled Brat,'" *Politico*, May 27, 2016, https://www.politico.com/story/2016/05/martin-shkreli-endorses-trump-223644.

7. Zoe Thomas and Tim Swift, "Who Is Martin Shkreli—'the Most Hated Man in America'?," *BBC News*, August 4, 2017, https://www.bbc.com/news/world-us-canada-34331761.

8. Jazz Monroe, "Wu-Tang Clan's Once Upon a Time in Shaolin Bought by Pharmaceuticals CEO Martin Shkreli," *Pitchfork*, December 9, 2015, https://pitchfork.com/news/62465-wu-tang-clans-once-upon-a-time-in-shaolin-bought-by-pharmaceuticals-ceo-martin-shkreli/.

9. Movieclips, "Wall Street (4/5) Movie CLIP—Greed Is Good (1987) HD," Video, YouTube, October 9, 2015, 2 min., 5 sec., https://www.youtube.com/watch?v=VVxYOQS6ggk.

10. Alan Nasser, "The Myth of the American Middle Class: Have Most Americans Always Been Poor?," *Counterpunch*, August 28, 2015, https://www.counterpunch.org/2015/08/28/the-myth-of-the-middleclass-have-most-americans-always-been-poor/.

11. Although Karl Marx did not coin the term "false consciousness," his 1867 work, *Das Kapital, Volume 1,* outlines it as what has come to be one among many classic Marxist theories. See Ashley Crossman, "Understanding Karl Marx's Class Consciousness and False Consciousness," *ThoughtCo*, https://www.thoughtco.com/class-consciousness-3026135 (accessed November 18, 2024).

12. Jeffrey B. Wenger and Melanie A. Zaber, "Who Is Middle Class?," RAND Corporation, February 25, 2021, https://www.rand.org/pubs/perspectives/PEA1141–3.html.

13. Jesse Bennett, Richard Fry, and Rakesh Kochhar, "Are You in the American Middle Class? Find Out with Our Income Calculator," *Pew Research Center* (blog), accessed May 9, 2023, https://www.pewresearch.org/short-reads/2020/07/23/are-you-in-the-american-middle-class/.

14. Wenger and Zaber, "Who Is Middle Class?"

15. Christopher Rugaber, "Soaring Wealth During Pandemic Highlights Rising Inequality," *AP News*, September 21, 2020, https://apnews.com/article/lifestyle-business-us-news-virus-outbreak-ap-top-news-28a44dd1a025d9b9af5a8d4ff8c5a033.

16. Amanda Dixon, "Survey: 1 in 5 Working Americans Aren't Saving Anything at All | Bankrate.Com," Bankrate, March 14, 2019, https://www.bankrate.com/banking/savings/financial-security-march-2019/; Yaël Bizouati-Kennedy, "Most Americans Have $1,000 or Less in Savings—How to Increase That Amount | Nasdaq," Nasdaq, 2023, https://www.gobankingrates.com/saving-money/savings-advice/most-americans-have-1000-or-less-in-savings/.

17. Kathy E. Gill, "Will Rogers on 'Trickle Up' Economics," *WiredPen*, January 30, 2015, https://wiredpen.com/2015/01/30/will-rogers-trickle-economics/.

18. See Harvey Cox, *The Market as God* (Cambridge: Harvard University Press, 2016), 2–3.

19. Katrine Marcal, *Who Cooked Adam Smith's Dinner?: A Story of Women and Economics* (New York: Pegasus Books, 2016), 10.

20. See George Kelsey, *Racism and the Christian Understanding of Man* (New York: Charles Scribner's Sons, 1965).

21. What follows is a summary of Cannon's analysis and extrapolation of both George Kelsey's and Oliver C. Cox's theories. See "Chapter 12: Racism and Economics," in *Katie's Canon: Womanism and the Soul of the Black Community, Revised and Expanded 25th Anniversary Edition* (Minneapolis: Fortress Press, [1995] 2021), 143–64.

22. Cox, *The Market as God*, 4.

23. See Douglas B. Holt, *How Brands Become Icons: The Principles of Cultural Branding* (Cambridge: Harvard Business Press, 2014).

24. "'When I Shop, the World Gets Better, and the World Is Better, but Then It's Not, and I Need . . . '—Confessions of a Shopaholic," video, Clip-Cafe, November 17, 2022, https://clip.cafe/confessions-of-a-shopaholic-2009/because-i-shop-the-world-gets-better/.

25. Susan Ratcliffe, ed., "W. Edwards Deming," in *Oxford Essential Quotations*, accessed November 23, 2024, https://www.oxfordreference.com/display/10.1093/acref/9780191866692.001.0001/q-oro-ed6-00019739.

26. See Greg Depersio, "What Are Arguments in Favor of Privatizing Public Goods?," *Investopedia*, June 20, 2021, https://www.investopedia.com/ask/answers/040615/what-are-main-arguments-favor-privatization-public-goods.asp.

27. Zachary Wolf, "The Worst Drug Dealers in History Are Getting Away with Billions," *CNN.com*, September 3, 2021, https://www.cnn.com/2021/09/02/politics/what-matters-sackler-opioid-purdue-pharma/index.html.

28. Wolf, "The Worst Drug Dealers."

29. As an extrapolation of this concept, Marcella Maria Althaus-Reid examines the connections between a theory of redemption as indebtedness and the wider political/economic realities of indebtedness. In order to illustrate the argument, Althaus-Reid demonstrates why it is necessary to even question the roots of theories since they too carry a wider agenda. She contrasts a debt economy with an economy of love. Althaus-Reid, "Queering the Cross: The Politics of Redemption and the External Debt," *Feminist Theology* 15, 3 (May 2007): 289–301.

30. See "Consumer Education: Payday Loans," Consumer Financial Protection Bureau, https://www.consumerfinance.gov/consumer-tools/payday-loans/.

31. See, for example, Cynthia Enloe, *Bananas, Beaches and Bases: Making Feminist Sense of International Politics* (Berkeley: University of California Press, 2014 [1990]); Pierre Bourdieu, *The Social Structures of the Economy* (Malden, MA: Polity, 2005); David Harvey, *A Brief History of Neoliberalism* (New York: Oxford University Press, 2007); and Nancy Fraser, *Fortunes of Feminism: From State-Managed Capitalism to Neoliberal Crisis* (Brooklyn: Verso Books, 2020).

32. For critical overviews of the term and the field, see Stephanie Mudge, "The State of the Art: What Is Neoliberalism?," *Socio-Economic Review* 6 (2008):

703–31; James Ferguson, "The Uses of Neoliberalism," *Antipode* 41:1 (2009): 166–84; Terry Flew, "Six Theories of Neoliberalism," *Thesis Eleven* 122:1 (2014): 49–71. Gary Gerstle has recently argued that it is problematic to use neoliberalism as a synonym for rightwing or conservative politics. See Gerstle, "The Rise and Fall(?) of America's Neoliberal Order," *Transactions of the Royal Historical Society* 28 (2018): 241–64.

33. Harvey, *Brief History of Neoliberalism*; see also Gérard Duménil and Dominique Levy, *The Crisis of Neoliberalism* (Cambridge: Harvard University Press, 2011).

34. Harvey, *Brief History of Neoliberalism*.

35. The revisionist dimension of recent works on the limits of liberalism since the New Deal is extensive in scope. Influential books include Ira Katznelson, *When Affirmative Action Was White* (New York: W. W. Norton, 2011); Kim Philips-Fein, *Invisible Hands: The Making of the Conservative Movement from the New Deal to Reagan* (New York: W. W. Norton, 2009); Thomas J. Sugrue, *The Origins of the Urban Crisis: Race and Inequality in Postwar Detroit* (Princeton: Princeton University Press, 1996); Robert O. Self, *American Babylon: Race and the Struggle for Postwar Oakland* (Princeton: Princeton University Press, 2003); Alice Kessler-Harris, *In Pursuit of Equity: Women, Men, and the Quest for Economic Citizenship in 20th-Century America* (New York: Oxford University Press, 2001); Margot Canaday, *The Straight State: Sexuality and Citizenship in Twentieth-Century America* (Princeton: Princeton University Press, 2009); and Linda Gordon, *Pitied but Not Entitled: Single Women and the History of Welfare* (New York: Free Press, 1994). For a historical viewpoint more compatible with Harvey's, see Jefferson Cowie, *The Great Exception: The New Deal and the Limits of American Politics* (Princeton: Princeton University Press, 2016). See also Jefferson Cowie and Nick Salvatore, "The Long Exception: Rethinking the Place of the New Deal in American History," *International Labor and Working-Class History* 74 (2008), 3–32, with commentary by Kevin Boyle, Michael Kazin, Jennifer Klein, Nancy MacLean, and David Montgomery, and a response by Cowie and Salvatore, 33–69.

36. Julia Ott, "Words Can't Do the Work for Us," *Dissent*, January 28, 2018, https://www.dissentmagazine.org/blog/neoliberalism-forum-julia-ott. On the importance of the local, see Thomas J. Sugrue, "All Politics Is Local: The Persistence of Localism in Twentieth-Century America," in *The Democratic Experiment*, ed. Meg Jacobs, William J. Novak, and Julian Zelizer (Princeton: Princeton University Press, 2003).

37. Wendy Brown, "American Nightmare: Neoliberalism, Neoconservatism, and De-Democratization," *Political Theory* 34 (December 2006): 694.

38. See, for example, Lisa McGirr, *Suburban Warriors: The Origins of the New American Right* (Princeton: Princeton University Press, 2001); Matthew D. Lassiter, *The Silent Majority: Suburban Politics in the Sunbelt South* (Princeton: Princeton University Press, 2007); Kevin Kruse, *White Flight: Atlanta and the Making of Modern American Conservatism* (Princeton: Princeton University Press,

2007); Bruce Schulman and Julian E. Zelizer, eds., *Rightward Bound: Making America Conservative in the 1970s* (Cambridge: Harvard University Press, 2011). Neoliberalism does not appear in major overviews of political history in twentieth-century America such as Julian E. Zelizer, *Governing America: The Revival of Political History* (Princeton: Princeton University Press, 2012).

39. See Corey Robin, "The First Neoliberals," *Jacobin*, April 28, 2016, https:// www.jacobinmag.com/2016/04/chait-neoliberal-new-inquirydemocrats socialism/. Important starting points are Lily Geismer, "Agents of Change: Microenterprise, Welfare Reform, the Clintons, and Liberal Forms of Neoliberalism," *Journal of American History* (2020), and especially Stephanie L. Mudge, *Leftism Reinvented: Western Parties from Socialism to Neoliberalism* (Cambridge: Harvard University Press, 2018).

40. D. G. Hart, *That Old-Time Religion in Modern America: Evangelical Protestantism in the Twentieth Century*, reprint edition (Chicago: Ivan R. Dee, 2003); William Martin, *With God on Our Side: The Rise of the Religious Right in America* (New York: Broadway Books, 2005); Chris Hedges, *American Fascists: The Christian Right and the War on America* (New York: Free Press, 2008); Axel Schäfer, *Countercultural Conservatives: American Evangelicalism from the Postwar Revival to the New Christian Right* (Madison: University of Wisconsin Press, 2011); Darren Dochuk, *From Bible Belt to Sun Belt: Plain-Folk Religion, Grassroot Politics, and the Rise of Evangelical Conservatism* (New York: W. W. Norton, 2012); Daniel K. Williams, *God's Own Party: The Making of the Christian Right* (New York: Oxford University Press, 2012); Matthew Sutton, ed., *Jerry Falwell and the Rise of the Religious Right: A Brief History with Documents* (Boston: Bedford/St. Martin's Press, 2012); Michael Sean Winter, *God's Right Hand: How Jerry Falwell Made God a Republican and Baptized the American Right* (New York: Harper One, 2012); Axel Schäfer, *American Evangelicals and the 1960s* (Madison: University of Wisconsin Press, 2013); David Swartz, *Moral Minority: The Evangelical Left in an Age of Conservatism*, reprint edition (Philadelphia: University of Pennsylvania Press, 2014); Lisa McGirr, *Suburban Warriors: The Origins of the New American Right*, rev. ed. (Princeton: Princeton University Press, 2015); Kevin M. Kruse, *One Nation Under God: How Corporate America Invented Christian America* (New York: Basic Books, 2016); Angela Denker, *Red State Christians: Understanding the Voters Who Elected Donald Trump* (Minneapolis: Fortress Press, 2019); Ben Howe, *The Immoral Majority: Why Evangelicals Chose Political Power over Christian Values* (New York: Broadside Books, 2019); Sarah Posner, *Unholy: Why White Evangelicals Worship at the Altar of Donald Trump* (New York: Random House, 2020), and Juan Floyd-Thomas, "The Donald Went Down to Georgia: The GOP from God's Own Party to the Party of Trump," Miguel De La Torre, ed., *Faith and Reckoning After Trump* (Maryknoll, NY: Orbis, 2021), 13–24.

41. See Julian E. Zelizer, ed., *The Presidency of Barack Obama: A First Historical Assessment* (Princeton: Princeton University Press, 2018); Reed Hundt, *A Crisis Wasted: Barack Obama's Defining Decisions* (New York: Rosetta Books, 2019).

42. David J. Roberts and Minelle Mahtani, "Neoliberalizing Race, Racing

Neoliberalism: Placing Race in Neoliberal Discourse," *Antipode* 42:2 (2010): 248, 250; see also Juan Floyd-Thomas, "Deep in the Heart of Texas: Race, Religion, and Rights in the COVID-19 Era," Stacey Floyd-Thomas, ed., *Religion, Race and COVID-19: Confronting White Supremacy in the Pandemic* (New York: New York University Press, 2021), 185–214.

43. See Mike Davis, *City of Quartz: Excavating the Future in Los Angeles* (London: Verso, 1990); Thomas J. Sugrue, *The Origins of the Urban Crisis* (Princeton: Princeton University Press, 1996); Robin D. G. Kelley, *Yo' Mama's Disfunktional!: Fighting the Culture Wars in Urban America* (Boston: Beacon Press, 1997); Andrew J. Diamond, *Chicago on the Make: Power and Inequality in a Modern City* (Berkeley: University of California Press, 2017); Maurice J. Hobson, *The Legend of the Black Mecca: Politics and Class in the Making of Modern Atlanta* (Chapel Hill: University of North Carolina Press, 2017); and Andrew J. Diamond and Thomas J. Sugrue, eds., *Neoliberal Cities: The Remaking of Postwar Urban America* (New York: New York University Press, 2020).

44. Marisa Chappell, *The War on Welfare: Family, Poverty, and Politics in Modern America* (Philadelphia: University of Pennsylvania Press, 2010); Julilly Kohler-Hausmann, *Getting Tough: Welfare and Imprisonment in 1970s America* (Princeton: Princeton University Press, 2017); Joe Soss, Richard C. Fording, and Sanford Schram, *Disciplining the Poor: Neoliberal Paternalism and the Persistent Power of Race* (Chicago: University of Chicago Press, 2011).

45. Walter Benjamin, *Selected Writings Vol. 1*, trans. Rodney Livingstone (Belknap Harvard Press, [1921], 1996), 288–91.

46. For discussion on Galbraith, see Joerg Rieger, *No Rising Tide: Theology, Economics, and the Future* (2009), 5.

47. Adam Kotsko, *Neoliberalism's Demons: On the Political Theology of Late Capital* (Palo Alto: Stanford University Press, 2018).

48. See Simone de Beauvoir, *Ethics of Ambiguity*, trans. Bernard Frechtman (New York: Open Road Integrated Media, 2018), 52.

49. Heather McGhee, "The Way Out of America's ZeroSum Thinking on Race and Wealth," *New York Times*, February 13, 2021, https://www.nytimes.com/2021/02/13/opinion/race-economy-inequality-civil-rights.html?referringSource=articleShare.

50. See "Chapter 2: Big Business," in Juan Floyd-Thomas, Stacey Floyd-Thomas, and Mark Toulouse, *The Altars Where We Worship* (Louisville: Westminster John Knox Press, 2016) 41–67.

51. Jane Knodell and Stephanie Seguino, "Austerity Is Dad Economics," *VTDigger*, May 26, 2020, https://vtdigger.org/2020/05/26/jane-knodell-stephanie-seguino-austerity-is-bad-economics/.

52. Natalia A. Kolesnikova and Yang Liu, "Jobless Recoveries: Causes and Consequences," Federal Reserve Bank of St. Louis, April 1, 2011, https://www.stlouisfed.org/publications/regional-economist/april-2011/jobless-recoveries-causes-and-consequences#_blank.

53. *1923*, season 1, episode 2, 43 minutes and 2 seconds into the episode.

Chapter 3. The Myth of the Good Life

1. Aisha Harris, host, *Pop Culture Happy Hour*, podcast, "'Succession': Mogul Money, Mogul Problems," NPR, August 14, 2019, https://www.npr.org/2019/08/13/750872902/succession-mogul-money-mogul-problems; Aisha Harris, host, Pop Culture Happy Hour, podcast, "Where We Stand (and Fall) With 'Succession' Season 3," NPR, December 8, 2021, https://www.npr.org/transcripts/1061883229; Emily St. James, "Nothing Changed and Everything Changed in Succession's Third Season," Vox, December 13, 2021, https://www.vox.com/culture/22831645/succession-finale-season-3-recap-review-all-the-bells-say-kendall-roman-shiv-tom; Rachel Connolly, "What Succession Gets Right About the Rich," *The Guardian*, October 7, 2021, https://www.theguardian.com/commentisfree/2021/oct/07/succession-right-rich-white-lotus-logan-roy; Erin Schwartz, "Eat the Rich," The Nation, https://www.thenation.com/article/archive/succession-hbo-tv-review/.

2. John Pearson, *Painfully Rich: The Outrageous Fortune and Misfortunes of the Heirs of J. Paul Getty* (New York: St. Martin's Press, 1995).

3. See, for example, Stacey M. Floyd-Thomas, ed., *Religion, Race, and COVID-19: Confronting White Supremacy in the Pandemic* (New York: New York University Press, 2022).

4. Joseph Campbell, *The Power of Myth* (New York: Anchor Books, 1991), 4–5.

5. Robert Wuthnow, *American Mythos: Why Our Best Efforts to Be a Better Nation Fall Short* (Princeton: Princeton University Press, 2006), 3.

6. Christopher Driscoll, *White Lies: Race and Uncertainty in the Twilight of American Religion* (New York: Routledge, 2016), 79.

7. Cheryl I. Harris, "Whiteness as Property," *Harvard Law Review* 106, no. 8 (1993): 1707–91, https://doi.org/10.2307/1341787.

8. Cheryl I. Harris, "Whiteness as Property," in *Critical Race Theory: The Key Writings That Formed the Movement*, ed. Kimberlé Crenshaw, Gary Peller, Kendall Thomas, and Neil Gotanda (New York: The New Press, 1995), 279.

9. Harris, "Whiteness as Property," in *Critical Race Theory*, 281.

10. Harris, "Whiteness as Property," in *Critical Race Theory*, 290.

11. George Tinker, "John Locke on Property," in *Beyond the Pale: Reading Ethics from the Margins*, ed. Stacey Floyd-Thomas and Miguel De La Torre (Louisville: Westminster John Knox Press, 2011), 49–58.

12. Tinker, "John Locke on Property," 49–58.

13. Toni Morrison, *Playing in the Dark: Whiteness and the Literary Imagination* (Cambridge: Harvard University Press, 1992), 90.

14. Zeus Leonardo, "Reading Whiteness: Antiracist Pedagogy Against White Racial Knowledge," in *Handbook of Social Justice in Education*, ed. William Ayers, Therese Quinn, and David Stovall (Routledge: New York, 2009), 236; Manning Marable, *The Great Wells of Democracy: The Meaning of Race in American Life* (Basic Civitas: New York, 2002), 320.

15. Edward Bonilla-Silva, *White Supremacy and Racism in the Post-Civil Rights Era* (Boulder: Lynne Rienner Publishers 2001), 153.

16. Bonilla-Silva, *White Supremacy and Racism*, 143.

17. David R. Roediger, *The Wages of Whiteness: Race in the Making of the American Working Class* (London: Verso, 2007), 3.

18. This is a commonly held biblical definition of "faith" from Hebrews 11:1.

19. Patricia J. Williams, "Metro Broadcasting, Inc. v. FCC: Regrouping in Singular Times," in *Critical Race Theory: The Key Writings That Formed the Movement*, ed. Kimberlé Crenshaw, Gary Peller, Kendall Thomas, and Neil Gotanda (New York: The New Press, 1995), 197.

20. Joe Pinsker, "The Real Reasons Legacy Preferences Exist," *The Atlantic*, April 4, 2019, https://www.theatlantic.com/education/archive/2019/04/legacy-admissions-preferences-ivy/586465/.

21. See Nelson George's powerful critique of the music industry's treatment of R&B, which traces its cultural decline through economic shifts and corporate exploitation. George, *The Death of Rhythm and Blues* (New York: National Geographic Books, 2003).

22. As argued by William C. Rhoden, *$40 Million Slaves: The Rise, Fall, and Redemption of the Black Athlete* (New York: Crown Publishers, 2006).

23. See Greg Tate, *Everything But the Burden: What White People Are Taking from Black Culture* (New York: Harlem Moon, 2003), and especially note Vernon Reid's "Steely Dan Understood as the Apotheosis of 'The White Negro,'" Carl Hancock Rux's "The Beats: America's First 'Wiggas,'" and Greg Tate's own introductory essay "Nigs 'R Us."

24. bell hooks, *Black Looks: Race and Representation* (New York: Routledge, 2015), 21.

25. See Yi-Fu Tuan, *Space and Place: The Perspective of Experience* (Minneapolis: University of Minnesota Press, 1977).

26. Jonathan Walton, *Watch This!: The Ethics and Aesthetics of Black Televangelism* (New York: New York University Press, 2009), 180.

27. Wuthnow, *American Mythos*, 3.

28. Toni Morrison, "The Pain of Being Black," interview by Bonnie Angelo, *Time*, May 22, 1989.

29. William Julius Wilson and Richard Taub, *There Goes the Neighborhood: Racial, Ethnic, and Class Tensions in Four Chicago Neighborhoods and Their Meaning for America* (New York: Vintage, 2007). See also George Lipsitz, *How Racism Takes Place* (Philadelphia: Temple University Press, 2011).

30. See Robert Bullard, ed., *Unequal Protection: Environmental Justice and Communities of Color* (San Francisco: Sierra Club Books, 1994).

31. See Sarah Maslin Nir, "How 2 Lives Collided in Central Park, Rattling the Nation," *New York Times*, June 14, 2020, updated October 14, 2020, https://www.nytimes.com/2020/06/14/nyregion/central-park-amy-cooper-christian-racism.html.

32. Ninian Smart, *Worldviews: Crosscultural Explorations of Human Beliefs* (Hoboken: Prentice Hall, 2000), 75.

33. Megan McCluskey, "The Significance of Bran Stark's Cryptic Conversation with Littlefinger on *Game of Thrones*," *Time*, August 6, 2017, https://time.com/4889240/game-of-thrones-bran-stark-littlefinger-chaos-conversation/.

34. Hortense J. Spillers, "Mama's Baby, Papa's Maybe: An American Grammar Book," *Diacritics*, vol. 17, no. 2, Culture and Countermemory: The "American" Connection (Summer 1987): 68.

35. As discussed in Tara J. Yosso, "Whose Culture Has Capital? A Critical Race Theory Discussion of Community Cultural Wealth," *Race Ethnicity and Education,* vol. 8, no. 1 (March 2005): 70.

36. Charles Taylor, *Sources of the Self: The Making of Modern Identity* (Cambridge: Harvard University Press, 1989), 15.

37. Laura Mulvey, *Visual and Other Pleasures* (Bloomington: Indiana University Press, 1989).

38. Maslin Nir, "How 2 Lives Collided in Central Park."

39. See Robin DiAngelo, *White Fragility: Why It's So Hard for White People to Talk About Racism* (Boston: Beacon Press, 2018).

40. Kimberly Jones, *How We Can Win: Race, History and Changing the Money Game That's Rigged* (New York: Henry Holt, 2021), 8.

41. Jones, *How We Can Win*, 8–10.

42. Debarati Sanyal, "The Social Contract and the Game of Monopoly: Listening to Kimberly Jones on Black Lives," *Critical Times: Interventions in Global Critical Theory*, June 29, 2020, https://ctjournal.org/2020/06/29/the-social-contract-and-the-game-of-monopoly-listening-to-kimberly-jones-on-black-lives/.

43. See Trevor Noah, "George Floyd, Minneapolis Protests, Ahmaud Arbery & Amy Cooper | The Daily Social Distancing Show," YouTube, May 29, 2020, https://www.youtube.com/watch?v=v4amCfVbA_c.

44. Zora Neale Hurston is often quoted as having said or written this, but there is no evidence of this quote in any of her writings or published interviews.

45. Eddie S. Glaude Jr., *Democracy in Black: How Race Still Enslaves the American Soul* (New York: Broadway Books, 2016), 6.

Chapter 4. Doctrine of the Good Life

1. See Joseph Campbell, *The Power of Myth* (New York: Anchor Books, 1991); Ninian Smart, *Worldviews: Crosscultural Explorations of Human Beliefs* (New Jersey: Prentice Hall, 1981); Carl G. Jung, *Man and His Symbols* (New York: Dell Publishing, 1968).

2. Jennifer J. Freyd, "What Is DARVO?," https://dynamic.uoregon.edu/jjf/defineDARVO.html.

3. "Governor DeSantis Announces Legislative Proposal to Stop W. O. K. E. Activism and Critical Race Theory in Schools and Corporations," Florida Government, press release, December 15, 2021, https://www.flgov.com/2021/12/15/governor-desantis-announces-legislative-proposal-to-stop-w-ok-e-activism-and-critical-race-theory-in-schools-and-corporations/.

4. The Stop Wrongs Against Our Kids and Employees Act (W.O.K.E.) Act, Fla. Stat. § 1000.05, https://laws.flrules.org/2022/72.

5. Geoff Bennett and Jess Conciatori, "DeSantis Defends Blocking African American Studies Course in Florida Schools," *PBS News Hour*, January 23, 2023, https://www.pbs.org/newshour/show/desantis-defends-blocking-african-american-studies-course-in-florida-schools.

6. "Governor Ron DeSantis Signs Legislation to Protect Floridians from Discrimination and Woke Indoctrination," https://www.flgov.com/2022/04/22/governor-ron-desantis-signs-legislation-to-protect-floridians-from-discrimination-and-woke-indoctrination/.

7. "Open Letter on Fighting 'Anti-Woke' Censorship of Intersectionality and Black Feminism," The African American Policy Forum, https://www.aapf.org/freedomtolearn.

8. Derrick A Bell, "David C. Baum Memorial Lecture: Who's Afraid of Critical Race Theory?" *University of Illinois Law Review*, no. 4 (1995): 898–899.

9. Bell, "Who's Afraid of Critical Race Theory?", 901.

10. Hebrews 11:1 (New Revised Standard Version).

11. David Hume, *Treatise* 2.1.5.1, https://davidhume.org/texts/t/2/1/5.

12. Stacey M. Floyd-Thomas, "Introduction," in *Deeper Shades of Purple: Womanism in Religion and Society*, ed. Stacey M. Floyd-Thomas (New York: New York University Press, 2006), 2.

13. Katie Cannon, "Structured Academic Amnesia: As If This True Womanist Story Never Happened," in *Deeper Shades of Purple: Womanism in Religion and Society*, ed. Stacey M. Floyd-Thomas (New York: New York University Press, 2006), 20.

14. G. W. F. Hegel, *The Philosophy of History* (Mineola, NY: Dover Publications, 2004), 99.

15. David Hume, "Of National Characters," in *The Philosophical Works*, Vol III, ed T. H. Green and T. H. Grose (Aalen, Scientia Verlag, [1748] 1964), 252; Voltaire, "Essai sur lesmoeurs," in *The Works of Voltaire: A Contemporary Version* vol XIX, part II, ed John Morely, trans William F. Fleming (New York: Dingwall-Roch, ltd., 1927) 240-241; Immanuel Kant, *Observations on the Feeling of the Beautiful and the Sublime* (Berkeley, CA: University of California Press, [1764] 1960); Thomas Jefferson, *Notes on the State of Virginia*, ed. William Peden (Chapel Hill, NC: University of North Carolina Press, 1954), 138-139; Louis Agassiz quoted by Stephen Jay Gould, *The Mismeasure of Man* (New York: W. W. Norton & Company, 1981), 44-45; Roger Taney quoted by Benjamin Munn Ziegler, *Desegregation and the Supreme Court* (Boston: D.C. Heath, 1958), 37; Abraham Lincoln quoted by Roy P. Basler, ed. *The Collected Works of Abraham Lincoln*, vol. III (New Brunswick, NJ: Rutgers University Press, 1953), 145-146; Edward Drinker Cope quoted by Naomi Zack, *Race and Mixed Race* (Philadelphia: Temple University Press, 1993), 119; E. A. Freeman quoted by Andrew Greeley, *The Irish Americans: The Rise to Money and Power* (New York: Harper and Row, 1981), 88; and Theodore Roosevelt quote by "White Supremacists Who

Once Occupied the White House." *The Journal of Blacks in Higher Education* 24 (Summer 1999): 76-77.

16. See Richard Delgado, "The Imperial Scholar: Reflections on a Review of Civil Rights Literature," *University of Pennsylvania Law Review* 132, no. 3 (March 1984): 563.

17. M. Shawn Copeland, *Enfleshing Freedom* (Minneapolis: Fortress Press, 2010), 9.

18. Paul Lauter, "Race and Gender in the Shaping of the American Literary Canon: A Case Study from the Twenties," *Feminist Studies* 9, no. 3 (Autumn 1983): 435.

19. See Richard Delgado and Jean Stafancic, *Critical Race Theory: An Introduction*, 3rd ed. (New York: New York University Press, 2017).

20. See Michael Eric Dyson, *Pride* (New York: Oxford University Press, 2006).

21. The term "epistemic solipsism" speaks both to a condition of whiteness as well as a reification of the same. The definition itself is greatly influenced by the significant theories of social construction, as it has been espoused by sociologist Peter Berger and critical theorist Michel Foucault. Both scholars deal specifically with the institutions of religion (Berger) and education (Foucault) as the contested space wherein reality is made. Berger refers to religion and world construction as a dialectic phenomenon that is an absolute human product that continuously acts back upon its producer. To this end, he adds that religion is the audacious attempt to conceive of the entire universe as being humanly significant. In this regard, he states that the threefold process of the construction of a normative worldview is a reabsorption into the consciousness of the objectivated world in such a way that the structures determine the subjectivity of consciousness itself. This takes place through first, externalization, wherein society is a human product; second, objectivation, wherein society become a *sui generis* reality; and third, internalization, wherein humanity is a product of society. Thereby, in an attempt to catch up with one's self, a human world is created and the individual produces themself in the world and religion becomes the divine legitimation for such a thoroughgoing process. For further explanation, see Berger, *The Sacred Canopy: Elements of a Sociological Theory of Religion* (New York: Anchor Books, 1967). In a similar fashion, Foucault states that education is a "learning machine" that constructs subjugated knowledges wherein historical contents have been buried and disguised in a functionalist coherence and formal systemization of learning one's self and place in a space that governs one's knowledge and role in society. Education in this regard projects identities, histories, knowledge, and narratives onto individuals while disregarding their moral agency or personal experience. See Foucault, "About the Beginning of the Hermeneutics of the Self: Two Lectures at Dartmouth," *Political Theory* 21, no. 2 (1993): 202, and *Discipline and Punish: The Birth of the Prison* (New York: Vintage Books, 1977). Both of these scholars, as white male authorities in critical theory, espouse and debunk the normative gaze of white Eurocentric thought, which speaks to the urgency of the interrogation of whiteness as the epistemic

solipsism that influences the realities and moral agency of Black individuals in American society. Epistemic solipsism couches itself as universal and ephemeral, when in fact whiteness imbricates itself into every fiber of society and being. Therefore, epistemic solipsism denotes the ways in which white prerogatives are camouflaged within plain sight of the racial "other."

22. Emilie M. Townes, *Womanist Ethics and the Cultural Production of Evil* (New York: Palgrave McMillian, 2006), 7.

23. Townes, *Womanist Ethics*, 59.

24. See Foucault, *Discipline and Punish*; Michel Foucault, *The History of Sexuality vol. 1* (New York: Vintage Books, 1981); Anthony Giddens, *The Consequences of Modernity* (Stanford: Stanford University Press, 1990); Anthony Giddens, *Modernity and Self-Identity: Self and Society in the Late Modern Age* (Stanford: Stanford University Press, 1991); Erving Goffman, *The Presentation of Self in Everyday Life* (New York: Anchor Books, 1959); Erving Goffman, *Relations in Public* (London: Allen Lane, 1971); Christopher Lasch, *The Culture of Narcissism* (London: Abacus, 1980); Christopher Lasch, *The Minimal Self* (London: Picador, 1985).

25. According to Giddens, a sequestration of experience is the actual separation of an individual or group from the full immersion and real contact of day-to-day reality. This results in a state of social and moral impoverishment that increases ambivalence about one's identity and ontological insecurity without the institutional validation.

26. Caitlin Flanagan, "Private Schools Have Become Truly Obscene," *The Atlantic*, April 2021, https://www.theatlantic.com/magazine/archive/2021/04/private-schools-are-indefensible/618078/.

27. Flanagan, "Private Schools."

28. Flanagan, "Private Schools."

29. Anthea Butler, *White Evangelical Racism: The Politics of Morality in America* (Chapel Hill: The University of North Carolina Press, 2021), 58.

30. Butler, *White Evangelical Racism,* 4.

31. Dianna Douglas, "Are Private Schools Immoral?: A Conversation with Nikole Hannah-Jones About Race, Education, and Hypocrisy," *The Atlantic*, December 14, 2017, https://www.theatlantic.com/education/archive/2017/12/progressives-are-undermining-public-schools/548084/.

32. For further discussion, see John Higham, *Strangers in the Land: Patterns of American Nativism, 1860–1925* (New Brunswick: Rutgers University Press, 1992).

33. See Joy James and Ruth Farmer, eds., *Spirit, Space and Survival: African-American Women in (White) Academe* (New York: Routledge, 1993).

34. See Foucault, *Discipline and Punish*, 195–308.

35. Foucault, *Discipline and Punish*, 14, 52.

36. Giddens, *Modernity and Self-Identity*, 52.

37. This direct quote is often attributed to Paulo Freire but the exact quote is not found in any of his books. The theme of the liberating education of the

oppressed can be found in his seminal text, *Pedagogy of the Oppressed, 50th Anniversary Edition* (New York: Bloomsbury Academic, 2018).

38. Giddens, *Modernity and Self-Identity*, 19.

39. W. E. B. Du Bois, *The Souls of Black Folk* (New York: Dover Publications, [1903] 1993), 2.

40. Helen M. Lynd, *Shame and the Search for Identity* (London: Routledge, 1958), 46–47, as quoted in Giddens, *Modernity and Self-Identity*, 66.

41. See Noam Chomsky, *The Common Good* (Tucson: Odonian Press, 1998).

42. Nicholas Confessore, "What to Know About Tucker Carlson's Rise," *New York Times*, April 30, 2022, https://www.nytimes.com/2022/04/30/business/media/tucker-carlson-fox-news-takeaways.html.

43. See Neil Postman, *Amusing Ourselves to Death: Public Discourse in the Age of Show Business* (New York: Penguin Books, 2006); and Noam Chomsky and Edward Herman, *Manufacturing Consent: The Political Economy of the Mass Media* (New York: Pantheon Books, [1988] 2002).

44. Ashley Cullins, "Fox News Argues Viewers Don't Assume Tucker Carlson Reports Facts," *Hollywood Reporter*, June 17, 2020, https://www.hollywoodreporter.com/business/business-news/fox-news-defends-tucker-carlson-karen-mcdougal-slander-suit-1298999/.

45. Jacob Knutson, "New Criminal Charges Haven't Changed Republicans' View of Trump, Polls Say," Axios, June 12, 2023, https://www.axios.com/2023/06/12/trump-classified-documents-indictment-republican-voters-surveys.

Chapter 5. Material of the Good Life

1. Mary Shelley, *Frankenstein: or, The Modern Prometheus* (Peterborough, Canada: Broadview, 2012), 37.

2. Shelley, *Frankenstein*, 83.

3. See Albert Camus, *The Myth of Sisyphus and Other Essays* (New York: Alfred A. Knopf, 1955).

4. Josephine Johnston, "Traumatic Responsibility: Victor Frankenstein as Creator and Causality," *Frankenbook*, April 30, 2018, https://www.frankenbook.org/pub/traumatic-responsibility.

5. See Bertram J. Cohler and Robert Galatzer-Levy, "Freud, Anna, and the Problem of Female Sexuality," *Psychoanalytic Inquiry 28* (January 2008), https://doi.org/10.1080/07351690701787085.

6. See Karen Horney, *Feminine Psychology* (New York: Norton, 1967); Linda Brannon, *Gender: Psychological Perspectives*, 7th ed. (New York: Routledge, 2017). Analyzing Freud's "penis envy" theory, Horney reasoned that his theory was better understood when taken as a metaphor, in that penis envy symbolized women's yearning for the social prestige and position that men have. Freud actually responded to Horney in his own work, writing, "We shall not be very greatly surprised if a woman analyst who has not been sufficiently convinced of

the intensity of her own wish for a penis also fails to attach proper importance to that factor in her patients." See Duane P. Schultz and Sydney E. Schultz, *Theories of Personality* (Belmont, CA: Wadsworth, 2009), 148.

7. Nina Totenberg and Sarah McCammon, "Supreme Court Overturns Roe v. Wade, Ending Right to Abortion Upheld for Decades," *NPR.org*, June 24, 2022, https://www.npr.org/2022/06/24/1102305878/supreme-court-abortion-roe-v-wade-decision-overturn.

8. Sabrina Tavernise, "Citizens, Not the State, Will Enforce New Abortion Law in Texas," *New York Times*, September 9, 2021, https://www.nytimes.com/2021/07/09/us/abortion-law-regulations-texas.html.

9. See "Genetic Engineering," National Human Genome Research Institute, accessed June 16, 2022, https://www.genome.gov/genetics-glossary/Genetic-Engineering.

10. Owen Dyer, "Researcher Who Edited Babies' Genome Retreats from View as Criticism Mounts," *BMJ Clinical Research*, November 30, 2018, https://doi.org/10.1136/bmj.k5113.

11. Juan M. Floyd-Thomas, Stacey M. Floyd-Thomas, and Mark G. Toulouse, *The Altars Where We Worship: The Religious Significance of Popular Culture* (Louisville: Westminster John Knox Press, 2016), 183.

12. See "The Legacy of Henrietta Lacks," Johns Hopkins Medicine, accessed June 22, 2022, https://www.hopkinsmedicine.org/henriettalacks/.

13. "Henrietta Lacks: Science Must Right a Historical Wrong," *Nature*, September 1, 2020, https://www.nature.com/articles/d41586-020-02494-z.

14. Ewen Callaway, "HeLa Publication Brews Bioethical Storm," *Nature*, March 27, 2013, https://www.nature.com/articles/nature.2013.12689.

15. "The Tuskegee Timeline," Centers for Disease Control and Prevention, accessed June 22, 2022, https://www.cdc.gov/tuskegee/timeline.htm.

16. See Cynthia Prather et al., "Racism, African American Women, and Their Sexual and Reproductive Health: A Review of Historical and Contemporary Evidence and Implications for Health Equity," *Health Equity* 2 (September 2018): 249–59.

17. For an extensive history of medical experimentation on African Americans, see Harriet A. Washington, *Medical Apartheid* (New York: Random House, 2019). See also Rolanda Donelson, "Misogynoir in Medicine: How Bias in the Medical Field Places Black Women's Lives at Risk," *O'Neill Institute*, February 22, 2024, https://oneill.law.georgetown.edu/misogynoir-in-medicine-how-bias-in-the-medical-field-places-black-womens-lives-at-risk/.

18. "Henrietta Lacks," *Nature*.

19. Aviad Kleinberg, *7 Deadly Sins: A Very Partial List* (Cambridge: Belknap/Harvard University Press, 2008), 48.

20. Colin McEvoy, "Why President Harry Truman Didn't Like J. Robert Oppenheimer," *Biography*, November 28, 2023, https://www.biography.com/political-figures/a44361438/why-harry-truman-didnt-like-oppenheimer-atomic-bombs.

21. See "J. Robert Oppenheimer Explains How He Recited a Line from Bhagavad Gita—'Now I Am Become Death, the Destroyer of Worlds'—upon Witnessing the First Nuclear Explosion," *Open Culture*, September 4, 2020, https://www.openculture.com/2020/09/j-robert-oppenheimer-explains-how-he-recited-a-line-from-bhagavad-gita.html.

22. J. Robert Oppenheimer, "The Open Mind," *The Atlantic Monthly*, February 1949, https://www.theatlantic.com/magazine/archive/1949/02/the-open-mind/305431/.

23. "People: September 29, 1961," *Time*, September 29, 1961, http://content.time.com/time/subscriber/article/0,33009,895704-2,00.html.

24. "J. Robert Oppenheimer," *Atomic Heritage Foundation*, accessed June 22, 2022, https://www.atomicheritage.org/profile/j-robert-oppenheimer#:~:text=Robert%20Oppenheimer%20(1904%2D1967),father%20of%20the%20atomic%20bomb.%22.

25. See "The Franck Report," *Atomic Heritage Foundation*, accessed June 22, 2022, https://www.atomicheritage.org/key-documents/franck-report.

26. Quoted in Moya Sumner, "The Age of Envy: How to Be Happy When Everyone Else's Life Looks Perfect," *The Guardian*, October 9, 2019, https://www.theguardian.com/lifeandstyle/2018/oct/09/age-envy-be-happy-everyone-else-perfect-social-media.

27. "The Atom Bomb, Einstein and Me," interview by Simon Rodgers, *The Guardian*, January 19, 2005, https://www.theguardian.com/education/2005/jan/20/science.highereducation2.

28. Mark Toulouse, *The Transformation of John Foster Dulles: From Prophet of Realism to Priest of Nationalism* (Macon, GA: Mercer University Press, 1985), 111.

29. Sadly, the so-called destroyer of worlds was now persona non grata in the new world order he helped create. See Kai Bird and Martin J. Sherwin, *American Prometheus: The Triumph and Tragedy of J. Robert Oppenheimer* (New York: Alfred A. Knopf, 2005).

30. See Mary Bellis, "Who Invented the Microchip?," *ThoughtCo*, January 10, 2021, https://www.thoughtco.com/what-is-a-microchip-1991410.

31. Pew Research Center, "Code-Dependent: Pros and Cons of the Algorithm Age," February 8, 2017, https://www.pewresearch.org/internet/2017/02/08/code-dependent-pros-and-cons-of-the-algorithm-age/.

32. Pew Research Center, "Code-Dependent."

33. Ben Dickson, "What Makes AI Algorithms Dangerous," *TechTalks*, June 10, 2020, https://bdtechtalks.com/2020/06/10/ai-weapons-of-math-destruction/#:~:text=The%20dangers%20of%20AI%20algorithms,to%20the%20criminal%20justice%20system; see also Cathy O'Neil, *Weapons of Math Destruction: How Big Data Increases Inequality and Threatens Democracy* (New York: Broadway Books, 2016).

34. Quoted in Pew Research, "Code-Dependent;" see also Andrew Tutt, "An FDA for Algorithms," 69 *Administrative Law Review*, March 15, 2016, http://dx.doi.org/10.2139/ssrn.2747994.

35. Erving Goffman, *The Presentation of Self in Everyday Life* (New York: Anchor Books, 1959).

36. Tom Huddleston Jr., "How Instagram Influencers Can Fake Their Way to Online Fame," *CNBC Make It*, February 4, 2021, https://www.cnbc.com/2021/02/02/hbo-fake-famous-how-instagram-influencers-.html#:~:text=Buying%20followers&text=The%20bot%20followers%20are%20%E2%80%9Can,photos%2C%20names%20and%20bios.%E2%80%9D.

37. See Christopher Lasch, *The True and Only Heaven: Progress and Its Critics* (New York: W. W. Norton, 1991).

38. Quoted in Rob Pegoraro, "From Russia with Lure: Why We're Still Beset by Bots and Trolls Pushing Disinformation," *Forbes*, August 7, 2020, https://www.forbes.com/sites/robpegoraro/2020/08/07/from-russia-with-lure-why-were-still-beset-by-bots-and-trolls-pushing-disinformation/?sh=35192fbb5542.

39. Drew Harwell, "Ukraine Is Scanning Faces of Dead Russians, Then Contacting the Mothers," *Washington Post*, April 15, 2022, https://www.washingtonpost.com/technology/2022/04/15/ukraine-facial-recognition-warfare/. For Clearview AI's own description of its mission, see its website: https://www.clearview.ai/overview.

40. Kashmir Hill, "The Secretive Company That Might End Privacy as We Know It," *New York Times*, January 18, 2020, updated November 2, 2021, https://www.nytimes.com/2020/01/18/technology/clearview-privacy-facial-recognition.html.

41. Joseph Epstein, *Envy: The Seven Deadly Sins* (Oxford: Oxford University Press, 2003), 93.

Chapter 6. Ritual of the Good Life

1. Augustine, *Confessions*, 1.1.5, trans. F. J. Sheed (Indianapolis: Hackett Publishing, 2006).

2. Emma Court, "A Weight Loss Program by Any Other Name Is Still a Diet," *Bloomberg US Edition*, July 12, 2020, https://www.bloomberg.com/news/articles/2022-07-12/noom-surges-in-weight-loss-market-at-dieting-s-expense. Fatness is not necessarily a reflection of gluttony any more than thinness is necessarily a reflection of health and self-discipline.

3. Christine Burne, "Weight Isn't the Problem with COVID-19. How We Talk About It Is," *Huffpost.com*, October 1, 2020, https://www.huffpost.com/entry/fat-covid-19-pandemic-obesity_1 _5f736f60c5b6e99dc3336e3e.

4. See Andrew Lisa, "50 Ways Food Has Changed in the Last 50 Years," *Stacker.com*, September 15, 2021, https://stacker.com/stories/2500/50-ways-food-has-changed-last-50-years.

5. Brian Bartels, "The History of the Buffet, an American Institution," *Vinepair.com*, May 23, 2017, https://vinepair.com/articles/the-buffet-a-cultural-history-of-an-american-institution/.

6. Bartels, "The History of the Buffet."

7. Sabrina Strings, *Fearing the Black Body: The Racial Origins of Fat Phobia* (New York: New York University Press, 2019), 205.

8. Strings, *Fearing the Black Body*, 207.

9. As much as the Western world has disparaged other cultures for their fetishes, its objectification of the world as something that can be consumed and controlled amounts to a type of fetishization, a reduction of that which is powerful in and of itself to a mere byproduct of desire.

10. Ninian Smart, *Worldviews: Crosscultural Explorations of Human Beliefs*, 2nd ed. (Englewood Cliffs, NJ: Prentice Hall, 1995), 123.

11. "The topic of the 'use' of fiction . . . opens both the problems and the possibilities of appropriation and reciprocity in womanist and feminist ethics. 'Use' is an appropriately ambiguous word, on the one hand, suggesting that we rarely get anywhere, least of all to wisdom and humanity, without help, and, on the other hand, whispering 'abuse.' We do learn by 'appropriating' the work of others. What, then, constitutes the difference between being mentored by a text—that is, learning from it by thinking along with it—and, to use Adrienne Rich's image, 'vampirizing' a text? To what extent is the difference between being mentored and 'vampirizing' constituted more by who is 'using' the text than how it is being 'used'? What follows are some observations, thoughts, and questions that emerge from my own practices of 'using' or, to choose a less laden term, engaging African American women's novels in teaching and scholarly reflection and construction." Katie Cannon, "Appropriation and Reciprocity in the Doing of Feminist and Womanist Ethics," *The Annual of the Society of Christian Ethics*, vol. 13 (1993): 198.

12. See Vincent Woodward, *The Delectable Negro: Human Consumption and Homoeroticism Within US Slave Culture* (New York: New York University Press, 2014).

13. Anne B. McGinness, "Christianity and Cannibalism: Three European Views of the Tupi in the Spiritual Conquest of Brazil, 1557–1563," *World History Connected*, October 2010, https://worldhistoryconnected.press.uillinois.edu/7.3/mcginness.html. For further conversations regarding cannibalism and Christianity, see Kelly L. Watson, *Insatiable Appetites: Imperial Encounters with Cannibals in the North Atlantic World* (New York: New York University Press, 2015), and Carla Cevasco, "This Is My Body: Communion and Cannibalism in Colonial New England and New France," *The New England Quarterly*, vol. LXXXIX, no. 4 (December 2016): 556–86. For conversations regarding "fetish," see David Chidester, "The Church of Baseball, the Fetish of Coca-Cola, and the Potlatch of Rock 'n' Roll: Theoretical Models for the Study of Religion in American Popular Culture," *Journal of the American Academy of Religion* LXIV, issue 4 (Fall 1996): 743–65, and Johan M. Strijdom, "The Material Turn in Religious Studies and the Possibility of Critique: Assessing Chidester's Analysis of 'The Fetish,'" *HTS Theological Studies* 70, no. 1 (2014): 1–7.

14. For a sound introduction to Paul Tillich's thought, see *Ultimate Concern:*

Paul Tillich in Dialogue, ed. D. Mackenzie Brown (New York: Harper and Row, 1965), and James Luther Adams, *Paul Tillich's Philosophy of Culture, Science, and Religion* (New York: Harper and Row, 1965).

15. Tara Isabella Burton, "The Prosperity Gospel, Explained: Why Joel Osteen Believes That Prayer Can Make You Rich," *Vox*, September 1, 2017, https://www.vox.com/identities/2017/9/1/15951874/prosperity-gospel-explained-why-joel-osteen-believes-prayer-can-make-you-rich-trump.

16. Martin Luther King Jr., "Facing the Challenge in a New Age (1957)," in *A Testament of Hope: The Essential Writings and Speeches of Martin Luther King, Jr.*, ed. James Melvin Washington (San Francisco: Harper, 1986), 138.

17. Thomas Hobbes, *Leviathan* (Indianapolis: Hackett Publishing, 1994), 76.

18. David I. Green, "Pain-Cost and Opportunity-Cost," *The Quarterly Journal of Economics (1886–1906)* (January 1894): 218.

19. Pope Gregory I, as translated in Aviad Kleinberg, *7 Deadly Sins: A Very Partial List,* (Cambridge: Belknap/Harvard Press, 2008), 81.

20. Thomas Aquinas, "Question 148: Gluttony," in *Summa Theologica.*

21. Seneca, "Consolation to Helvia," in *On the Shortness of Life*, trans. C. D. N. Costa (Harmondsworth: Penguin, 1997), 48–49.

22. Philippians 3:19 (New Revised Standard Version).

23. St. John of the Cross, *Dark Night of the Soul* (Mineola, NY: Dover Publications, 2003), 16.

24. See Thomas Aquinas, "Question V: Article 1," in *On Evil*, trans. Richard Regan (Oxford: Oxford University Press, 2003).

25. Carol Roth, "The Greatest Transfer of Wealth from the Middle Class to the Elites in History," Brownstone Institute, November 1, 2021, https://brownstone.org/articles/the-greatest-transfer-of-wealth-from-the-middle-class-to-the-elites-in-history/.

26. Kate Bowler, *Blessed: A History of the American Prosperity Gospel* (New York: Oxford University Press, 2013), 8.

27. "About Lakewood Church," Joel Osteen Ministries, accessed February 27, 2022, https://www.joelosteen.com/our-ministry/about-lakewood.

28. "Lakewood Church," accessed February 26, 2022, https://www.lakewoodchurch.com/.

29. Edward Luce, "A Preacher for Trump's America: Joel Osteen and the Prosperity Gospel," *Financial Times.com*, April 17, 2019, https://www.ft.com/content/3990ce66-60a6-11e9-b285-3acd5d43599e.

30. Christine Miller and Nathan Carlin, "Joel Osteen as Cultural Selfobject: Meeting the Needs of the Group Self and Its Individual Members in and from the Largest Church in America," *Pastoral Psychology* 59, no. 1 (February 2010): 30, http://dx.doi.org/10.1007/s11089-009-0197-7.

31. "The Lakewood Experience," accessed February 27, 2022, https://www.lakewoodchurch.com/lakewood-experience.

32. "The Lakewood Experience."

33. Luce, "A Preacher for Trump's America."

34. "Lakewood Church."

35. Luce, "A Preacher for Trump's America"; "Lakewood Church and Subsidiaries Consolidated Financial Statements," https://s3.documentcloud.org/documents/4489169/2017-Financial-Statements-for-Lakewood-Church.pdf.

36. "Texas Megachurch Pastor Kirbyjon Caldwell Sentenced to Prison for Fraud Scheme," *CBS News*, January 14, 2021, https://dfw.cbslocal.com/2021/01/14/texas-megachurch-pastor-kirbyjon-caldwell-sentenced-prison-fraud-scheme/.

37. Derek Hawkins, "Kirbyjon Caldwell, Famed Houston Megachurch Pastor, Sold Millions in Worthless Bonds, Feds Charge," *Washington Post*, March 30, 2018, https://www.washingtonpost.com/news/morning-mix/wp/2018/03/30/kirbyjon-caldwell-famed-houston-megachurch-pastor-sold-millions-in-worthless-bonds-feds-charge/.

38. Eric Gorski, "'Gospel of Wealth' Facing Scrutiny," *Associated Press*, December 27, 2007, https://perma.cc/NRF5-9TKY.

39. "A Prayer for Pastor Kirbyjon Caldwell and Family," *Windsor Village* (blog), February 23, 2022, https://www.kingdombuilders.com/prayer/a-prayer-for-pastor-kirbyjon-caldwell-and-family-5/.

40. WFAA, "News 8 Reporting Featured in 'Last Week Tonight' Segment | WFAA.Com," WFAA 8 ABC, accessed February 27, 2022, https://perma.cc/VB6Z-MG7G.

41. Laura Nickas, "Bellevue Baptist Church," *Tennessee Encyclopedia*, March 1, 2018, https://tennesseeencyclopedia.net/entries/bellevue-baptist-church/.

42. Nickas, "Bellevue Baptist Church."

43. "Missions: Bellevue Loves Memphis," *Bellevue Baptist Church.com*, accessed June 27, 2022, https://www.bellevue.org/bellevue-loves-memphis.

44. Matt Stroud, "Spiritual Warriors," *Guru: The Dark Side of Enlightenment*, podcast audio, July 1, 2020, https://podcasts.apple.com/us/podcast/spiritual-warriors/id1518839824?i=1000552748226. Brandy Amstel now works to raise awareness of what she's learned from this experience and the ways people give up their power to people of authority.

45. Valerie Taliman, "Selling the Sacred," *Indian Country Today*, October 15, 2009, https://indiancountrytoday.com/archive/selling-the-sacred.

46. Taliman, "Selling the Sacred."

47. The quotes from James Arthur Ray in this section are from Christopher Goodwin, "At the Temple of James Arthur Ray," *The Guardian*, July 8, 2011, https://www.theguardian.com/world/2011/jul/08/james-arthur-ray-sweat-lodge-arizona.

48. See Tina Rodia, "Is It a Cult, or a New Religious Movement?," *Penn Today*, August 29, 2019, https://penntoday.upenn.edu/news/it-cult-or-new-religious-movement. Not only are so-called cults alternately considered new emergent religions, various established religions like Judaism, Christianity, Islam, etc., were also once considered to fall within modern parameters of "cult." The Troeltschian view (from the German theologian Ernst Troelt) situated these groups as

competition versus comparison for the Church. Additionally, it is important to highlight that there is problematic and pejorative discourse regarding the term "cult" that is deeply yoked to white supremacy, patriarchy, and imperialism.

49. Marica R. Rudin, "Cults and Satanism: Threats to Teens," *NASSP Bulletin* 74, 46.

50. See David Chidester, *Salvation and Suicide: An Interpretation of Jim Jones, the Peoples Temple, and Jonestown* (Bloomington: Indiana University Press, 2003), and Rebecca Moore, Anthony Pinn, and Mary Sawyer, eds., *Peoples Temple and Black Religion in America* (Bloomington: Indiana University Press, 2004).

51. See Julia Scheeres, *Thousand Lives: The Untold Story of Hope, Deception, and Survival at Jonestown* (New York: Free Press, 2012).

52. For an earlier example of such scholarship, see David Chidester, *Salvation and Suicide: Jim Jones, the Peoples Temple, and Jonestown* (Bloomington: Indiana University Press, 1991).

53. Catherine Barrett Abbott, "The Reverend Jim Jones and Religious, Political, and Racial Radicalism in Peoples Temple," *Theses and Dissertations*, 2017, 1037, https://dc.uwm.edu/etd/1037.

54. Michael Luo, "The Wasting of the Evangelical Mind," *The New Yorker*, March 4, 2021, https://www.newyorker.com/news/daily-comment/the-wasting-of-the-evangelical-mind.

55. Beginning in the mid-eighteenth century with "The Great Awakening," a revival during "The Second Great Awakening" of the early nineteenth century, and the rapid growth of Pentecostalism in the twentieth century, the trend toward privileging emotive responses and religious "enthusiasm" over cognitive engagement within Christian religious ceremony created the foundations for modern evangelical Christianity. See Thomas S. Kidd, *The Great Awakening: The Roots of Evangelical Christianity in Colonial America* (New Haven: Yale University Press, 2009).

56. Matthew Rozsa, "Survey: Religion, Right-Wing News Consumption Are Strong Predictors of QAnon Beliefs," *Salon*, May 27, 2021, https://www.salon.com/2021/05/27/survey-religion-rightwing-news-consumption-are-strong-predictors-of-qanon-beliefs/.

57. Luo, "The Wasting of the Evangelical Mind."

58. Robert Jones, *White Too Long: The Legacy of White Supremacy in American Christianity*, (New York: Simon and Schuster, 2020), 171–72.

59. Holly Stallcup, "Why the Passion Conference Was Bad News for Public Health," *Sojourners*, January 10, 2022, https://sojo.net/articles/why-passion-conference-was-bad-news-public-health.

60. Stallcup, "Why the Passion Conference Was Bad News."

61. See the Passion Church website, https://passioncitychurch.com.

62. Joseph Hudak, "Jesus Christ, Superspreader?," *Rolling Stone*, October 12, 2020, https://www.rollingstone.com/culture/culture-news/sean-feucht-preacher-covid-1074213/.

63. See Chris Driscoll, "Live and Let Die: Spirits of White Christian Male Defiance in the Age of COVID-19," in *Religion, Race, and COVID-19: Confronting White Supremacy in the Pandemic*, ed. Stacey M. Floyd-Thomas (New York: New York University Press, 2022), 78–102.

64. Joan Cocks, *The Oppositional Imagination: Feminism, Critique, and Political Theory* (Oxon, England: Routledge, 1989), 141, https://doi.org/10.4324/9780203093924.

65. See chapter 2, "Eating the Other," in bell hooks, *Black Looks: Race and Representation* (Boston: South End Press, 1992), 21–40.

66. Claire Gecewicz, "'New Age' Beliefs Common Among Both Religious and Nonreligious Americans," *Pew Research Center*, accessed February 27, 2022, https://www.pewresearch.org/fact-tank/2018/10/01/new-age-beliefs-common-among-both-religious-and-nonreligious-americans/.

67. Jenna Koch, "Explore Religions, Don't Culturally Appropriate Them," *Marquette Tribune*, February 16, 2021, https://issuu.com/marquettetribune/docs/2–16_tribune_online.

68. Koch, "Explore Religions, Don't Culturally Appropriate Them."

69. Koch, "Explore Religions, Don't Culturally Appropriate Them."

70. "Tourist and Visitor Information," *Abyssinian Baptist Church*, accessed February 27, 2022, https://abyssinian.org/contact-us/visitors/.

71. *The Devil's Advocate*, directed by Taylor Hackford (Warner Bros., 1997), 1:31:26.

Chapter 7. Legality of the Good Life

1. Michael Torny, *Malign Neglect: Race, Crime, and Punishment in America* (New York: Oxford University Press, 1995); Michelle Alexander, *The New Jim Crow: Mass Incarceration in the Age of Colorblindness* (New York: Free Press, 2012); Christina Beltran, *Cruelty as Citizenship: How Migrant Suffering Sustains White Democracy* (Minneapolis: University of Minnesota Press, 2020); Stacey Floyd-Thomas, ed., *Religion, Race and COVID-19: Confronting White Supremacy in the Pandemic* (New York: New York University Press, 2021).

2. Thomas Frank, *What's the Matter with Kansas?: How Conservatives Won the Heart of America* (New York: Henry Holt, 2005); Dominic Sandbrook, *Mad as Hell: The Crisis of the 1970s and the Rise of the Populist Right* (New York: Anchor Books, 2012); Carol Anderson, *White Rage: The Unspoken Truth of Our Racial Divide* (London: Bloomsbury, 2016); Jonathan M. Metzl, *Dying of Whiteness: How the Politics of Racial Resentment Is Killing America's Heartland* (New York: Basic Books, 2020).

3. Hillary Hanson, "Former GOP Missouri Gov. Blasted for 'RINO Hunting' Senate Campaign Ad," *Huffpost.com*, June 20, 2022, https://www.huffpost.com/entry/eric-greitens-rino-hunting-ad_n_62ab9451e4b06594c1d3f516.

4. David Moye, "GOP Senate Candidate's Old Friend Begs Him to End

Campaign," *Huffpost.com*, June 6, 2022, https://www.huffpost.com/entry/ken-harbaugh-eric-greitens-twitter-video_n_62c5da09e4b0d740197e70be.

5. The source of this quote is unverifiable, but it became popular when President Jimmy Carter used it in a speech. See Katherine Lucky, "What Would Niebuhr Say? An American Conscience: The Reinhold Niebuhr Story," *Commonweal.org*, February 15, 2017, https://www.commonwealmagazine.org/what-would-niebuhr-say/.

6. Charles M. Blow, "Trump Reflects White Male Fragility," *New York Times*, August 4, 2016, https://www.nytimes.com/2016/08/04/opinion/trump-reflects-white-male-fragility.html?_r=0/.

7. Christopher Anders, "What Is an Executive Order? How Is It Different from a Law?," ACLU, February 4, 2025, https://www.aclu.org/news/privacy-technology/what-is-an-executive-order-and-how-does-it-work.

8. Eric Tucker, "About 500 Law Firms Sign Brief Challenging Trump's Executive Orders Targeting the Legal Community," *AP News*, April 4, 2025, https://apnews.com/article/trump-law-firms-threats-executive-order-1ed67d108ff4dc311c907b96c465dbe5; Jude Joffe-Block, "19 States Sue over Trump's Voting Executive Order, Arguing It's Unconstitutional," *NPR*, April 3, 2025, https://www.npr.org/2025/04/03/nx-s1-5351751/voting-executive-order-lawsuit.

9. James Oliphant and Jeff Mason, "Trump Uses Power Against Foes Unlike Any Other Modern US President," *Reuters*, April 2, 2025, https://www.reuters.com/world/us/trump-uses-power-against-foes-unlike-any-other-modern-us-president-2025-04-02/; David A. Super, "The Hidden Patterns in Trump's Executive Orders," *The Hill*, https://thehill.com/opinion/white-house/5230090-the-hidden-patterns-in-trumps-executive-orders/.

10. Charlie Savage, Maggie Haberman, and Jonathan Swan, "Sweeping Raids, Giant Camps and Mass Deportations: Inside Trump's 2025 Immigration Plans," *New York Times*, November 11, 2023, https://www.nytimes.com/2023/11/11/us/politics/trump-2025-immigration-agenda.html.

11. Aaron Blake, "Trump's Dark 'I Am Your Retribution' Pledge—and How GOP Enabled It," *Washington Post*, March 6, 2023, https://www.washingtonpost.com/politics/2023/03/06/trumps-dark-i-am-your-retribution-pledge-how-gop-enabled-it/.

12. Joy Ann Reid (@joyreidofficial), 2023, "Are y'all paying attention yet??? #trumpisdangerous #fascism," TikTok, June 23, 2023, https://www.tiktok.com/@joyreidofficial/video/7250703498055126314?_op=1&_r=1&_t=8dd7GygUHDG/.

13. Paul Blumenthal, "The Supreme Court's Conservative Supermajority Continues Its Work Rolling Back the 20th Century," *Huffpost.com*, June 30, 2023, https://www.huffpost.com/entry/supreme-court-2023-term_n_649f25b7e4b030efa12065d4/.

14. In fact, in his concurring opinion, Clarence Thomas appears to indicate that he believes issues regarding contraception and marriage equality should also be revisited. He wrote, "In future cases, we should reconsider all of this Court's substantive due process precedents, including *Griswold*, *Lawrence*, and *Obergefell*

. . . because any substantive due process decision is 'demonstrably erroneous,' [. . .] we have a duty to 'correct the error' of those precedents." See Madeline Carlisle and Julia Zorthian, "Clarence Thomas Signals Same-Sex Marriage and Contraception Rights at Risk After Overturning Roe v. Wade," *Time*, June 24, 2022, https://time.com/6191044/clarence-thomas-same-sex-marriage-contraception-abortion/; https://www.supremecourt.gov/opinions/21pdf/19–1392_6j37.pdf.

15. Trump v. United States, 144 S. Ct. 2312 (2024).

16. Adam Liptack and Jason Kao, "The Major Supreme Court Decisions in 2022," *New York Times*, June 21, 2022, https://www.nytimes.com/interactive/2022/06/21/us/major-supreme-court-cases-2022.html.

17. Brett Murphy and Alex Mierjeski, "Clarence Thomas' 38 Vacations: The Other Billionaires Who Have Treated the Supreme Court Justice to Luxury Travel," *ProPublica*, August 10, 2023, https://www.propublica.org/article/clarence-thomas-other-billionaires-sokol-huizenga-novelly-supreme-court.

18. Kevin Breuninger, "Supreme Court Justice Clarence Thomas Accepted Gifts Worth Millions of Dollars over 20 Years, Analysis Finds," *CNBC*, June 6, 2024, https://www.cnbc.com/2024/06/06/supreme-court-justices-millions-dollars-gifts-clarence-thomas.html/.

19. Jodi Kantor, "At Justice Alito's House, a 'Stop the Steal' Symbol on Display," *New York Times*, May 16, 2024, https://www.nytimes.com/2024/05/16/us/justice-alito-upside-down-flag.html/.

20. Robert Barnes, "Alito Says Congress Has No Authority to Police Supreme Court," *Washington Post*, July 28, 2023, https://www.washingtonpost.com/politics/2023/07/28/alito-ethics-supreme-court-congress/. On November 13, 2023, in light of increased public scrutiny, the Supreme Court announced that it had adopted a code of ethics. However, it is unclear who would enforce the code. Abbie VanSickle and Adam Liptak, "Supreme Court Adopts Ethics Code After Reports of Undisclosed Gifts and Travel," *New York Times*, November 13, 2023, https://www.nytimes.com/2023/11/13/us/politics/supreme-court-ethics-code.html.

21. Randall Kennedy, "More Foe Than Friend: The Supreme Court and the Pursuit of Racial Equality," *The Nation*, August 9, 2021, https://www.thenation.com/article/society/justice-deferred-racial-equality-supreme-court/.

22. See also Orville Vernon Burton and Armand Derfner, *Justice Deferred: Race and the Supreme Court* (Cambridge: Belknap Press, 2021); Elie Mystal, *Allow Me to Retort: A Black Guy's Guide to the Constitution* (New York: New Press, 2022).

23. See Darryl M. Trimiew, "America, Land of the Free and Home of the Poor: Inequality as a Way of Life," in *Spirit and the Age of Inequality*, ed. Robert P. Jones and Ted A. Smith (New York: Routledge, 2018), 211–26.

24. *Students for Fair Admissions, Inc. v. President and Fellows of Harvard College*, 600 U. S. 181 (2023).

25. *Students for Fair Admissions, Inc.*, 600 U. S. 181. For further information, see Tr. of Oral Arg. 19.

26. See Philip A. Klinkner and Rogers M. Smith, *The Unsteady March: The*

Rise and Decline of Racial Equality in America (Chicago: University of Chicago Press, 2002), and John Higham, *Civil Rights and Social Wrongs: Black-White Relations Since World War II* (University Park: Penn State University, 1999).

27. James Davison Hunter, *Culture Wars: The Struggle to Define America* (New York: Basic Books, 1992), 249.

28. Maya Angelou, "These Yet to Be United States," in *I Shall Not Be Moved* (New York: Random House, 1990); also see Andrew Walker, "These Yet to Be United States by Maya Angelou," Poem Analysis, November 18, 2021, https://poemanalysis.com/maya-angelou/these-yet-to-be-united-states/.

29. Over the past twenty years, dozens of documentaries have been released about 9/11; some of the most noteworthy films and miniseries include *Fahrenheit 9/11*; *Faith and Doubt at Ground Zero*; *The Man Who Knew*; *9/11: Phone Calls from the Towers*; *The 26th Street Garage: The FBI's Untold Story of 9/11*; *No Responders Left Behind*; CBS's *The CIA: Race Against Time—The True Story of the CIA and 9/11*; *Rise and Fall: The World Trade Center*; *9/11: The Legacy*; *9/11: Four Flights*; *9/11: I Was There*; and *NYC Epicenters 9/11→2021½*.

30. See Chris Hedges, *American Fascists: The Christian Right and the War on America* (New York: Free Press, 2006), and Sheldon S. Wolin, *Democracy Incorporated: Managed Democracy and the Specter of Inverted Totalitarianism* (Princeton: Princeton University Press, 2008).

31. James Traub, "The Way We Live Now: 06-01-03; Weimer Whiners," *New York Times Magazine*, June 1, 2003, https://www.nytimes.com/2003/06/01/magazine/the-way-we-live-now-6-01-03-weimar-whiners.html; Paul Krugman, "Going to Extreme," *New York Times*, May 16, 2010, https://www.nytimes.com/2010/05/17/opinion/17krugman.html; Tony Judt, "Bush's Useful Idiots," *London Review of Books*, September 21, 2006, https://www.lrb.co.uk/the-paper/v28/n18/tony-judt/bush-s-useful-idiots.

32. Arthur M. Schlesinger Jr., *The Imperial Presidency* (Boston: Houghton Mifflin, 1973), x; Thomas Cronin, "A Resurgent Congress and the Imperial Presidency," *Political Science Quarterly* 95, no. 2 (1980): 211.

33. Henry A. Giroux, *Zombie Politics and Culture in the Age of Casino Capitalism* (New York: Peter Lang, 2011), 4.

34. Hina Shamsi, "Trump's Secret Rules for Drone Strikes and Presidents' Unchecked License to Kill," *Just Security*, May 3, 2021, https://www.justsecurity.org/75980/trumps-secret-rules-for-drone-strikes-and-presidents-unchecked-license-to-kill/.

35. See Jürgen Habermas, *The Structural Transformation of the Public Sphere: An Inquiry into a Category of Bourgeois Society* (Cambridge: MIT Press, 1989); Evelyn Brooks Higginbotham, *Righteous Discontent: The Women's Movement in the Black Baptist Church, 1880–1920* (Cambridge: Harvard University Press, 1993), 7–13; Nancy Fraser, "Rethinking the Public Sphere: A Contribution to the Critique of Actually Existing Democracy," in Craig Calhoun, ed., *Habermas and the Public Sphere* (Cambridge: MIT Press, 1992), 109–42; Craig Calhoun, "Civil Society and the Public Sphere," *Public Culture* 5 (1993): 267–80; Jef-

frey Alexander and Philip Smith, "The Discourse of American Civil Society: A New Proposal for Cultural Studies," *Theory and Society* 22 (1993): 151–207; Adam B. Seligman, *The Idea of Civil Society* (Princeton: Princeton University Press, 1992); Marshall Battani et al., "Cultures' Structures: Making Meaning in the Public Sphere," *Theory and Society* 26 (December 1997): 781–812; Earl Lewis, *In Their Own Interests: Race, Class, and Power in Twentieth-Century Norfolk, Virginia* (Berkeley: University of California Press, 1991), 5–6, 81–84, 188–94; and Carl Boggs, "The Great Retreat: Decline of the Public Sphere in Late Twentieth-Century America," *Theory and Society* 26 (December 1997): 741–80.

36. Ruth Ben-Ghiat, *Strongmen: Mussolini to the Present* (New York: W. W. Norton, [2020] 2021), 9.

37. Ben-Ghiat, *Strongmen*, 29.

38. Zachary Wolf, "The 5 Key Elements of Trump's Big Lie and How It Came to Be," *CNN Politics.com*, May 19, 2021, https://www.cnn.com/2021/05/19/politics/donald-trump-big-lie-explainer/index.html.

39. Ben-Ghiat, *Strongmen*, 93.

40. Ben-Ghiat, *Strongmen*, 13.

41. https://www.nybooks.com/articles/1978/10/26/hannah-arendt-from-an-interview/.

42. Fyodor Dostoevsky, *The Brothers Karamazov*, trans. Constance Garnett (New York: Barnes and Noble, 1995), 37.

43. Jen Kirby, "Trump's Own Officials Say 2020 Was America's Most Secure Election in History," *Vox.com*, November 13, 2020, https://www.vox.com/2020/11/13/21563825/2020-elections-most-secure-dhs-cisa-krebs; "It's Official: The Election Was Secure," Brennan Center for Justice, December 11, 2020, https://www.brennancenter.org/our-work/research-reports/its-official-election-was-secure; "Joint Statement from Elections Infrastructure Government Coordinating Council and the Election Infrastructure Sector Coordinating Executive Committees," *Cybersecurity and Infrastructure Security Agency*, November 12, 2020, https://www.cisa.gov/news/2020/11/12/joint-statement-elections-infrastructure-government-coordinating-council-election.

44. Amanda Holpuch, "William Barr: No Evidence of Voter Fraud That Would Change Election Outcome," *The Guardian*, December 1, 2020, https://www.theguardian.com/us-news/2020/dec/01/william-barr-no-evidence-voter-fraud.

45. "National Terrorism Advisory System Bulletin—January 27, 2021," *Homeland Security*, https://www.dhs.gov/ntas/advisory/national-terrorism-advisory-system-bulletin-january-27–2021.

46. Richard Cowen, "Trump Attempt at a Coup to Be a Focus of U. S. House Hearings, Lawmaker Raskin Says," *Reuters*, April 19, 2022, https://www.reuters.com/world/us/trump-attempt-coup-be-focus-us-house-hearings-lawmaker-raskin-says-2022-04-18/.

47. Jonathan Weisman and Reid Epstein, "GOP Declares Jan. 6 Attack 'Legitimate Political Discourse,'" *New York Times*, February 4, 2022, https://www

.nytimes.com/2022/02/04/us/politics/republicans-jan-6-cheney-censure.html?smid=url-share.

48. Tom Dreisbach, "Criminal Records of Jan. 6 Rioters Pardoned by Trump Include Rape, Domestic Violence," *NPR*, January 30, 2025, https://www.npr.org/2025/01/30/nx-s1–5276336/donald-trump-jan-6-rape-assault-pardons-rioters. The United States Attorney's Office, District of Columbia, "One Year Since the Jan. 6 Attack on the Capitol," *United States Department of Justice*, January 6, 2022, https://www.justice.gov/usao-dc/one-year-jan-6-attack-capitol. A Department of Justice summary of the investigation as of December 30, 2021, is no longer available as a published webpage, but it is viewable via the Internet Archive's Wayback Machine: https://web.archive.org/web/20250124124556/https://www.justice.gov/usao-dc/one-year-jan-6-attack-capitol#expand.

49. See Isabel Wilkerson, *Caste: The Origins of Our Discontents* (New York: Random House, 2020).

50. George Orwell, *1984* (New York: Penguin, 1950), 263.

51. See Jonathan Swan, Charlie Savage, and Maggie Haberman, "Trump and Allies Forge Plans to Increase Presidential Power in 2025," *New York Times*, July 17, 2023, https://www.nytimes.com/2023/07/17/us/politics/trump-plans-2025.html, and Andrew Chung and John Kruzel, "Federal Agency Powers in the Crosshairs at the US Supreme Court," *Reuters*, July 5, 2023, https://www.reuters.com/legal/federal-agency-powers-crosshairs-us-supreme-court-2023-07-04/.

52. Ruth Ben-Ghiat, "Trump's Plans for 2025 Sound Like a Vengeful Disaster," *MSNBC*, July 19, 2023, https://www.msnbc.com/msnbc/amp/rcna95098. For more on Project 2025, see Elena Shao and Ashley Wu, "The Many Links Between Project 2025 and Trump's World," *New York Times*, October 22, 2024, https://www.nytimes.com/interactive/2024/10/22/us/politics/project-2025-trump-heritage-foundation.html. To access Project 2025's "fourth pillar," a "180-day Transition Playbook [that] includes a comprehensive, concrete transition plan for each federal agency," access the Heritage Foundation's webpage: https://www.project2025.0rg/playbook/.

53. Ben-Ghiat, *Strongmen*, 271.

54. Aysha Bagchi, "'We Are Just Going to Stay in Power': New Revelations in Trump's Georgia Case," *USA Today*, November 14, 2023, https://www.usatoday.com/story/news/politics/2023/11/14/trump-georgia-election-case-president-wouldnt-leave-office/71577950007/. Nia Prater, "The Case(s) Against Donald Trump," *Intelligencer*, August 29, 2023, https://nymag.com/intelligencer/article/what-are-the-legal-cases-against-donald-trump.html. For additional summaries of Trump's legal troubles, see https://www.reuters.com/world/us/legal-troubles-former-us-president-donald-trump-2023-08-15/ and https://apnews.com/article/donald-trump-investigations-other-charges-b8b064a00caad4306fb54d2f6a320468.

55. https://www.cnn.com/2024/03/25/politics/trump-civil-fraud-trial-bond/index.html.

56. Carrie Johnson, "Trump Election Interference Case Returns to D. C. After Immunity Ruling," *NPR*, August 2, 2024, https://www.npr.org/2024/08/02/g-s1-15083/trump-election-interference-case-returns-to-dc-after-immunity-ruling.

57. Adam Serwer, "The Cruelty Is the Point," *The Atlantic*, October 3, 2018, https://www.theatlantic.com/ideas/archive/2018/10/the-cruelty-is-the-point/572104/?utm_medium=social&utm_term=2018-10-03T20%3A43%3A10&utm_content=edit-promo&utm_campaign=the-atlantic&utm_source=facebook&fbclid=IwAR30cI9zsdp2NVmqxJnP3UnVJbQz0IxrHhoAGdWocfNLBeswdLp1M6KhwP0.

58. Aaron Blake, "Judge Clarifies: Yes, Trump Was Found to Have Raped E. Jean Carroll," *Washington Post*, July 19, 2023, https://www.washingtonpost.com/politics/2023/07/19/trump-carroll-judge-rape/?utm_source=rss&utm_medium=referral&utm_campaign=wp_politics, and Jim Sergent and George Petras, "19 Women Have Accused Trump of Sexual Misconduct. Carroll Verdict Bolsters Their Claims," *USA Today*, May 9, 2023, https://www.usatoday.com/in-depth/graphics/2023/05/09/trump-carroll-sexual-assault-similar-patterns-19-women/70197377007/.

59. Matthew Gilbert, "With Donald Trump in Charge, 'Apprentice' Isn't Business as Usual," *Boston Globe*, January 8, 2004, https://archive.boston.com/ae/tv/articles/2004/01/08/with_donald_trump_in_charge_apprentice_isnt_business_as_usual/.

60. Zach Everson, "Trump's Properties Charged Defense Department $1 Million, New Documents Reveal," *Forbes*, June 8, 2023, https://www.forbes.com/sites/zacheverson/2023/06/08/trumps-properties-charged-defense-department-1-million-new-documents-reveal/?sh=528c8da05901.

61. Rebecca Davis O'Brien, "How Trump Uses Supporters' Donations to Pay His Legal Bills," *New York Times*, August 17, 2023, https://www.nytimes.com/article/trump-donations-legal-bills.html/.

62. John Nichols, "Trump Got Rich by Screwing Over Workers—Of Course He's Doing It Again as President," *The Nation*, January 11, 2019, https://www.thenation.com/article/archive/donald-trump-government-shutdown-screwing-workers/.

63. Jill Colvin, "Trump Is Selling 'God Bless the USA' Bibles for $59.99 as He Faces Mounting Legal Bills," *Associated Press*, March 26, 2024, https://apnews.com/article/trump-god-bless-usa-bible-greenwood-2713fda3efdfa297d0f024efb1ca3003.

64. Claudia Lauer and Jill Colvin, "Trump Hawks $399 Branded Shoes at 'Sneaker Con,' a Day After a $355 Million Ruling Against Him," *Associated Press*, February 17, 2024, https://apnews.com/article/trump-sneakers-sneaker-con-philadelphia-4de093eda6f8d1c68baf8fe8095f777b/.

65. Steve Contorno and Scott Glover, "CNN Tried to Find the Makers of Trump's New 'Swiss-Made' Watches. We Ended Up at a Shopping Center in Wyoming," *CNN*, October 17, 2024, https://www.cnn.com/2024/10/17/politics/trump-watches-wyoming-invs/index.html/.

66. David A. Graham, "The President Who Doesn't Read," *The Atlantic*, January 5, 2018, https://www.theatlantic.com/politics/archive/2018/01/americas-first-post-text-president/549794/.

67. McKay Coppins, "Trump Secretly Mocks His Christian Supporters," *The Atlantic*, September 29, 2020, https://www.theatlantic.com/politics/archive/2020/09/trump-secretly-mocks-his-christian-supporters/616522/.

68. Thomas B. Edsall, "The Deification of Donald Trump Poses Some Interesting Questions," *New York Times*, January 17, 2024, https://www.nytimes.com/2024/01/17/opinion/trump-god-evangelicals-anointed.html/.

69. Anthony Salvanto et al., "CBS News Poll Finds Trump's Big Lead Grows, as GOP Voters Dismiss Indictments," *CBS News*, August 20, 2023, https://www.cbsnews.com/news/trump-poll-indictments-2023-08-20/.

70. Scott Detrow, Gabriel J. Sánchez, and Sarah Handel, "He Was a Top Church Official Who Criticized Trump. He Says Christianity Is in Crisis," *NPR*, August 8, 2023, https://www.npr.org/2023/08/08/1192663920/southern-baptist-convention-donald-trump-christianity.

71. Bill Barrow and Jeff Amy, "Democratic Sen. Warnock Wins Georgia Runoff Against Walker," *Associated Press*, December 7, 2022, https://apnews.com/article/2022-midterm-elections-walker-warnock-runoff-3d4e4d1ab1760792454e1cbd618ce332. Jack Jenkins, "The Insurrectionists' Senate Floor Prayer Highlights a Curious Trumpian Ecumenism," *Religion News Service*, February 25, 2021, https://religionnews.com/2021/02/25/the-insurrectionists-senate-floor-prayer-highlights-a-curious-trumpian-ecumenism/.

72. Alexander Hamilton, "Objections and Answers Respecting the Administration of the Government," August 18, 1792.

Conclusion

1. Frederick Douglass, "If There Is No Struggle, There Is No Progress: West India Emancipation Speech," delivered at Canandaigua, New York, on August 3, 1857.

2. Reinhold Niebuhr, *Moral Man and Immoral Society: A Study in Ethics and Politics* (Louisville: Westminster John Knox Press, 2001).

3. Martin L. King Jr., as quoted in Deborah Ellis, "The Arc of the Moral Universe Is Long, But It Bends Toward Justice," *White House Archives*, October 21, 2011, https://obamawhitehouse.archives.gov/blog/2011/10/21/arc-moral-universe-long-it-bends-toward-justice#:~:text=Home,%E2%80%9CThe%20Arc%200f%20the%20Moral%20Universe%20is%20Long,But%20it%20Bends%20Toward%20Justice.%E2%80%9D.

4. Micah 6:8 (New Revised Standard Version).

5. Matthew 20:1–16 (New Revised Standard Version).

6. Martin Luther King Jr., "A Christmas Sermon on Peace," 1967, http://www.leighb.com/MLK_Interrelated.htm; see also Richard Bernstein, *The Revolution*

of Values: The Origins of Martin Luther King Jr.'s Moral and Political Philosophy (New York: Rowman and Littlefield, 2018).

7. See Martin Buber and Walter Arnold Kaufman, *I and Thou* (New York: MacMillan, 1988).

8. Cornel West, *Democracy Matters: Winning the Fight Against Imperialism* (New York: Penguin, 2005), 208.

9. Stacey Abrams, as quoted in Linda Kramer Jenning, "Stacey Abrams Wants You to Upend the Status Quo, Too," *Yes!: Socialism to Journalism*, May 24, 2018, https://www.yesmagazine.org/democracy/2018/05/24/stacey-abrams-wants-you-to-upend-the-status-quo-too/.

10. Marla Frederick, "Religion, Inequality, and the Will 'To Stop,'" American Academy of Religion (AAR) presidential plenary address, AAR annual meeting, San Antonio, Texas, November 20, 2021.

11. Toni Morrison, *Beloved* (New York: Knopf, 1987), 87.

12. Stephen Stills, "Love the One You're With," Crosby, Stills, Nash & Young, *Déjà Vu* (1970).

13. Martin Luther King, Jr., "Loving Your Enemies," in *A Gift of Love* (Beacon Press, 2012).

14. Gary Dorrien, "How History Has Shaped Us," as quoted in Stacey Floyd-Thomas, "Got Ethics?: Envisioning and Evaluating the Future of Our Guild," *Journal of the Society of Christian Ethics*, vol. 36, no. 2 (Fall/Winter 2016): 196.

15. Gloria Albrecht, "Is There a Common Good Anymore? A Candid Look at the Opposing Wills of Race, Religion, and Gender at Work," as quoted in Floyd-Thomas, "Got Ethics?," 196.

16. Miguel De La Torre, "WTF, What Gives and Who Cares? The Hopelessness or Our Discipline and Future," as quoted in Floyd-Thomas, "Got Ethics?," 197.

17. Quoted in "Toni Morrison: 'Goodness Lurks Backstage,'" *Harvard Magazine*, August 9, 2023, https://www.harvardmagazine.com/2012/12/toni-morrison-goodness-lurks-backstage.

18. With apologies to Reinhold Niebuhr's "Serenity Prayer," which can be found as an epigraph to Elisabeth Sifton, *The Serenity Prayer: Faith and Politics in Times of Peace and War* (New York: W. W. Norton, 2005). I began sharing my revision of Niebuhr's prayer years ago, one earlier instance being my 2015 presidential address for the University of Denver and Iliff School of Theology, "What's the Matter with US?: Intersectionality, Culture Wars and the Growing Edges of Womanist Thought." Another response to the Serenity Prayer, commonly attributed to the Black feminist scholar and activist Angela Davis, says, "I am no longer accepting the things I cannot change. I am changing the things I cannot accept." See "The New McCarthyism: Angela Davis Speaks in New York After Critics Shut Down Two Events," *Democracy Now!*, December 2, 2022, https://www.democracynow.org/2022/12/2/angela_davis_rockland_speech_protests.

Index

STACEY M. FLOYD-THOMAS is the E. Rhodes and Leona B. Carpenter Professor of Ethics and Society at Vanderbilt University and has served as the executive director of both the Society of Christian Ethics, the Black Religious Scholars Group and is co-founder of the Society of Race, Ethnicity, and Religion. She has published ten books including *Religion, Race, and COVID-19: Confronting White Supremacy in the Pandemic* and *The Altars Where We Worship: The Religious Significance of Popular Culture.*

The University of Illinois Press
is a founding member of the
Association of University Presses.

Composed in 11.5/13
with Caecilia display
by Jim Proefrock
at the University of Illinois Press
Manufactured by Sheridan Books, Inc.

University of Illinois Press
1325 South Oak Street
Champaign, IL 61820-6903
www.press.uillinois.edu